Orson Pratt

**A Series of Pamphlets on the Doctrines of the Gospel**

Orson Pratt

**A Series of Pamphlets on the Doctrines of the Gospel**

ISBN/EAN: 9783337280666

Printed in Europe, USA, Canada, Australia, Japan

Cover: Foto ©Lupo / pixelio.de

More available books at **www.hansebooks.com**

# A SERIES OF PAMPHLETS.

## ON THE

# DOCTRINES OF THE GOSPEL

BY THE LATE

ELDER ORSON PRATT.

*One of the Twelve Apostles of the Church of Jesus Christ of Latter-day Saints.*

---

GEORGE Q. CANNON & SONS COMPANY,
PUBLISHERS,
SALT LAKE CITY, UTAH:
1891.

# PREFACE.

THE labors of the late respected and beloved Orson Pratt, some of whose writings we herewith present to the public, are too well known to require any extended comments from us. His voice has been heard in various parts of the earth bearing a faithful testimony to the truth of the gospel, and in many places where he never was seen, his precious writings have been perused with pleasure and profit by the honest in heart. Thus has his name become familiar and honored among the people of God.

The first edition of his "Works," published in England, have, of late years, been very scarce, and this is one reason why we have been led to republish them. We trust that this book will find a place in every home and be studied by both old and young, so that all may see the beauty of the truths therein explained.

That the Spirit of God may enlighten the minds of those into whose hands this work may come so that they may comprehend and heed its teachings, and that Brother Pratt, though dead, may yet live in the hearts of the people, are the sincere desires of

THE PUBLISHERS.

# DIVINE AUTHORITY,

### OR THE QUESTION,

## WAS JOSEPH SMITH SENT OF GOD?

#### BY ORSON PRATT,

ONE OF THE TWELVE APOSTLES OF THE CHURCH OF JESUS CHRIST OF LATTER-DAY SAINTS.

A FEW days since, Mrs. Pratt and myself, together with some others, were kindly invited to take tea with a very respectable gentleman of this town (Liverpool), who, though not connected with our Church, yet was, with his family sincerely enquiring after the truth. They seemed to be fully convinced in relation to the most important features of our doctrine, and were desirous of extending their investigations still further. We hope that their researches may happily result in a full conviction of the truth, and that they may obtain that certainty, so much to be desired, as to the *divine* authority of the great and important message *now* revealed from heaven—a message which must assurdly prove a savor of *life* or *death* to the generations now living. This message is beginning to awake the attention of the honest, virtuous and upright among all classes of society. They seem to be aroused from the slumber of ages.

A message of simple truth, when sent from God—when published by divine authority, through divinely inspired men, penetrates the mind like a sharp two-edged sword, and cuts asunder the deeply-rooted prejudices, the iron-bound sinews of ancient error and tradition, made sacred by age and rendered popular by human wisdom. It severs with undeviating exactness between truth and falsehood—between the doctrine of Christ and the doctrines of men; it levels with the most perfect ease every argument that human learning may array against it. Opinions, creeds invented by uninspired men, and doctrines originated in schools of divinity, all vanish like the morning dew—all sink into insignificance when compared with a message direct from heaven. Such a message shines upon the understanding like the splendors of the noon-day sun; it whispers in the ears of mortals, saying, "This is the way, walk ye in it." Certainty and assurance are its constant companions; it is entirely unlike all plans or systems ever invented by human authority, it has no alliance, connection or fellowship with any of them; it speaks with divine authority, and all nations, without an exception, are required to obey. He that receives the message and endures to the end will be saved; he that rejects it will be damned. It matters not what his former righteousness may have been—none can be excused.

As a specimen of the anxious inquiry which now pervades the minds of many in relation to this Church, we publish the following extract from a letter, which was kindly read to us during our afore-mentioned visit, by the gentleman who received it from his friend in London. We were struck with the apparent candor, the sound judgment, and the correct conclusions of the author of the letter, and earnestly solicited the privilege of publishing it. Permission was granted on condition that we would withhold names. We here present it to our readers, and shall endeavor, in the same spirit of candor, to answer the all-important inquiries contained in it.

*July 15th* 1848.

My Dear Sir:—I have been expecting, time after time, to be able to return you the "Letters" you so kindly left with me. As I informed you in my last, I cursorily read through the letters, and then handed the book to Mr. ———. With him it is at the present time. The impression made thereby on his mind is very remarkable, and he requests me to inform you, that if you will allow him, he means to keep the book, if you will please to let him know the price thereof. He and I concur in our views of "Mormonism" at present. Do you inquire what those views are? I will then proceed to state them. We consider that the proofs which "Mormonism" gives of the apostasy are, without question, clear and demonstrative; we entirely concur also in the personal appearance and reign of our Lord; we are persuaded that all the preachers and teachers of the day are without *authority*—that their teachings and interpretations are uncertain as to the truth—that the translations of the scripture, being done without inspiration, are also uncertain. All is uncertain! melancholy thought. a deplorable picture but a true one!—the different teachers doing the best they can!—all jarring—all contending! The result— division. multiplied division! And they have a right if they think proper to divide from an authority *merely human*. But their multiplied division is a multiplied proof that they are wrong— that they are without that SPIRIT who guides into truth, and *truth is* ONE.

My dear sir, the Saints have made out a strong and irrefragable case to show that 'authority to teach" is nowhere, if not with them; but the proposition that *they have authority to teach, interpret*, etc., is one that at present does not create a conviction in Mr. ——— or my mind. We admit that it is very reasonable to suppose that, under such circumstances, God would raise up and send *one invested with authority*. Whether Joseph Smith was such a one is the all-important question. I also admit. that so far as I am acquainted with his history, there is something very remarkable about him: perhaps I should be fully convinced if I were more fully read in writings relating to him. I wish I lived near to you. and then I would read more fully on the subject; I confess my mind is much concerned to arrive at a clear conclusion upon the point.

Mr.——— wishes you, if you will be so good, to select a few books that you think clearly prove the divine mission of Joseph Smith, and send them in a parcel to him with the prices. he will feel much obliged, and will send you a post-office order for the amount; he believes your selection will be a judicious one. I have heard Mr. Banks twice since I saw you, and other individual teachers also. There is much in their public services I approve. I am struck with the simplicity of their celebration of the ordinances. * * One result of my conversation with you and Banks, and perusing the letters, is, that I can be no longer connected with any sect. So far as I see, I can without difficulty confound in argument—plain scriptural argument —any into whose company I am at any time thrown. The Methodist *system* I am convinced is the worst, because its pretensions are highest. I stand, therefore, fully alone. I declare I should be glad to be convinced that "Mormonism" is what it professes to be; I would join it to-day if my mind could be convinced that its Elders had *authority to baptize me for the remission of sins, and lay hands on me for the gift of the Holy Ghost.* These sacred ordinances I would obey gladly, if I knew men having authority to administer them. To have these ordinances administered without divine authority is mere child's play. Thus you see my position. A Methodist leader, an old friend, said to me the other day, "Are you connected with the church of Christ now?—I hear you are not with us now." I answered, Where is the church of Christ?" He replied it is found among the different sects. I then inquired, "Are you in the church of Christ? for if you are, you must be a member of all the sects." This rather puzzled him. I then asked him "Show me the sect that resembles the church at the beginning; does any one of them, or do they all put together resemble the church at the beginning?" He said certainly not. I enquired why not. He was shrewd enough to be silent and to see that his own mouth must condemn his sect and all the sects. Observe, in the absence of the spirit, men must do as well as they can. This I am trying to do, only I confess that I am poor, and blind, and naked, bereft of the glory of the *certainty of the authority and truth of the church of Christ.* The sects, however, are satisfied, though "poor, blind, and naked," to boast of increase of goods, chapels, rich friends, preachers, etc., etc. So much for my present views and standing. I suppose by this time you have acted on your convictions, and are joined to the Saints; in all honesty you ought, I confess. The moment the conviction that *divine authority and certainty of teaching* is with them, that moment will I join them. * * * Farewell. My respectful regards to Mrs.———, and ever believe me, my dear sir,-yours very truly,

FIRST.—The author of the above letter has carefully examined the present state of the world, and declares himself fully convinced of the awful apostasy which now so universally prevails. He unhesitatingly admits that all authority to teach —to administer ordinances—to build up the church of Christ, has entirely ceased from the earth—that "all is uncertain." He also admits that "it is very reasonable to suppose that under such circumstances, God would raise up and send one *invested with authority.* Whether Joseph Smith was such a one is the all-important question." Yes, indeed, it is an important question, and one that involves the fate of the present generation. If Joseph Smith was not sent of God, this Church cannot be the Church of God, and the tens of thousands who have been baptized into this Church are yet in their sins, and no better off than the millions that have gone before them. *The form*, without the power and authority, is no better than the hundreds of human forms that have no resemblance to the ancient pattern; indeed, it is more dangerous, because better calculated to deceive. Other churches do not profess to have inspired apostles, prophets, prophetesses, evangelists, etc., hence we *know*, if the New Testament be true, that they cannot be the church of God. But the Latter-day Saints profess to have all these officers and gifts among them, and profess to have authority to administer in every form, ordinance and blessing of the ancient church; hence we know, that so far as the officers, doctrines, ordinances, and ceremonies are evidence, this Church can exhibit a perfect pattern. In these things, then, both ancient and modern Saints are exactly alike. By the New Testament then we cannot be condemned.

If the Latter-day Saints are not what they profess to be, one thing is certain, that no one ever will be able to confute their doctrine by the scriptures; however, imperfect the people may be, their doctrine is *infallible.* Can this be said of any other people who have existed on the eastern hemisphere during the last 1700 years? No. Their doctrines have been a heterogenous mixture of truth and error, that would not stand the test one moment when measured by a pattern of inspiration; some disparity could be seen and pointed out—some deviation either in the organization or in the ordinances of the gospel could be shown to exist. And now after so many centuries have elapsed, and when human wisdom has been exerted to its utmost strength, and the most exalted and gigantic talents displayed to lay a stable foundation whereon to build, we awake and behold all an empty bubble—a vain show —a phantom of man's creation, with scarcely a vestige of the ancient *form*, to say nothing of the *power*. In the midst of all this thick darkness, a young, illiterate, obscure and inexperienced man announces a message from heaven, before which darkness flees away; human dogmas are overturned; the traditions of ages are uprooted; all forms of church government tremble like an aspen leaf at its approach, and the mighty fabric of popular sectarianism is convulsed and shaken to its very foundation. How happens all this? If Joseph Smith were an impostor, whence his superior wisdom? What power inspired his mind in laying the foundation of a church according to the ancient order? How could an impostor so far surpass the combined wisdom of seventeen centuries as to originate a system diverse from every other system under heaven, and yet harmonize with the system of Jesus and His apostles in every particular? What! an impostor discover the gross darkness of ages, and publish a doctrine perfect in every respect, against which not one scriptural argument can be adduced! The idea is perposterous! The *purity* and *infallibility* of the doctrine of this great modern prophet is a presumptive evidence of no small moment in favor of his divine mission.

We do not pretend that a *perfect doctrine* is an *infallible* evidence in favor of the *divine authority* of the one who teaches it. We can conceive it possible, though not probable, for a man to teach a doctrine unmixed with error, and yet be without authority to administer its ordinances. Swedenborg, Irving and many others, taught, doctrines in some respects true, in other respects false: hence their authority should be rejected, even though they should perform miracles. We have no examples on the records of history, of a doctrine perfect in every respect, being taught by any person or persons, unless they were inspired with divine authority. If Joseph Smith taught a doctrine in any respect false, he should be rejected as an impostor, though he should, like the magicians of Egypt, turn rivers of water into blood, or create frogs in abundance, or even raise the dead like the witch of Endor. On the other hand, if he taught a true and perfect doctrine, he might be sent of God, though he himself should perform no miracle, like John the Baptist, or the Prophet Noah, or many other prophets of the Old Testament.

In ancient times, many great prophets were sent of God, and we have no record of their doing miracles, yet their respective messages were of infinite importance, and could not be rejected without condemnation. Where is there a man, no matter how great his attainments, that can show Mr. Smith's doctrine to be false? Did the ancient saints teach baptism to the penitent believer for the remission of sins? So did Mr. Smith. Did they teach the laying on of hands for the gift of the Holy Spirit? So did Mr. Smith. Did the former-day saints teach that apostles, prophets, evangelists, pastors, teachers, deacons, bishops, elders, etc., all inspired of God, were necessary in the church? So did Mr. Smith. Did the ancient saints teach that dreams, visions, new revelations, ministering of angels, healings, tongues, interpretations, and all other spiritual gifts were necessary in the church? So did this modern prophet. Where, then, is the discrepancy between the ancient and modern teachings? Nowhere. The teaching of the one is as perfect as the other; and we again assert that this perfect coincidence in teaching, in every point, is a strong presumptive evidence that *Mr. Smith was sent of God.*

SECOND —In what manner does Joseph Smith declare that a dispensation of the gospel was committed unto him? He testifies that an angel of God, whose name was Moroni, appeared unto him; that this angel was formerly an ancient prophet among a remnant of the tribe of Joseph on the continent of America. He testifies that Moroni revealed unto him where he deposited the sacred records of his nation some fourteen hundred years ago; that these records contained the "everlasting gospel" as it was anciently taught and recorded by this branch of Israel. He gave Mr. Smith power to reveal the contents of those records to the nations of the earth. Now how does this testimony of Joseph Smith agree with the book of John's prophecy given on the Isle of Patmos? John testifies that when the dispensation of the gospel is again committed to the nations, it shall be through the medium of an *angel* from heaven. Joseph Smith testifies that a dispensation of the gospel for all nations has been committed to him by an *angel*. The one uttered the prediction; the other testifies its fulfillment. Though Mr. Smith had taught a perfect doctrine, yet if he had testified that his doctine was not restored by an angel, all would at once have known him to be an impostor. How came Mr. Smith, if an impostor, to not only discover a perfect doctrine, but also to discover the precise medium through which that doctrine should be restored to the earth? Did Swedenborg, Irving, Wesley, or any other person, not only teach a pure system, but at the same time did they declare that it was committed to them by an angel from heaven? If not, however pure and holy their teaching, they were not divinely authorized to administer in ordinances. If Mr. Smith had professed to have accidentally discovered those records, and that he was inspired to reveal their contents through the Urim and Thummim; or if he had professed to have received a message of the gospel through the inspiration of the Holy Ghost, or the Urim and Thummim, or in any other way but that of the ministering of an angel, we should, without further inquiry, have known him to be without authority. How came Mr. Smith, if a deceiver, to think of all this? Did Martin Luther, Wesley, Whitfield, Swedenborg, or Irving think of this? Whence his superior intellect—his depth of understanding—his extensive foresight—that he should so far surpass all former impostors for 1700 years? John testifies that when the everlasting gospel is restored to the earth it shall be by an *angel*. Mr. Smith testifies that it was restored by an *angel*, and in no other way. *This is another presmptive evidence that he was sent of God.*

THIRD.—A revelation and restoration to the earth of the *everlasting gospel* through the angel Moroni would be of no benefit to the nations, unless some one should be ordained with authority to preach it and administer its ordinances. Moroni might reveal a book containing a beautiful and glorious system of salvation, but no one could obey even its first principles without a legally authorized administrator, ordained to preach, baptize, lay on hands for the gift of the Holy Ghost, etc. Did Moroni ordain Mr. Smith to the apostleship, and command him to administer ordinances? No, he did not. But why not confer authority by ordination, as well as reveal the everlasting gospel? Because in all probability he had not the right so to do. All angels have not the same authority—they do not all hold the same keys. Moroni was a prophet, but we have no account of his holding the office of an apostle; and if not, he had no right to ordain Mr. Smith to an office which he himself never possessed. He no doubt went as far as he was authorised, and that was to reveal the "stick of Ephraim"—the record of his fathers containing the "everlasting gospel." How then did Mr. Smith obtain the office of an apostle, if Moroni had no authority to ordain him to such office? Mr. Smith testifies that Peter, James and John came to him in the capacity of ministering angels, and by the laying on of hands ordained him an apostle, and commanded him to preach, baptize, lay on hands for the gift of the Holy Ghost, and administer all other ordinances of the gospel as they themselves did in ancient days. Did Swedenborg—did Irving's apostles—or did any other impostors during the long age of darkness—profess that the apostleship was conferred upon them by those who held it last—by any angel who held the office himself? No: and therefore they are not apostles, but deceivers. If Mr. Smith had pretended that he received the apostleship by the revelation of the Holy Ghost, without an ordination under the hands of an apostle, we should at once know that his pretensions were vain, and that he was a deceiver. If an impostor, how came Mr. Smith to discover this? Why did he not, like the Irvingites, assume the apostleship without an apostle to ordain him? How came he to possess so much more wisdom than Irving, as to discover that he could not be an apostle without being ordained under the hands of an apostle? If Mr. Smith be a false apostle, it must be confessed that he has exhibited far more judgment than all the false apostles who have preceded him, learned and talented as they were. Is not this another presumptive evidence of *Joseph Smith's divine mission?* Such a correctness upon matters of so great a moment, and upon subjects on which millions have heretofore erred, indicates something more than *human*—it indicates inspiration of the Almighty. The purity of Mr. Smith's doctrine—the perfect coincidence of his testimony with that of

John's, in relation to the manner of the restoration of the everlasting Gospel to the earth, and the consistency of his testimony in relation to the manner of the restoration of the apostleship, are strong presumptive evidences that beautifully harmonize with and strengthen each other; the evidence is therefore accumulative, and increases with every additional condition or circumstance in a multiplied ratio, and seems almost irresistibly to force conviction upon the mind.

Fourth.—Joseph Smith not only professes, through the medium of angels, to have received a dispensation of the gospel, and the power and authority of the apostleship, but he also professes to have received through *revelation* and *commandment* from God, a dispensation for the gathering of the Saints from all nations. Now the doctrine of the gathering of the Saints in the last days must either be *false* or *true;* if false, then Joseph Smith must be an impostor. It matters not how correct he may have been in all other points of his system, if this one point—the doctrine of the gathering be false, he *must* be a deceiver. Why? Because he professes to have received *this doctrine* by direct *revelation* and *commandment.* On the other hand, if the doctrine of the gathering of the Saints be a *true* doctrine and scriptural, this will be another presumptive evidence that Mr. Smith was sent of God.

Now a doctrine may be *true* and not be *scriptural;* as for example, Newton's doctrine or law of universal gravitation is a *true* doctrine, but not a *scriptural* one; that is, it can neither be proved nor disproved by the scriptures. So, Noah's doctrine of gathering into an ark—Lot's doctrine of fleeing out of Sodom—Christ's doctrine to depart out of Jerusalem and flee to the mountains to escape destruction, were all *true;* but neither of them could be proved or disproved by any scripture given to any of the former prophets. So likewise Mr. Smith's doctrine of the gathering of the Saints in the last days might be *true*, even though there should be no former scripture that predicted such an event; but in this case such a doctrine would be no evidence that Mr. Smith, who advocated it, was sent of God; but if such a doctrine can be proved to be a *scriptural* doctrine, that is, if the gathering of the Saints was predicted in ancient scriptures as an event to take place in a certain age, in a certain way, and through certain means, and Mr. Smith comes in *that age,* professing to have a message to gather the Saints in *such way,* and by *such means* as the scriptures have foretold, then the exact and perfect agreement between the professed message of Mr. Smith, and the scriptural predictions relating to such a message or work, would be a presumptive evidence of great weight in favor of his divine mission.

The doctrine of the gathering of the people of God, including Israel, is one so clearly predicted by the inspired writers, that it seems almost superfluous to refer to the numerous passages relating to it. The dispensation in which the people of God were to be gathered in one, is called by the apostle Paul, "the dispensation of the fullness of times;" which he represents as being an event then in the future. John, nearly one hundred years after the birth of our Savior, saw the wonderful events and sceneries of unborn generations displayed in majestic and awful grandeur before him. He saw the churches of Asia, then under his own personal watch-care, lukewarm, corrupted, and about ready to be moved out of their place. He saw the universal apostasy that was soon to succeed and hold dominion for ages over all kindred and tongues, under the name of the Mother of Harlots—the great Babylon that should make all nations drunk with her wickedness. He saw that after the nations had been thus overwhelmed in thick darkness for ages, without the church of God, without apostles, without prophets, without the ministering of angels, without one cheering message from heaven, that there would be one more proclamation of mercy made to all people—one more dispensation of glad tidings from the heavens, to be ushered in by an angel restoring the everlasting gospel, which was to receive a universal proclamation to all the inhabitants of the earth, followed with a loud cry, that the hour of Gods jugdment is come. He saw the universal proclamation of this warning message immediately followed by another angel, proclaming the complete overthrow and downfall of Babylon. Between the interval of the flying of these two angels, he "heard another voice from heaven, saying, *Come out of her, my people, that ye be not partakers of her sins, and that ye receive not of her plagues. For her sins have reached unto heaven, and God* hath remebered her iniquities." Remember, that this voice, commanding the people to come out of Babylon, was to be a "voice from heaven." It was not to be a cunningly devised plan of uninspired man, brought about by human ingenuity, but it was to be a voice from heaven—a message sent from God—a new revelation, commanding the Saints to come out of Babylon previous to its downfall. How came Mr. Smith, if an impostor, to get, not only all the other particulars which we have mentioned, perfectly exact, but also to discover that there must be a gathering of the Saints out of Babylon, and that that work must immediately follow the introduction of the gospel by an angel? Why did he not say, my doctrine is true, and if you will embrace it you can be saved, and still remain where you are? It matters not how correct this doctrine might have been in all other points, if he had told his disciples to remain among the corrupt nations, and not gather together—this alone would have exposed the cloven foot, and proved him to be a deceiver. Swedenborg, Wesley, Irving and a numerous host of others, during the last seventeen hundred years, have entirely neglegted the gathering, which proves that they were without authority—that a dispensation of the gospel was never committed to them—that the voice from heaven to come out of Babylon had never saluted their ears. Previous to the restoration of the *gospel* by an angel, God had no people in Babylon, and therefore he could not call them out. An unauthorized uninspired priesthood, preaching a perverted gospel, never could raise up a people of God in Babylon; for they themselves are Babylon, and all their converts or children are begotten after their own likeness with Babylonish inscriptions upon their foreheads. It is only when the gospel, apostleship, and power are again restored in the way and manner predicted, that a people of God can be raised up among the nations. It is then, and not till then, that the voice is heard from heaven, calling that people out from among the nations. Mr. Smith did not forget this. It is marvellously strange, indeed, that he should be an impostor, and yet embrace in his system every particular that was to characterize the great dispensation of the latter times. It matters not how diverse the points of his doctrine were to the popular current among the great modern systems of religion. He seems to have introduced his system without paying the least regard as to what would be popular or unpopular—as to whether it would suit the learned or the unlearned—as to whether it would suit the temporal circumstances of man or not. He did not stop to make the inquiry whether the gathering of the Saints would be congenial to the feelings of those who occupied splendid mansions, upon fine farms, surrounded with every luxury of life. He did not stop to consider any of those things, but spoke as one having authority; saying, "thus saith the Lord," upon every point of doctrine which he promulgated. Now, for a young man, inexperienced and illiterate, to profess to give the word of the Lord upon subjects of so great a moment—to reveal doctrines which were directly opposed, not only to his own traditions, but to the teachings and doctrines of the most popular, numerous, and powerful sects of the day, and at the same time have those doctrines exactly accord, not only with the ancient gospel, but with every minute prediction relative to the dispensation of the last days, is an evidence that carries TRUTH upon the face of it, and leaves a deep and lasting impression upon every reflecting mind, and we can hardly refrain from assenting in our hearts, that surely *he must have been sent of God.*

FIFTH.—What else besides the "everlasting gospel" does the Book of Mormon profess to contain? It professes to contain a brief but faithful history of a small branch, of the *tribe of Joseph,* and the revelations given to them both before and after Christ, written by a succession of prophets who were the literal descendants of Joseph; hence it professes to be, in the full sense of the word, the *writings or records of the tribe of Joseph.* It contains numerous and pointed predictions, showing expressly that the age in which their records should, by the power of God, be revealed to the nations, should also be the day in which Israel should be gathered; and that their records in conjunction with the records of the Jews, should be the powerful instruments in the hands of the servants of God in bringing about that great work. Now, how does this accord with the word of the Lord to Ezekiel upon the same subject? Ezekiel was commanded to write upon two sticks, one for

Judah and the other for Joseph; after which he was commanded to join them together into one. And when the children of Israel should make inquiry what these two united writings of Judah and Joseph meant, he was to say unto them, that the Lord God would join the writings of Joseph with those of Judah; immediately after which He would take the children of Israel from among the heathen, whither they were gone, and would gather them on every side, and bring them into their own land: and that He would make them one nation in the land upon the mountains of Israel; and that one king should be king to them all; and that they should no more be two nations or kingdoms. Ezekiel testifies that the *writings of Joseph* should be joined with the *writings of Judah.* Mr. Smith presents this generation with a book, consisting of several hundred pages, professing to be the sacred writings of the inspired prophets of the tribe of Joseph, who anciently inhabited the great western hemisphere. Ezekiel testifies that Israel should be gathered, never again to be scattered, immediately after the union of these two records. The professed record of Joseph, brought to light by Mr. Smith, testifies in the most positive language, that this is the age in which Israel shall be gathered through the instrumentality of the word and power of God, contained in the two records. Ezekiel uttered the prediction. Mr. Smith presents a professed fulfillment. This is another presumptive evidence in favor of the divine authority of his mission; for if the gathering of Israel had not been included in the mission of Mr. Smith, as an important part of the great work of the last dispensation, all would have had good reason for rejecting him without further inquiry. The ministering of an angel—the restoration of the gospel—the conferring of the apostleship—the setting up of the kingdom of God—the gathering of the Saints—the revelation of the record of Joseph, and its union with the Jewish record—and the restoration of all the house of Israel to their own lands, are the wonderful events to be fulfilled in the great "dispensation of the fullness of times." Whatever person or persons are divinely commissioned to usher in that dispensation, must have the keys of authority to perform every work pertaining thereunto. If Joseph Smith had included all these remarkable events in his mission, *excepting one;* then that one exception would be sufficient to prove him to be acting without authority. But where, we ask, is there one exception? What particular event or circumstance pertaining to the dispensation, of which he professed to hold the keys, has he excluded from his system? Did John predict the restoration of the gospel by an angel? It is included in Mr. Smith's system. Did John predict that the Saints should receive a message from heaven, commanding them to come out of Babylon? It also is included in the system of Joseph Smith, and the Saints are now obeying it. Did Ezekiel predict the final gathering of Israel as an immediate result of the union of the two records of Joseph and Judah? Mr. Smith also includes that in his system. The two records are already united in their testimony, and will soon accomplish the purpose for which they were sent forth. What then is lacking? Is there any of the prophets, or inspired writers of ancient times, who have pointed out some other way for the latter-day dispensation to be brought about? Can any man show that the gospel will not be restored by an angel, or that the Saints will not be called out of Babylon by a message from heaven? or that the record of the tribe of Joseph will not be joined with the Jewish record—the Bible? or that Israel will not be gathered to their own lands through the istrumentality of more revelation? or that the kingdom of God will not be set up in the latter days to break in pieces all other kingdoms? or that apostles and prophets will not be restored to the earth as in ancient times? If all these things are possible, probable, and scriptural—if all these events must come to pass in their time, and in the manner predicted—can any one show that this is not the time? that the Book of Mormon is not the record of Joseph, about which Ezekiel prophesied? Can any one show any cause why Joseph Smith should not receive the ministering of an angel? why he should not be ordained an apostle, or prophet, or receive revelations and commandments from God? If the gospel is to be restored by an angel, it must be restored at the first to some person. Why not that person be Mr. Smith? If the records of two different tribes are to be joined in one, why not the Book of Mormon and the Bible be the two records? and why not Mr. Smith be the instrument in the hands of God in fulfilling this prophecy? If these things are not the fulfillment of those ancient predictions, will the generations that live when they do come to pass be any more believing than they are at present in this work? Will they be any more ready to receive new revelations, visions, angels, or ancient sacred records than they are now? When God sets up His kingdom, will mankind be any more willing to receive the apostles, prophets, and inspired officers of that kingdom, than they are now? One thing is certain; if the angel has not come—if the gospel is not restored—if the records of Joseph are not revealed—then there is no kingdom of God on the earth, no authority to preach or administer the ordinances among men; all is gross darkness—all is uncertainty—and our only alternative is to wait till the voice of the angel is heard, till the great work of the last dispensation is ushered in. But will we then receive it? Will not our prejudices be as great then as they are now against Mr. Smith? Are there any qualifications that Mr. Smith should possess that he did not possess? Were there any doctrines which he advocated adverse to scriptural doctrine? Were there any principles connected with his system inconsistent with the prophecies? If then perfection characterizes every doctrine embraced in the great scheme of this modern prophet, who can say that he was not sent of God? Who dare oppose so great and perfect a system, without the least shadow of evidence to prove its falsity? Who so lost to every sense of reason and sound judgement, as not to perceive an overwhelming evidence flowing in from every quarter to establish the divine mission of Joseph Smith? Who that has examined his mission or system impartially, can bring even one evidence against it? Are we not bound then to yield, at least, our faith on the side of evidence? What excuse then can the learned, and great and wise of the earth, render for opposing a work of so great importance with nought but ridicule, and slander, and vile reproaches? Let them bring forth their strong reasonings, or else let them hear, and say it is TRUTH.

SIXTH.—The perfect agreement between the prediction of Isaiah (chap. xxix.) and Mr. Smith's account of the finding and translation of the Book of Mormon, is another collateral proof that he was divinely commissioned. Mr. Smith testifies that the plates from which that book was translated were taken *out of the ground*, from where they were originally deposited by the prophet Moroni; that the box containing them was composed of stone, so constructed as to exclude, in a great degree, the moisture of the soil; that with the plates he discovered a Urim and Thummim, through the aid of which he afterwards was enabled to translate the book into the English language. Soon after obtaining the plates, a number of the characters were correctly transcribed, and sent to some of the most learned individuals in the United States, to see if they could translate them. Among the rest, they were presented to Professor Anthon, of New York city. But no man was found able to read them by his own learning or wisdom. Mr. Smith, though an unlearned man, testifies that he was commanded to translate them, through the inspiration of the Holy Ghost, by the aid of the Urim and Thummim, and that the Book of Mormon is that translation. Now, Isaiah says to Israel, "Thou shalt be brought down, and shalt speak out of the ground, and thy speech shall be low out of the dust, and thy voice shall be, as of one that hath a familiar spirit, out of the ground, and thy speech shall whisper out of the dust."

Who cannot perceive the perfect harmony between Isaiah's prediction and Mr. Smith's testimony? Isaiah, as if to impress it upon the minds of those who should live in future generations, gives no less then four repetitions of the same prediction in the same passage, informing us, in the most definite language, that after Israel should be brought down, they should speak in a very familiar manner "out of the ground," and "whisper low out of the dust." Mr. Smith has been an instrument in the hands of God of fulfilling this prediction to the very letter. He has taken "out of the ground" the ancient history of one half of our globe—the sacred records of a great nation of Israel—the writings of a remnant of the tribe of Joseph, who once flourished as a great and powerful nation on the western hemisphere. The mouldering ruins of their ancient forts, and towers, and cities, proclaim their former greatness, in mournful contrast with their present sad condition. They have been brought down like all the rest of Israel; but the words of their ancient prophets "speak out of the ground, and "whisper out of the dust" to the ears of the present generation, revealing in a very "familiar" manner the history of ancient America, which before was entirely unknown to the nations. Isaiah says, that Israel should "speak out of the ground." Mr. Smith says that he obtained the writings of Joseph from "out of the ground." Now, if Mr. Smith had professed that he had got his book as Swedenborg obtained his, or as the Shakers obtained theirs; that is, if he had professed to have obtained this book to usher in this last dispensation in any other way but "out of the ground," we should have had reason to suppose him a deceiver, like Swedenborg and thousands of others. Again, Isaiah says that "the vision of all is become unto you as the words of a book that is sealed, which men deliver to one that is learned, saying, Read this, I pray thee: and he saith, I cannot; for it is sealed: And the book is delivered to him that is not learned, saying, Read this, I pray thee: and he saith, I am not learned. Wherefore the Lord said, Forasmuch as this people draw near me with their mouth, and with their lips do honor me, but have removed their heart far from me, and their fear toward me is taught by the precept of men: Therefore, behold, I will proceed to do a marvellous work among this people, even a marvellous work and a wonder: for the wisdom of their wise men shall perish, and the understanding of their prudent men shall be hid." All this was fulfilled before Mr. Smith was aware that it had been so clearly predicted by Isaiah. He sent the "WORDS of a book" which he found, as before stated, to Professor Anthon. But it was a sealed writing to the learned professor—the aboriginal language of ancient America could not be deciphered by him. He was as much puzzled as the wise men of Babylon were to interpret the unknown writing upon the wall. Human wisdom and learning, in this case, were altogether insufficient. It required another Daniel, who was found in the person of Mr. Smith. What a marvellous work! What a wonder! How the wisdom of the wise and learned was made to perish by the gift of interpretation given to the unlearned! If the Book of Mormon is what it professes to be—a sacred record—then it must be the very book mentioned in Isaiah's prediction; for the

Prophet Nephi, one of the writers of the Book of Mormon, who lived upwards of 2,400 years ago, informs us that their writings should be brought to light in the last days, in fulfillment of Isaiah's prediction; he also delivers a prophecy in relation to the same book, and predicts many events in connenction therewith, which are not mentioned by Isaiah. We here give an extract from his prediction, as also his quotations from Isaiah:

"Behold, in the last days, or in the days of the Gentiles; yea, behold all the nations of the Gentiles, and also the Jews, both those who shall come upon this land, and those who shall be upon other lands; yea, even upon all the lands of the earth; behold, they will be drunken with iniquity, and all manner of abominations; and when that day shall come, they shall be visited of the Lord of Hosts, with thunder, and with earthquake, and with a great noise, and with storm, and with tempest, and with the flame of devouring fire; and all the nations that fight against Zion, and that distress her, shall be as a dream of a night vision; yea, it shall be unto them, even as unto a hungry man which dreameth, and behold he eateth, but he awaketh and his soul is empty; or like unto a thirsty man which dreameth, and behold he drinketh, but he awaketh, and behold he is faint, and his soul hath appetite: yea, even so shall the multitude of all the nations be that fight against mount Zion: for behold, all ye that do iniquity, stay yourselves and wonder, for ye shall cry out, and cry; yea, ye shall be drunken, but not with wine; ye shall stagger, but not with strong drink: for behold, the Lord hath poured out upon you, the spirit of deep sleep. For behold, ye have closed your eyes, and ye have rejected the prophets; and your rulers, and the seers hath He covered because of your iniquity.

"And it shall come to pass, that the Lord God shall bring forth unto you the words of a book, and they shall be the words of them which have slumbered And behold the book shall be sealed: and in the book shall be a revelation from God, from the beginning of the world to the ending thereof. Wherefore, because of the things which are sealed up, the things which are sealed shall not be delivered in the day of the wickedness and abomination of the people. Wherefore the book shall be kept from them. But the book shall be delivered unto a man, and he shall deliver the words of the book, which are the words of those who have slumbered in the dust; and he shall deliver these words unto another; but the words which are sealed he shall not deliver, neither shall he deliver the book. For the book shall be sealed by the power of God, and the revelation which was sealed shall be kept in the book until the own due time of the Lord, that they may come forth; for, behold, they reveal all things from the foundation of the world unto the end thereof. And the day cometh that the words of the book which were sealed, shall be read upon the house-tops; and they shall be read by the power of Christ: and all things shall be revealed unto the children of men which ever have been among the children of men, and which ever will be, even unto the end of the earth. Wherefore at that day when the book shall be delivered unto the man of whom I have spoken, the book shall be hid from the eyes of the world, that the eyes of none shall behold it save it be that three witnesses shall behold it, by the power of God, besides him to whom the book shall be delivered; and they shall testify to the truth of the book, and the things therein. And there is none other which shall view it, save it be a few, according to the will of God, to bear testimony of his word unto the children of men; for the Lord God hath said, that the words of the faithful should speak as if it were from the dead. Wherefore, the Lord God will proceed to bring forth the words of the book; and in the mouth of as many witnesses as seemeth him good, will he establish his word; and wo be unto him that rejecteth the word of God

"But behold, it shall come to pass that the Lord God shall say unto him to whom He shall deliver the book, take these words which are not sealed and deliver them to another, that he may show them unto the learned, saying, read this, I pray thee. And the learned shall say, bring hither the book, and I will read them: and now, because of the glory of the world, and to get gain will they say this, and not for the glory of God. And the man shall say, I cannot bring the book, for it is sealed. Then shall the learned say, I cannot read it. Wherefore it shall come to pass, that the Lord God will deliver again the book and the words thereof to him that is not learned; and the man that is not learned shall say, I am not learned. Then shall the Lord God say unto him, the learned shall not read them, for they have rejected them, and I am able to do mine own work; wherefore, thou shalt read the words which I shall give unto thee. Touch not the things which are sealed, for I will bring them forth in my own due time; for I will show unto the children of men that I am able to do mine own work. Wherefore, when thou hast read the words which I have commanded thee, and obtained the witnesses which I have promised unto thee, then shalt thou seal up the book again, and hide it up unto me, that I may preserve the words which thou hast not read, until I shall see fit in mine own wisdom, to reveal all things unto the children of men. For behold, I am God; and I am a God of miracles: and I will show unto the world that I am the same yesterday, to-day, and for ever; and I work not among the children of men, save it be according to their faith.

"And again it shall come to pass, that the Lord shall say unto him that shall read the words that shall be delivered him, forasmuch as this people draw near unto me with their mouth, and with their lips do honor me, but have removed their hearts far from me, and their fear towards me is taught by the precepts of men, therefore, I will proceed to do a marvellous work among this people, yea, a marvellous work and a wonder; for the wisdom of the wise and learned shall perish, and the understanding of their prudent shall be hid. * * * * * * And in that day shall the deaf hear the words of the book, and the eyes of the blind shall be set out of obscurity and out of darkness; and the meek also shall increase, and their joy shall be in the Lord, and the poor among men shall rejoice in the Holy One of Israel. For assuredly as the Lord liveth they shall see that the terrible one is brought to nought, and the scorner is consumed, and all that watch for iniquity are cut off; and they that make a man an offender for a word, and lay a snare for him that reproveth in the gate, and turn aside the just for a thing of nought. Therefore thus saith the Lord, who redeemed Abraham, concerning the house of Jacob, Jacob shall not now be ashamed, neither shall his face now wax pale. But when he seeth his children, the work of my hands, in the midst of him, they shall sanctify my name, and sanctify the Holy One of Jacob, and shall fear the God of Israel. They also that erred in spirit shall come to understanding, and they that murmured shall learn doctrine."

Here it will at once be perceived that the Book of Mormon is actually the book predicted by Isaiah, or else it must be an imposture. The book mentioned by Isaiah was to have every characteristic which seems to accompany the Book of Mormon. Did Isaiah predict that the "deaf should hear the words of the book, and the eyes of the blind see out of obscurity, and out of darkness?" It has been fulfilled by the coming forth of the Book of Mormon. Did Isaiah say that in the day his predicted book should speak out of the ground, then those who "erred in spirit should come to understanding, and they that murmured should learn doctrine?" It has been fulfilled to the very letter through the instrumentality of the Book of Mormon. Tens of thousands of honest men, who erred in spirit because of the doctrines and precepts of men, have come to understanding. Many points of doctrine which had been in controversy for ages are made perfectly plain in the Book of Mormon; hence those who have murmured because of the darkness and obscurity thrown over the scriptures by human wisdom and learning, have "learned doctrine." Did Isaiah prophesy that when the predicted book should make its appearance, that then "the house of Jacob should no longer be made ashamed, neither should the face of Jacob any more wax pale?" The Book of Mormon has come, declaring that the time is at hand for the gathering of the house of Jacob, no more to be scattered. Did Isaiah perdict that in the day of the revelation of a certain book, "the terrible one should be brought to nought, the scorner be consumed, and all that watch for iniquity be cut off;" and finally, that "all the nations who should fight against Mount Zion, should pass away as the dream of a ngiht vision, and be destroyed by earthquake and the flame of devouring fire?" The Book of Mormon comes testifying that the hour of these judgments is at hand. And finally, there is no circumstance mentioned by Isaiah, connected with the revelation and translation of the book he mentions, but what is connected with the Book of Mormon. If Joseph Smith was an impostor, and wished to palm himself off upon the world as the great prophet who was to usher in the preparatory dispensation for the coming of the Lord, how came he to discover all these minute particulars contained in Isaiah's prophecy, so as to so exactly and perfectly incorporate in his great scheme of imposture each and every one of them? If this illiterate youth was a deceiver, he has far outstretched all the learned divines or impostors of the last eighteen hundred years—he has made his great and extended scheme to harmonize in every particular, not only with the ancient gospel but with the ancient prophecies, and this, too, so perfectly, that no one can detect the delusion. Reader, does not such a scheme savor very strongly of the truth? Does it not require a greater effort of mind to disbelieve such a scheme than it does to believe it? If such a scheme cannot be credited, where is there a scheme or system in the whole world that can be credited? Can you find a scheme more perfect than the one introduced by Mr. Smith? Can you find one equal to it in perfection? Can you find one that contains one-twentieth part of the truth which his system contains? If, then, you doubt the authority of Mr. Smith, how much more ought you to doubt the authority of every other man now on the earth? If Mr. Smith's perfect scheme should be rejected, surely all other schemes or doctrines which can be shown to be ten times more imperfect, should also be rejected. If any are to be received, surely that one should be received which seems to contain all the elements of a true doctrine, and in which there cannot be detected the least evidence of imposture. To invent a scheme apparently every way suited to the last dispensation or preparatory work for the second advent of our Lord—to have that scheme agree in every minute particular with the endless circumstances and numberless events predicted by the ancient prophets, bespeaks a wisdom far superior to that of man: it bespeaks the wisdom of God. This endless train of circumstances—all harmonizing—all combining—all concentrating as it were into one focus—carries with it such irresistible evidence of truth that it is almost impossible for the careful investigator to reject the divinity of Joseph Smith's mission. Like investigating the works of nature, the more he examines the more he perceives the wisdom of the Deity e stamped upon every sentence.

SEVENTH.—According to the Book of Mormon, all of the great western continent, with all the valleys, hills and mountains, riches and resources pertaining thereunto, was given to the remnant of Joseph, as their "land of promise." The Almighty sealed this covenant and promise by an oath, saying, that the land should be given unto them for ever. The western world, including both North and South America, is the "land of promise," to the remnant of Joseph, in the same sense that the land of Palestine is a promised land unto the twelve tribes of Israel. Now this testimony of the Book of Mormon agrees most perfectly with the prophetic blessing placed upon the head of Joseph by the patriarch Jacob; who, just previous to his death, called together his sons and predicted upon each what should befall them or their tribes "in the last days." The blessing upon the tribe of Joseph is as follows:—(*Gen. xlix chap.*) "Joseph is a fruitful bough, even a fruitful bough by a well, whose branches run over the wall: the archers have sorely grieved him, and shot at him, and hated him: but his bow abode in strength, and the arms of his hands were made strong by the hands of the mighty God of Jacob; (from thence is the shepherd, the stone of Israel:) even by the God of thy father, who shall help thee; and by the Almighty, who shall bless thee with blessings of heaven above, blessings of the deep that lieth under, blessings of the breast and of the womb: *the blessings of thy father have prevailed above the blessings of my progenitors, unto the utmost bound of the everlasting hills:* they shall be on the head of Joseph, and on the crown of the head of him that was separate from his brethren." In the preceeding chapter, when blessing the two sons of Joseph, he says, "let them grow into a multitude in the midst of the earth." And again, "his seed shall become a multitude of nations." From this predictions it will be perceived that Jacob prevailed with God, and obtained a greater blessing in behalf of the tribe of Joseph than what Abraham and Isaac, his progenitors, had obtained. While the blessing of Jacob's progenitors was limited to the land of Palestine, Joseph had confirmed upon him a blessing, or country, above, or far greater than Palestine—a country at a distance, represented by "the utmost bounds of the everlasting hills. Some of the "branches" of the "fruitful bough" of Joseph were to spread far abroad from the parent tree—they were to "run over the wall" of the mighty ocean—they were to "become a multitude of nations in the midst of the earth." There, among the "everlasting hills," they were to be "made strong by the hands of the mighty God of Jacob." It was to be there among the "multitude of nations" of the posterity of Joseph, that the "Shepherd—the stone of Israel" was to establish a kingdom, which should break in pieces all other kingdoms, and "fill the whole earth."

In America there is "a multitude of nations," called by us "Indians." These Indians evidently sprang from the same source as is indicated by their color, features, customs, dialects, traditions, etc.; that they are of Israelitish origin is also evident from their religious ceremonies, their language, their traditions, and the discovery of Hebrew inscriptions, etc. If America is not the land given to a branch of Joseph, where or in what part of the globe shall that tribe receive the fulfillment of Jacob's prediction? where, if not in America, has a land been peopled by a multitude of the nations of Joseph? Can a multitude of the nations of Joseph be found in Europe, Asia, or Africa, or in any of the adjoining islands? If not, then America seems to be the only place where that great prediction could receive its accomplishment. The Book of Mormon testifies that America is "the land of Joseph," given to them by promise. Is not this an additional evidence that *Mr. Smith was sent of God?* If Mr. Smith was an impostor, how came he to discover that the tribe of Joseph was to be favored so much above all the other tribes of Israel? Perhaps it may be replied, that it was easy to discover *that* from the scriptures; but, we ask, why did not Swedenborg, Wesley, Irving, or some of the other impostors of former times, make this scriptural discovery, and incorporate it in their pretended dispensations? It would be, at first, thought far more natural to suppose the American Indians to be the ten lost tribes of Israel; indeed, this is the opinion of many of the learned at the present day. Why did not this modern prophet, if a deceiver, form his deceptive scheme more in accordance with the opinions of the learned? or why should he choose a remnant of the tribe of Joseph to people ancient America? Out of the twelve tribes of Israel, why did he select only a branch of one tribe to people this vast continent? All can *now* perceive why the Book of Mormon should profess to be the history of a remnant of one tribe, instead of being the history of the ten tribes. All can see, why America should be represented as a promised land to Joseph, instead of being given to Reuben, Simeon, or any of the other tribes. All can *now* see, though it was not seen at first, that if the Book of Mormon was different from what it now is; that is, if it professed to contain a history of the ten lost tribes; or if it had given the great western continent to any other people, or to any other tribe than that of Joseph, that it would have proved itself false—it would not have been the book or record which the prophets predicted should come forth to usher in the great work of the last days. An impostor would be obliged to take into consideration all these minute circumstances, many of which are in direct opposition to the established traditions of the day, yet none of them could be neglected without proving fatal to his scheme. But Mr. Smith with all the accuracy of a profound mathematician, has combined all the minute elements of both doctrine and prophecy in his grand and wonderful scheme—nothing is wanting. Whatever department of his system is examined it will be found invulnerable. What an invaluable amount of evidence to establish the *divine mission of the Prophet Joseph Smith!*

EIGHTH.—In the Book of Mormon are given the names and locations of numerous cities of great magnitude, which once flourished among the ancient nations of America. The northern portions of South America, and also Central America, were the most densely populated. Splendid edifices, palaces, towers, forts and cities, were reared in all directions. A careful reader of that interesting book, can trace the relative bearings, and distances of many of these cities from each other, and if acquainted with the present geographical features of the country, he can, by the discriptions given in that book, determine, very nearly, the precise spot of ground they once occupied. Now since that invaluable book made its appearance in print, it is a remarkable fact, that the mouldering ruins of many splendid edifices and towers, and magnificent cities of great extent, have been discovered by Catherwood and Stephens in the interior wilds of Central America, in the very region where the ancient cities described in the Book of Mormon were said to exist. Here, then, is a *certain and indisputable evidence* that this illiterate youth—the translator of the Book of Mormon, was inspired of God. Mr. Smith's translation describes the region of country where great and populous cities anciently existed, together with their relative bearings and approximate distances from each other. Years after, Messrs. Catherwood and Stephens discovered the ruins of forty four of these very cities and in the very place described. What, but the power of God, could have revealed beforehand this unknown fact, demonstrated years after by actual discovery?

NINTH.—The fulfillment of a vast number of prophecies delivered by Mr. Smith is another infallible evidence of his divine 'mission. Out of the many hundreds of fulfilled predictions uttered by him, we select the following as examples:

1. Soon after Mr. Smith found the plates, he commenced translating them. He had not proceeded far before he discovered from his own translation of the prophecy of Nephi, as before quoted, the THREE WITNESSES, besides himself, should behold the book by the power of God, and should know and testify of its truth. Some length of time after this, or in the month of June, A. D. 1829, the Lord gave a revelation, through Mr. Smith, to Oliver Cowdery, David Whitmer and Martin Harris, promising them that if they would exercise faith, they should have a view of the plates, and also of the Urim and Thummim. This prediction was afterwards fulfilled; and these three persons send forth their written testimony, in connection with the Book of Mormon, to all nations, kindreds, tongues and people, declaring that an angel of God descended from heaven, and took the plates and exhibited them before their eyes; and that at the same time, the voice of the Lord from the heavens testified to them of the truth contained in Mr. Smith's translation of these records. Now an impostor might indeed predict the raising of THREE WITNESSES, but he could never call down an angel from heaven, in the presence of these WITNESSES, to fulfill his prediction.

2. Before the Church of Jesus Christ of Latter-day Saints had any existence upon the earth, the prophecy of Moroni was translated and printed in the Book of Mormon. It is expressly predicted in this prophecy, that in the day that that book should be revealed, "the blood of the Saints should cry unto the Lord from the ground," because of the wickedness of the people, and that the "time should soon come when," because of the cries and mourning of "widows and orphans," whose husbands and fathers should be slain by wicked hands, "the Lord should avenge the blood of his Saints." And again, in August, 1831, the word of the Lord came to Mr. Smith, saying that "the Saints should be scourged from city to city, and from synagogue to synagogue," and that but FEW of those then in the Church should "stand to receive an inheritance."—(*See Book of Doctrine and Cove-*

*nauts, page* 235.) The blood of many hundreds of Saints who have been slain and martyred in this Church, is an incontrovertible evidence of the truth of the prediction. Surely Mr. Smith must have been a prophet of God to have foreseen not only the rise of the Church of the Saints, but that their blood should cry aloud from the ground for vengeance upon the nation who should perpetrate these bloody deeds. No human foresight could have seen the bloody sceneries that were to take place after the rise of the Church. All natural appearances in the United States were against the fulfillment of this dreadful prediction. Every religious society throughout the whole country was strongly guarded against persecution and religious intolerance by the strong arm of the civil law. The glorious constitution of this great and free people proclaimed religious freedom to every son and daughter of Columbia's soil: yet, in the midst of this boasted land of freedom and religious rights, where universal peace seemed to have selected her quiet dwelling-place, the voice of the great prophet is heard predicting the rise of the Latter-day Church, and the bloody persecutions that should follow her "from city to city, and from synagogue to synagogue." Never were there any prophecies more literally and palpably fulfilled since the creation of the earth. If the foretelling of future events that could not possibly have been foreseen by human wisdom— events, too, that to all outward appearances were very unlikely to come to pass: if the predicting of such events and their subsequent fulfillment constitutes a true prophet, then Joseph Smith must have been a true prophet, and, if a true prophet, *he must have been sent of God.*

TENTH.—There are many thousands of living witnesses who testify that God has revealed unto them the truth of the Book of Mormon, by dreams, by visions, by the revelations of the Holy Ghost, by the ministering of angels, and by His own voice. Now, if Mr. Smith is an impostor, all these witnesses must be impostors also. Perhaps it may be said, that these witnesses are not impostors, but are deceived themselves. But, we ask, can any man testify that he KNOWS a false doctrine to be true, and still not be an impostor? Men frequently are deceived when they testify their *opinions* but never deceived when they testify they have a *knowledge*. Such must either be impostors, or else their doctrine must be true. Now, would it not be marvelously strange indeed, if even three or four men, who were entirely disconnected, being strangers to each other, should all undertake to deceive mankind by testifying that an angel of God had descended before them, or that a heavenly vision had been shown to them, or that God had in some other marvellous way manifested to them the divine authenticity of the Book of Mormon? If the testimony of three or four impostors would appear marvelous, how infinately more marvelous would appear the testimony of tens of thousands of impostors in different countries, widely separated from each other, and who never saw each others faces, and yet all endeavoring to palm upon the world the same great imposition! If many thousands of witnesses do testify boldly, with words of soberness, that God has revealed to them that this is His church or kingdom that was to be set up in the last days, then we have an overwhelming flood of collateral evidences to establish the divine mission of Joseph Smith.

ELEVENTH.—The miracles wrought by Joseph Smith are evidences of no small moment to establish his divine authority. In the name of the Lord he cast out devils, healed the sick, spoke with new tongues, interpreted ancient languages, and predicted future events. Many of these miracles were wrought before numerous multitudes of both believers and unbelievers, and upon persons not connected with our Church. And again, the numerous miracles wrought through the instrumentality of thousands of the officers and members of this Church, are additional evidences that the man who was instrumental in founding the Church *must have been sent of God*. The thousands of sick that have been miraculously healed in all parts of the world where this gospel is preached, give forth a strong and almost irresisitble testimony that Mr. Smith's authority is "from heaven." Although the great majority of mankind consider miracles to be an *infallible* evidence in favor of the divine authority of the one who performs them, yet we do most distinctly dissent from this idea. If miracles be admitted as an *infallible* evidence, then all that have ever wrought miracles must have been sent of God. The magicians of Egypt wrought some splendid miracles before that nation; they created serpents and frogs, and turned rivers of water into blood. If miraculous evidence is *infallible*, the Egyptians were bound to receive the contradictory messages of both Moses and the magicians as of divine authority. According to this idea, the witch of Endor must have established her divine mission beyond all controversy by calling forth a dead man from the grave in the presence of Saul, king of Israel. A certain wicked power described by John (*Rev. xiii. chap.*) was to do "great wonders" and "miracles," and cause "fire to come down from heaven on the earth in the sight of men." If miracles were infallible evidences, surely no one should reject the divine authority of John's beast. Again in (*Rev. xvi. chap.*) "John saw three unclean spirits like frogs," which he expressly says, *are the* SPIRITS OF DEVILS WORKING MIRACLES, *which go forth unto the kings of the earth and of the whole world to gather them to the battle of that great day of God Almighty.*" The learned divines and clergy of the nineteenth century boldly declare that "miracles are an INFALLIBLE evidence of the divine mission of the one who performs them." If so, who can blame "the kings of the earth," and these learned divines, and all their followers for embracing the message of these divinely inspired devils? For, according to their arguments, they should in no wise reject them, for they prove their mission by evidences which they say are infallible. We shall expect in a few years, to see an innumerable host of sectarian ministers as well as kings, taking up their line of march for the great valley of "Armageddon," near Jerusalem, and thus prove by their works that they do really believe in the *infallibility of miraculous evidence.* Devils can work miracles as well as God, and as they have already persuaded the religious world that miracles are infallible evidences of divine authority, they will not have much difficulty among the followers of modern christianity in establishing the divinity of their mission. But the Latter-day Saints do not believe in the infallibility of miraculous evidence. We believe the miraculous gifts are absolutely necessary in the church of Christ, without which it cannot exist on the earth. Miracles, when taken in connection with a pure, holy, and perfect doctrine, reasonable and scriptural, is a very strong collateral evidence in favor of that doctrine, and of the divine authority of those who preach it. But abstract miracles alone, unconnected with other evidences, instead of being *infallible* proofs are no proofs at all: they are as likely to be *false* as true. So baptism "for the remission of sins" is essential in the church of Christ, and when taken in connection with all other points of doctrine embraced in the gospel, is a presumptive evidence for the divine authority of the person who preaches it. But baptism "for the remission of sins," unconnected with other parts of the doctrine of Christ, would be no evidence either for or against the divine authority of any man. The many thousands of miracles wrought in this Church, being connected as they are with an infallible doctrine, and with a vast number of other proofs, have carried an almost irresistible conviction to the minds of vast multitudes, who have, in consequence, yielded obedience to the message, and become in their turn the happy recipients of the same power of God, by which they themselves can also heal the sick and work by faith in the name of the Lord; thus demonstrating to themselves the truth of the Savior's promise, viz:—that certain miraculous "signs shall follow them that believe."—(*See Mark, chapter xvi.*)

There is one thing connected with Joseph Smith's message which will at once prove him to be an impostor or else a true prophet. It is a certain promise contained in a revelation which was given through him to the apostles of this Church in the year 1832. It reads as follows

"Go ye into all the world, and whatsoever place ye cannot go into ye shall send, that the testimony may go from you into all the world unto every creature.

"And as I said unto mine apostles, even so I say unto you, for you are mine apostles, even God's High Priests; ye are they whom my Father hath given me—ye are my friends;

"Therefore, as I said unto mine apostles I say unto you again, that every soul who believeth on your words, and is baptized by water for the remission of sins, shall receive the Holy Ghost;

"And these signs shall follow them that believe.

"In my name they shall do many wonderful works;

'In my name they shall cast out devils;

'In my name they shall heal the sick ;

'In my name they shall open the eyes of the blind, and unstop the ears of the deaf,

"And the tongue of the dumb shall speak,

"And if any man shall administer poison unto them it shall not hurt them

"And the poison of a serpent shall not have power to harm them.   *   *   *   Verily, verily, I say unto you they who believe not on your words, and are not baptized in water, in my name, for the remission of their sins, that they may receive the Holy Ghost, shall be damned, and shall not come into my Father's kingdom, where my Father and I am

"And this revelation unto you, and commandment, is in force from this very hour upon all the world "  (*Doctrine and Covenants, page* 294, 295.)

Here, then, this great modern prophet has presented himself before the whole world with a bold unequivocal promise to every soul who would believe on his message—a promise, too, that no impostor would dare to make with the most distant hope of success.  An impostor might indeed make such a promise to his followers, but they never would realize a fulfillment of it.  If these miraculous signs have not followed according to the above promise, then the tens of thousands who have complied with the conditions would know Joseph Smith to be an impostor, and with one accord would turn away, and that would be the end of the imposition.  But the very fact that vast multitudes are annually being added to the Church, and continue therein year after year, is a demostrative evidence that the promise is fulfilled—that the Holy Ghost is given, and the miraculous signs also.  Dare any other societies in all the world make such a promise unto the believers in their respective systems?  No, they dare not; they know full well that it would be the speedy downfall and utter overthrow of their vain, unauthorized, and powerless religions.  O, what a wide and marked difference between the religion of Joseph Smith and that of Protestant and Catholic religion—between his authority and that of sectarian divines! The one promises all the miraculous gifts of the Holy Ghost, to his followers, the other is as powerless as the dry stubble prepared for the burning. While the followers of this great prophet cast out devils, speak with new tongues, heal the sick, open the eyes of the blind, cause the lame to walk, obtain heavenly visions, and converse with angels, the followers of those unauthorized, deluded and crafty sects not only deny these great and glorious gifts, or impute them in these days to the power of the devil, but they grasp the sword, and fire-arms, and deadly weapons, to kill off the Saints, and drive them from the face of what they call civilized society. While the one class are suffering martyrdom by scores for their testimony, the other class are rolling in all the luxuries and splendors of great Babylon, with fat salaries of from ten to twenty-seven thousand pounds sterling per annum.

As we have briefly examined into the nature of the evidences in favor of Joseph Smith's divine mission, it may be well at the close of this number to give a short summary of the proofs and arguments contained in the foregoing.

1. Joseph Smith's doctrine is reasonable, scriptural, perfect and infallible in all its precepts, commands, ordinances, promises, blessings and gifts. In his organization of the Church, no officer mentioned in the New Testament organization is omitted. Inspired apostles and prophets are considered as necessary as pastors, teachers, or any other officer.

2. Joseph Smith's account of the restoration of the gospel by an angel—of his taking out of the ground the sacred records of the tribe of Joseph—of their subsequent translation by the gift of God—and of the great western continent's being given to a remnant of Joseph, where they have grown into a multitude of nations, are all events clearly predicted by the ancient Jewish apostles and prophets, together with the minute circumstances connected therewith. The times and seasons in which these events should transpire, and the purposes which they should accomplish are also all plainly foretold. Joseph Smith presents the world with the fulfillment at the predicted time— in the predicted manner—and for the predicted purpose as anciently specified.

3. Joseph Smith incorporates in his mission the gathering of the Saints out of Babylon, and every other predicted event that was to characterize the great preparatory dispensation for the second advent of our Lord.

4. The revelation in the Book of Mormon, pointing out the location of many ancient cities, the ruins of which were subsequently discovered by Catherwood and Stephens—the direct and palpable fulfillment of many of the prophecies of Joseph Smith, which no human sagacity could have foreseen, all natural appearances and circumstances being entirely against their expected fulfillment—the raising up of numerous other witnesses who also testify to the ministering of angels and the manifestations of the power of God confirmatory of this message—the performance of many splendid miracles by Mr. Smith and his followers; and the bold unequivocal promise of the miraculous gifts to all who should believe and embrace this message, are all evidences such as no impostor ever has given, or ever can give. They are evidences such as will prove the salvation of every creature that receives the message, and the damnation of every soul that rejects it.

# THE KINGDOM OF GOD.

### BY ORSON PRATT,
ONE OF THE TWELVE APOSTLES OF THE CHURCH OF JESUS CHRIST OF LATTER-DAY SAINTS.

## CHAPTER I.

THE NATURE AND CHARACTER OF THE KING—THE CHARACTER AND REQUISITE QUALIFICATIONS OF THE SUBORDINATE OFFICERS.

THE kingdom of God is an order of government established by divine authority. It is the only legal government that can exist in any part of the universe. All other governments are illegal and unauthorized. God, having made all beings and worlds, has the supreme right to govern them by His own laws, and by officers of His own appointment. Any people attempting to govern themselves by laws of their own making, and by officers of their own appointment, are in direct rebellion against the kingdom of God. The antediluvians were overthrown by a flood, because they rejected the government of the Almighty, and instituted their own governments in its stead. Noah and his family were the only loyal and obedient subjects to the legal power: they alone were saved. The universal desolation and utter abolishment of all the unauthorized man-made governments of the old world, should have been an everlasting warning to all future generations to avoid the same rebellion, and to establish no governments on the earth of human origin. But alas! the posterity of Noah soon revolted from the only legal, rightful power, and set up for themselves forms of governments of their own inventions. The rebellion soon became so general, that all the inhabitants of the earth, except Melchizedek, Abraham, Lot, and a very few others, engaged themselves in it, supporting and upholding kings and other officers in their usurped authority, and suffering themselves to be governed by human laws, instead of revealed laws from God. From that time until the present, empires, kingdoms, principalites, republics, and numerous other corrupt, illegal, unauthorized powers, have multiplied themselves in the four quarters of the globe. At various times, during the last four thousand years, God has asserted His rights, and endeavored to establish His own authority, His own laws, and His own government among the children of men. But so great was the opposition manifested by those illegal, rebellious powers, that His government while on earth was exceedingly limited in numbers. The vast majority of mankind made war against it—overcame, killed, and destroyed its officers and loyal subjects, until not a vestige of it was left remaining on the earth. For seventeen hundred years the nations, upon the eastern hemisphere have been entirely destitute of the *kingdom of God*—entirely destitute of a true and legal government—entirely destitute of officers legally authorized to rule and govern. All the emperors, kings, princes, presidents, lords and rulers, during that long night of darkness, have acted without authority. Not one of them was called or anointed a king or a prince by the God of heaven—not one of them received his office or appointment by Him—not one of them has received revelations or laws from Him—not one of them has received any communication whatsoever from the rightful sovereign, the great King. Their authority is all assumed—it originated in man. Their laws are not from the great Lawgiver, but the production of their own false governments. Their very foundations were laid in rebellion, and the whole superstructure, from first to last, is a heterogeneous mass of discordant elements, in direct opposition to the kingdom of God, which is the only true government which should be recognized on earth or in heaven.

The kingdom of God is a theocracy. And as it is the only form of government which will redeem and save mankind, it is necessary that every soul should be rightly and thoroughly instructed in regard to its nature and general characteristics. The beauty, glory, power, wisdom and order of the kingdom of God may be more fully understood by a careful examination of the following subjects.

First.—*The nature and character of the King.*

Second.—*The character and requisite qualifications of the subordinate officers.*

Third.—*The nature and character of the laws of adoption, or the invariable rule by which aliens are admitted into the kingdom as citizens.*

Fourth.—*The nature and character of the laws given for the government of all adopted citizens.*

Fifth.—*The character, disposition, and qualifications necessary for every citizen to possess.*

Sixth.—*The rights, privileges, and blessings enjoyed by the subjects in this life.*

Seventh.—*The rights, privileges, and blessings promised to the faithful, obedient subjects in a future life.*

Dear reader, your future well-being in all time to come depends upon your rightly understanding these seven subjects. Read, therefore, with serious attention, and your mind shall be opened to see things that you never saw before; things too of infinite importance, without which you can in no wise be saved. Let us begin by examining—

First.—*The nature and character of the King.* God is the King. In Him exists all legal authority. He alone has the right of originating a system of government on the earth. He claims this right by virtue of His having made man and the earth he inhabits.. Man, therefore, is indebted to God for his own formation and for the formation of the planet on which he dwells. He also claims the right of establishing His government among men, by virtue of His superior wisdom and power. If God had sufficient wisdom and power to construct such a beautiful world as this, with all the infinite varieties of vegetables. and animals appended to it; if He could form such an intricate and complicated piece of machinery as the human tabernacle as a dwelling-place for the human spirit, then we must admit that His wisdom and power are immeasurably greater than that of man, and hence He is qualified to reign as king. An order of government, established by such an all-wise, powerful being, must be good and perfect, and must be calculated to promote the permanent peace, happiness, and well-being of all His subjects. The great King is a very amiable being, full of benevolence and goodness, and never turns any person away empty, that comes requesting a favor which He sees would be for his benefit.

The King occasionally visited His subjects in ancient times, and once tarried with them for several years but He received such cruel abuse from many of the people that He left them, and went to some other part of His dominions. Where the King is gone the people cannot tell. They have not heard one word from Him for upwards of seventeen hundred years. He has been absent so long, that some of the people have doubted even His extistence. They have argued that if He did exist, that some one would very likely have heard something from him in the course of so many centuries. Many millions however have some idea that He exists, and are constantly sending all kinds of petitions to Him; but for some reason He sends no word back. No messengers are dispatched to the petitioners, to give them any counsel upon any subject. It has become a very popular thing to send daily petitions to the King, and to appropriate one day out of seven for the especial purpose of sending in their petitions. The same petitions are frequently sent a great number of times. It is very unpopular however for any one to expect the King to make any reply to any petitions sent in. Any one pretending to have received a reply would be counted a base impostor; for, say they, the King has spoken to no one for the last seventeen hundred years; no one has heard from Him since He conversed with His servant John on the isle of Patmos. The King conversed very freely with His subjects in the early and middle ages; and some think it very strange that He has been silent so long. They have expended millions in building many costly and magnificent churches in honor of His name, but yet He has not deigned to grace one of them with a visit, neither has He condescended to send any tidings to them by a messenger or otherwise. He has not informed them whether He was pleased or displeased with their splendid edifices. His profound silence for so many centuries has caused many to think, that He was, for some reason, very angry with the people; yet they could not see why He should be angry when the people were doing so much honor to Him—when they were expending millions to hire learned men to preach and write in such an eloquent manner about Him.

Reader, can you tell why the King should be so distant? Why He holds no communication with any of the people? Why He has not sent one sentence of consolation or counsel to them? Why He has suffered some fifteen thousand millions of the human race to fall into their graves, in the latter ages without condescending to speak one word to any of them? There must be some cause for all this. There must be something wrong. The King never formerly served His people in this manner; and when He went away, He left word that if any of His people lacked wisdom or knowledge on any subject, they should send in their petition to Him, and He would liberally send them the requisite information.

I will now tell you the reason why the King has kept silence so long. It is because He has had no subjects to converse with; all have turned away from Him and advocated other governments as being the rightful and legal authority. They killed off, and utterly destroyed, every true subject of His kingdom, and left not a vestige of it upon the earth; and, to add to their guilt and wickedness, they have introduced idolatry in its worst forms, and utterly turned away from the true and living God. They have introduced a *God without* BODY, PARTS *or* PASSIONS. They have had the audacity to call this newly-invented god by the same name as the God of the ancient saints, although there is not the least resemblance between them. Indeed there could be no resemblance between them; for a bodiless god, without *parts or passions*, could resemble nothing in heaven, on earth, or in hell. This imaginary modern god has become exceedingly popular. It is to him that a vast number of churches have been erected. It is not to the true and living God that they send forth petitions, but it is to this imaginary being. No wonder that they have

The Godhead consists of the Father, the Son, and the Holy Spirit. The Father is a material being. The substance of which He is composed is wholly material. It is a substance widely different, in some respects, from the various substances with which we are more immediately acquainted. In other respects it is precisely like all other materials. The substance of His person occupies space the same as other matter. It has solidity, length, breadth, and thickness, like all other matter. The elementary materials of His body are not susceptible of occupying, at the same time, the same identical space with other matter. The substance of His person, like other matter, cannot be in two places at the same instant. It also requires *time* for Him to transport Himself from place to place. It matters not how great the velocity of His movements, *time* is an essential ingredient to all motion, whether rapid or slow. It differs from other matter in the superiority of its powers, being intelligent, all wise, and possessing the power of self-motion to a far greater extent than the coarser materials of nature. "God is a *spirit.*" But that does not make Him an immaterial being —a being that has no properties in common with matter. The expression *an immaterial being*, is a contradiction in terms. Immateriality is only another name for nothing. It is the negative of all existence. A *spirit* is as much *matter* as oxygen or hydrogen. It has many properties in common with all other matter. Chemists have discovered between fifty and sixty kinds of matter, and each kind has some properties in common with all other matter, and some properties peculiar to itself which the others do not inherit. Now, no chemist, in classifying his substances, would presume to say—This substance is material, but that one is immaterial, because it differs in some respects from the first. He would call them all material though they in some respect differed widely. So the substance called spirit is material, though it differs in a remarkable degree from other substances. It is only the addition of another element of a more powerful nature than any yet discovered. He is not a being "without *parts*," as modern idolators teach, for every whole is made up of parts. The whole person of the Father consists of innumerable parts; and each part is so situated as to bear certain relations of distance to every other part. There must also be, to a certain degree, a freedom of motion among these parts, which is an essential condition to the movement of His limbs, without which He could only move as a whole.

All the foregoing statements in relation to the person of the Father, are equally applicable to the person of the Son.

The Holy Spirit being one part of the Godhead, is also a material substance, of the same nature and properties in many respects, as the spirits of the Father and Son. It exists in vast immeasurable quantities in connection with all material worlds. This is called God in the scriptures, as well as the Father and Son. God the Father and God the Son cannot be everywhere present; indeed they cannot be even in two places at the same instant; but God the Holy Spirit is omnipresent—it extends through all space, intermingling with all other matter, yet no one atom of the Holy Spirit can be in two places at the same instant, which in all cases is an absolute impossiblity. It must exist in inexhaustible quantities, which is the only possible way for any substance to be omnipresent. All the innumerable phenomena of universal nature are produced in their origin by the actual presence of this intelligent, all-wise, and all-powerful material substance called the Holy Spirit. It is the most active matter in the universe, producing all its operations according to fixed definite laws enacted by itself, in conjunction with the Father and Son. What are called the laws of nature are nothing more or less than the fixed method by which this spiritual matter operates. Each atom of the Holy Spirit is intelligent, and, like all other matter, has solidity, form, and size, and occupies space. Two atoms of this Spirit cannot occupy the same space at the same time, neither can one atom, as before stated, occupy two separate spaces, at the same time. In all these respects it does not differ in the least from all other matter. Its distinguishing characteristics from other matter are its almighty powers and infinite wisdom, and many other glorious attributes which other materials do not possess. If several of the atoms of this Spirit should unite themselves together into the form of a person, then this person of the Holy Spirit would be subject to the same necessity as the two other persons of the Godhead,

that is, it could not be everywhere present. No finite number of atoms can be omnipresent; an infinite number of atoms is requisite to be *everywhere* in infinite space. Two persons receiving the gift of the Holy Spirit, do not each receive at the same time the same identical particles, though they each receive a substance exactly similar in kind. It would be as impossible for each to receive the same identical atoms at the same instant, as it would be for two men at the same time to drink the same identical pint of water. It is these three all-powerful substances that stand at the head of all legal government. All governments, not established by these three, will be ere long overthrown. They hold the supreme authority and power in heaven, and in the heaven of heavens, and throughout the wide expanse of universal nature. All principalities, powers, and kingdoms, whether in heaven or on earth, must yield to be instructed and controlled by the supreme power, or they cannot stand.

SECOND.—*The character and requisite qualifications of the subordinate officers in the kingdom of God* are now to be considered. As the persons of the Father and Son cannot be everywhere present, it is therefore impossible for them to attend in *person* to all the multiplied affairs of government among intelligent beings; therefore, God, in establishing a government among such beings, has always called persons of their own number to officiate in His name. The character of these persons, previously to their calling and appointment, has generally been that of honesty and sincerity; otherwise they have not differed materially from other men.

The various officers, called of God to administer the affairs of His government, are apostles, prophets, bishops, evangelists, elders, pastors, teachers, and deacons. God has only one way of calling these different officers, and that is by *new revelation*. No person was ever authorized to act in the name of the Lord, unless called by *new revelation*. Paul says (*Heb. v.* 4), "No man taketh this honor unto himself, but he that is called of God as was Aaron." Among the vast number of national governments now upon the earth, where is there one that even professes to be the kingdom of God, or that its officers were called of God as was Aaron?

Human authority and human calling are the only powers which any nation professes to have. But there are certain petty governments, called churches, organized within these national governments, which claim divine authority, and consider their officers authorized to act in the name of the Lord. But the great question is, have any of them been called as Aaron was? By *new revelation* Aaron was called. By *new revelation* the duties of his calling were made known. Have any of the Roman Catholic or Protestant officers been called by *new revelation?* Has God said one word to any of them? Do they not, with very few exceptions, declare that "There is no later revelation than the *New Testament?*" If the revelations contained in the New Testament are the last ones given, then the persons to whom they were given, were the last ones called of God. When *new revelation* ceases to be given, officers cease to be called of God. When the calling of officers cease, the kingdom of God ceases to be perpetuated upon the earth. Nothing is more certain than that the church of God ceased to exist on the earth when new revelation ceased to be given. All the modern Christian churches, who deny new revelation, have no more authority to preach, baptize, or administer any other ordinance of the gospel than the idolatrous Hindoos have; indeed all their administrations are worse than in vain—they are a solemn mockery in the sight of God. It is a grievous sin in the sight of God for any man to presume to baptize, unless God has authorized him by new revelation to baptize in His name. Saul, the king of Israel, lost his kingdom because he assumed the authority that did not belong to him (*I. Sam. xiii.* 8-15). Another king of Israel was smote with leprosy until the day of his death, because he attempted to administer an ordinance without being called and authorized (*II. Chron. xxvi.* 16-22). So all the baptisms and sacraments administered by modern Christian churches who have done away with new revelation, are an abomination in the sight of God. All persons who shall suffer themselves to be baptized, or partake of these ordinances through the administration of these illegal unauthorized persons, after having been duly warned of the evil thereof, will bring themselves under great condemnation before God, and unless they repent of that sin they can in nowise be saved. The twelve apostles were called by new revelation, but that did not authorize Paul, Barnabas, Timothy, or any other person. Each one had to receive a separate call by new revelation for himself. No one could lawfully act under a commission given to some other person. All the commissions recorded in the New Testament were given to individuals then living, and not to any individuals who should live in some future age. If any persons would have authority, let them obtain a new commission from God, as His servants always did in ancient times, and if they officiate without such new commission, then know assuredly that they are impostors.

The subordinate officers in the kingdom of God must not only be called of God, but qualified to act in their respective offices. The first qualification absolutely necessary for every officer in the kingdom is, *the gift of the Holy Spirit*. This is the most important qualfiication of all others. No man, without this qualification, can attain to an office in the kingdom of God; it matters not how great his other attainments are; though he has studied the scriptures from a child, and committed them all to memory—though he has carefully learned the original languages in which they were written—though he has made himself master of all sciences—grasped with a comprehensive mind all the arguments set forth in theological works, yet none of these attainments will qualify him for even the least office in the kingdom of God. The unlearned youth, who had not the knowledge of the English alphabet, if he were called of God, and qualified by the gift of the Holy Spirit, would have more power and authority, and could do more towards saving men, than all the theologians and doctors of divinity that the world affords, unless they also were called of God, and endowed with the gift of the Holy Ghost. No other qualification whatsoever can be substituted in the stead of the Holy Spirit. The Holy Spirit is the great distinguishing characteristic between the officers of the kingdom of God and impostors. Every officer sent of God has a qualification that no impostor ever had or ever can have.

The first officers placed in the kingdom of God are apostles. Let us inquire how in ancient times this office was conferred on man. Jesus said to His ancient apostles (*John xv.* 16),

"Ye have not chosen Me, but I have chosen you, and ordained you, that ye should go and bring forth fruit." Paul informs us (*Heb. iii.* 1) that Jesus Himself was an apostle. Holding the office Himself, He had the most perfect right to confer the same calling upon others; hence He first *chose* them, and then *ordained* them; after this He sent them forth to preach (*Matthew x.*), "and commanded them, saying, Go not into the way of the Gentiles, and into any city of the Samaritans, enter ye not: but go rather to the lost sheep of the house of Israel. And as ye go, preach, saying, The kingdom of heaven is at hand. Heal the sick, cleanse the lepers, raise the dead, cast out devils: freely ye have received, freely give." Although these apostles were chosen, ordained, and sent forth on a particuliar mission to the cities of Israel, with power to work mighty miracles, yet there was an essential qualification which they had not yet received. They had received power sufficient to qualify them to preach that the "kingdom of heaven" was at hand. But they had not yet received power sufficient to fully organize and build up that kingdom on the earth. They lacked one very important qualification, without which they could never establish the kingdom which they had already predicted "was at hand." What was this further qualification which these apostles had not yet received? It was the gift of the Holy Ghost, or the other Comforter which Jesus promised them. It is very remarkable that these apostles should have such great power, and yet not have the Holy Ghost. But hear what the scripture saith (*John vii.* 37, 38, 39), "In the last day, that great day of the feast, Jesus stood and cried, saying, If any man thirst, let him come unto Me, and drink. He that believeth on Me, as the scripture hath said, out of his belly shall flow rivers of living water. (But this spake He of the Spirit, which they that believe on Him should receive: *for the Holy Ghost was not yet given; because that Jesus was not yet glorified.*)" Mark the expression, *the Holy Ghost was not yet given.* This agrees with another saying of Jesus to His apostles (*John xvi.* 7). "Nevertheless, I tell you the truth; it is expedient for you that I go away: for if I go not away, the Comforter will not come unto you; but if I depart I will send Him unto you."

Jesus calls this Comforter the Holy Ghost (*John xiv.* 26). After the resurrection of Jesus, and as He was about to be taken up into heaven, He said to His apostles (*Luke xxiv.* 49), "Behold I send the promise of my Father upon you," (alluding to the Comforter or the Holy Ghost, which He promised several days before should be sent unto them from the Father after His glorification); "but," said He, "tarry ye in the city of Jerusalem, until ye be endued with power from on high." Thus you see, dear reader, that these apostles had power to "heal the sick, cleanse the lepers, raise the dead, and cast out devils," although the Holy Ghost was not yet given to them. A certain power was yet lacking. Jesus had commanded them, saying, "Go ye into all the world and preach the gospel to every creature." But He would not suffer them to commence this mission until the promise of the Father—the Holy Ghost—was given to them. They already had power to work mighty miracles, but had not the power to build up the kingdom of God. This power they were to tarry for in Jerusalem, and when they should receive it, they were then to commence the duties of their mission, first, in the city of Jerusalem, and afterwards extend their labors to all nations. The power to work miracles is entirely a different thing from the power to build up the kingdom of God: the latter power, however, always includes the former, but the former power does not always include the latter.

We now ask, Where is there a man among all the churches of modern times, who has been called to the office of an apostle by *new revelation?* Where is there a man among all the millions of modern Christians who has been ordained to the office of an apostle, under the hands of an apostle, as the twelve were anciently? Where is there a man to be found among all the Catholics or Protestants who has been endowed with even the power of working miracles, to say nothing of the still greater power communicated in the gift of the Holy Ghost? If the apostles in ancient days could not build up the kingdom of God, without being endowed with these two degrees of power, surely no one since their day could be authorized to build the church of God with any less qualification.

One of the important duties required of an apostle is to ADMINISTER THE SPIRIT. In II. Cor. iii. 6, we read that both Paul and Timothy were made able ministers of the Spirit. The ordinance through which the Spirit is ministered is THE LAYING ON OF HANDS. (*Acts viii.* and *xix. Heb. vi*) To the apostles were entrusted three very important ministrations for the salvation of man:—

First.—*The ministration of the word*

Second.—*The ministration of the baptism of water.*

And Third.—*The ministration of the baptism of the Spirit.*

While Jesus was with His apostles in person, they had power to minister the *word* and *water*, but not the *Spirit*, for they themselves had not yet been baptized with the Spirit, and they could not administer that which they were not in possession of. It was necessary that they should first receive the gift themselves, before they could confer it upon others. Hence we can perceive the propriety of Jesus commanding them to wait at Jerusalem until they should be "endued with power from on high;" for without this additional power they could neither save themselves nor others. Many persons have flattered themselves that they can be saved without the assistance of a minister sent of God. But this is a vain, delusive hope, for Jesus hath expressly said, "Except a man be born of water and of the Spirit he *cannot* enter the kingdom of God." Now as no man can be saved out of the kingdom, it is necessary that he should be "born" into the kingdom, and this would be impossible without an administrator sent of God, for the birth or baptism of water, and the birth or baptism of the Spirit, require some one legally authorized to officiate in behalf of the candidate.

Reader, have you ever received the Holy Ghost through the laying on of the hands of one sent of God? If not, you are not yet born of the Spirit. You are not yet a child of the kingdom. Know assuredly, that unless you find some man who has been sent by the command of God as was Aaron, and get him to remit your sins through your faith, repentance and baptism, and have him to minister to you the Holy Ghost, as did the ancient apostles—you need not flatter yourself that you can be saved. Do not deceive yourself upon this all-important subject. Do not suffer any man to baptize or minister unto you, unless God has spoken unto him by the voice of His servants, and authorized him to minister in His name. Do you inquire how you are to know an authorized man of God from one who has no authority? I will tell you how to discern the difference. A true servant of God will never teach a false doctrine. He will never deny new revelation. He never will tell you that the canon of scripture is full, or that the New Testament is the last revelation ever intended to be given to man. He never will tell you that miraculous gifts are no longer necessary in the Church of God. He never will tell you that inspired apostles, prophets and other officers are not requisite in the Church now. He never will tell you that the *ministration of the spirit*, by "the laying on of hands," is done away by God's appointment. But he will tell you that if you will receive his message, and be baptized by one having authority, that your *sins shall be remitted*, and that you shall be filled with the Holy Ghost by the laying on of hands; and that you shall know, by the teachings thereof, that his doctrine is true and of God. In this respect he will differ from all impostors; for an impostor never had power to *minister the spirit*. An impostor dare not promise you that you shall be filled with the Holy Ghost by the laying on of his hands, for he knows that such a promise would not be fulfilled—he knows that you would detect him to be a false teacher by complying with his conditions, and failing to receive his promise. An impostor, knowing that he has no power to give the Holy Ghost as the ancient apostles had, will endeavor to persuade you that such power is not necessary now. He knows very well, that if he cannot get the people to believe that such power is not necessary in these days, that his own unauthorized pretensions will be at once detected.

An impostor, like Simon Magus, may deceive ignorant people by witchcraft and sorcery, but he can never deceive them by pretending to give the Holy Ghost through prayer and laying on of hands. This is a power that none but a true minister of God possesses; it cannot be counterfeited by the devil. The devil can counterfeit the miracles of

Christ, but he cannot counterfeit the gift of the Holy Ghost. None but the lawful ministers of Christ can minister the spirit. This, then, is an infallible sign by which to distinguish true apostles from false ones. But does this infallible sign exist either among the Papists or Protestants? Can any of their ministers give the Holy Ghost by the laying on of hands? If not, they are not the church of God, and their ministers are unauthorized—all their ministrations are illegal and an abomination in the sight of God—salvation is not among them. Not one person among all these societies has been legally baptized. Reader, are you a member of any of these societies? if so, haste to withdraw yourself from them, that you partake not of their plagues, *for the hour of their judgment is come.* If you would be saved, seek after the apostles and prophets of the kingdom of God, and receive their ministrations, and you shall be filled with the Holy Ghost, and obtain eternal life.

## CHAPTER II.

### THE NATURE AND CHARACTER OF THE LAWS OF ADOPTION, OR THE INVARIABLE RULE BY WHICH ALIENS ARE ADMITTED INTO THE KINGDOM AS CITIZENS.

IN our examinations of the Kingdom of God, in Chapter I., we gave *the nature and character of the King;* and also *the qualifications of the subordinate officers.* We shall now proceed to examine,

Third.—*The nature and character of the laws of adoption, or the invariable rule by which aliens are admitted into the kingdom as citizens.*

Whenever the kingdom of God exists on the earth, all mankind are required, first, to become legal citizens thereof; and afterwards, to obey strictly all its laws unto the end of their days. To become a legal citizen in the kingdom is of infinite importance; for salvation is only to be obtained in the kingdom of God. All other kingdoms or governments will be broken to pieces and destroyed, while the kingdom of God will endure for ever.

During the first century of the Christian era, the servants of God preached and administered the law of adoption both to Jew and Gentile in all the world. But the nations soon made war upon them, and overcame and killed them, and destroyed the kingdom from the earth; since which time the law of adoption has not been administered until of late. The nations, remaining so long without the kingdom among them, became quite ignorant of its laws and characteristics, hence a vast number of opinions arose, and thick darkness overwhelmed all people.

The unchangeable law of adoption, however, is very clearly revealed in the New Testament, and may be easily understood and obeyed, when there are officers sent of God to administer it. This law was preached in great plainness to a very numerous multitude on the day of Pentecost. It was preached, too, by men who were filled with the Holy Ghost, and who had been commanded to commence their first proclamation in Jerusalem. The multitude to whom it was preached consisted of Jews who had come from all the surrounding nations to keep the great feast of Pentecost. They were not in the kingdom of God; but were all sinners in an unconverted state. They believed in the existence of God, and looked for a Messiah to come, but as for this Jesus of Nazareth, whom their nation had just crucified, they had no faith in Him, but considered Him as one of the greatest of impostors. Peter, with the rest of the disciples, commenced teaching them, proving from the scriptures of the Old Testament that Jesus was both Lord and Christ. So great were the evidences, and so powerfully did they affect the minds of that multitude, that they were pricked in their hearts, that is, they believed that Jesus was the Christ, and that their nation was under great condemnation for crucifying Him, and they knew not what the consequences would be; they were filled with alarm, and enquired of the apostles in the anguish of their souls, saying, "Men and brethren, what shall we do?" Then Peter said unto them, Repent, and be baptized every one of you in the name of Jesus

Christ *for the remission of sins*, and ye shall receive the gift of the Holy Ghost. For the promise is unto you, and to your children, and to all that are afar off, even as many as the Lord our God shall call." "Then they that gladly received his word were baptized: and the same day there were added unto them about three thousand souls." (*Acts ii.*, 37-39-41.) Here, reader, you will see the law of adoption as it was preached by the apostles at the commencement of their great mission to all nations. Here you have the example of three thousand sinners all complying with the law and becoming citizens in the kingdom of God in one day. When they came together in the morning they were all unconverted sinners, but before the day had passed, they were converted and made Saints. In the morning they were subjects of the kingdom of darkness, but in the evening they were citizens of the kingdom of God. Whatever the law was that wrought so great a change upon them in so short a time, the same law when administered by like authority, will produce like effects in all future ages.

It will be perceived that the great congregation of sinners to whom the apostles addressed themselves, were required—

First—To believe that Jesus Christ was the Son of God;

Secondly—To repent of their sins,

And, thirdly—To be baptized in the name of Jesus Christ.

And they were promised that, after attending to these three things, they should receive, first, A REMISSION OF THEIR SINS; and, secondly, THE GIFT OF THE HOLY GHOST. But are these all the rules necessary to be complied with in order to become legal heirs of the kingdom? No; there is one more condition which the sacred historian has neglected to mention in his history of the conversion of these three thousand; but as he has mentioned it in other parts of his history, in connection with the conversion of others, we are not left in ignorance of it. It is THE LAYING ON OF HANDS of the ministers of Christ for the gift of the Holy Ghost.

Faith, repentance, baptism and the laying on of hands, are the four rules of adoption. Remission of sins, and the gift of the Holy Ghost, are the two blessings of adoption which are inseparably connected with obedience to the rules. Both the rules and the blessings of adoption are the same in all ages and dispensations of the gospel. No man or woman ever entered into the Church or kingdom of God on this earth, and became a legal citizen thereof, without complying strictly with these rules. Indeed, it is the only door or entrance into the kingdom. Any persons attempting to get into the kingdom in any other way are called "thieves and robbers," and will be punished as such. Let the reader not be startled when I tell him that something like fifteen thousand millions of the human race have gone down to their graves without complying with these rules. Do not be angry nor prejudiced when I candidly inform you that no man nor woman on the great eastern hemisphere, during the long period of more than seventeen hundred years, has been legally adopted into the kingdom of God. No person among them, from the second to the ninteenth century of the Christian era has obeyed the gospel, or has been born into the kingdom. All have been aliens and strangers, and such a thing as the kingdom of God has not been known among them. Before we close our investigations relative to the kingdom of God, we shall demonstrate by the most incontrovertible evidence what we have now asserted.

FAITH being the first rule of adoption, we shall now proceed to show what faith is, and how it is obtained. The author of the epistle to the Hebrews says (*Heb. xi.*, 1) "Faith is the substance (assurance) of things hoped for, the evidence of things not seen." Faith, in a more extended sense, is the *assurance of the mind* in relation to what has been, what is or what will be. This *faith* or *assurance of the mind* is obtained only through evidence. It is not a *knowledge* of things, but the *belief* of things of which the mind has no certain knowledge. All belief is founded on evidence. A true faith is founded on true evidence; a false faith on false evidence. And in no case can a man have faith, either true or false, unless it is the result of true or false evidence. The greater the evidence, the greater will be the faith resulting from that evidence. Hence there are various degrees of faith both true and false; as for instance, when Europeans first discovered America, and came back and reported the same to the nations of the old world, they had a certain degree of faith in their testimony. When the discovery was confirmed by the additional testimony of numerous other witnesses, the faith of the nations was greatly increased: as evidences multiplied, faith was made perfect; so that in process of time, millions who never saw America, believed there was such a place, without the least shadow of a doubt. Those who visited America obtained a perfect knowledge of its existence through the evidence of their senses.

We will now relate an example of false faith:—When the American Indians first saw the powerful effects of gunpowder, they were anxious to procure large quantities of it. They were told by Europeans, that if gunpowder were sown in the earth, it would sprout up and grow, and yield an abundant harvest. The ignorant natives believing this false evidence, purchased, at high prices, large quantities of the supposed seed, and carefully sowed the same; but the result, like the result of all other false faiths, was disappointment. A person ignorant of geometrical reasoning may still have faith in many geometrical propositions; he believes the propositions on the testimony of geometricians, who declare that they have demonstrated to their own minds the truth of them; every additional geometrician who testifies to their truth increases his faith, yet he cannot know them to be true until he has put them to the test of geometrical reasoning for himself.

If a native of New Zealand were told by some person that light travels with a velocity of 192,000 miles every second, he would consider the statement incredible, if not impossible. If several respectable witnesses should tell him that it had been demonstrated, it might, perhaps, beget a very small degree of faith in his mind; if, still further, some of the steps of the demonstration were opened to his mind, and some of the phenomena resulting from the velocity of light were made known, his faith would become stronger; and pursuing the investigation of the evidences, he would, at length, demonstrate the fact to his own mind. and his faith would be swallowed up in knowledge.

When Copernicus asserted that the earth revolved in an orbit around the sun with a velocity of ninteen miles every second, his statements were considered visionary; but other evidences of a satisfactory nature being adduced, mankind began to exercise faith in the Copernican theory. As the evidences increased, their faith increased; and when the evidences became demonstrative, faith became knowledge.

On the morning of the day of Pentecost, the large multitude of the Jews who were assembled, considered Jesus an impostor, but after hearing the evidence of the Old Testament prophets, combined with the evidence of the apostles who stood as living witnesses of the resurrection of Jesus, three thousand of them believed that He was the Son of God; the faith of these three thousand was founded wholly upon the evidences then set before them. The faith they had in this fact, was not different from faith in any other fact. The faith that Jesus is the Son of God, is the same as the faith that Solomon is the son of David; faith in both of these facts comes by evidence, and in no other way. Devils, as well as man, believe that Jesus is the Son of God. Devils' faith is the result of evidence the same as men's; in this respect, the faith of devils and human beings is alike. But abstract faith alone can benefit no being. Devils believe that Christ is the Son of God, and tremble. Sinners may believe the same, and yet be damned. Saints may have the same faith, and yet, Judas like, become the sons of perdition; the angels of heaven may have strong faith, and yet be thrust down to hell: so that faith alone will save neither devils, angels, nor men. Faith is essential to salvation; without faith no one can be saved; no one can even repent without first having faith. If a man does not believe in the existence of God, he will not believe in His revealed laws; neither will he believe that it is sinful to disregard those laws; he will not believe himself to be a sinner, neither will he believe that he will be punished in a future state for transgressing laws which he does not believe emanated from God. Faith must, therefore, precede repentance. Before mankind can properly repent, there are several things necessary to be believed. they must believe not only in the existence of God, but in the revealed laws of God; that is, in the laws He has given against doing evil. If they believe in those laws, and compare their own conduct with them, they will perceive that in many instances they have transgressed them, and are, therefore, under the penalty of the same. They must believe that God would be just in executing the penalty of His own law, and that the law could not be sustained, or made honorable, unless justice should be satisfied. What effect, for instance, would the laws of England have, if the penalties were never to be inflicted? Stealing, robbing, murdering and the most savage acts of wickedness, would sweep through the land, depopulating whole cities and towns; that fair island would soon be transformed into one wide scene of desolation and ruin. So if the penalties affixed to the law of God should not be executed, order, peace and happiness, would vanish from all worlds, and naught but the most fearful anarchy, and the most direful confusion, would devastate the widely extended universe. Before sinners can repent acceptably before God, they must also believe that Jesus Christ, the Son of God, has voluntarily suffered the penalty of the law of His Father in behalf of man. If there had been no innocent being to suffer in the stead of man, then man, having once broken the law, must himself have suffered its penalty, or else God would have ceased to be a God of justice. Man, having once become guilty, could not atone for his own sins, and escape the punishment of the law, though he should ever afterwards strictly keep the law; for "By the works of the law," or, by obedience to the law, NO FLESH CAN BE JUSTIFIED. If a sinner, after having once transgressed the law, could purchase forgiveness by ever afterwards keeping the law, then there would have been no need of the atonement made by Christ. If the demands of justice could have been satisfied, and pardon granted, through repentance and good works, then the sufferings and death of Christ would have been entirely unnecessary. But if Christ had not suffered in our behalf, our faith, repentance, baptisms, and every other work, would have been utterly useless and in vain. Works, independently of Christ, would not atone even for the least sin.

Every man must perceive that before sinners can repent, they must believe, first, in the existence of God; secondly in His revealed law; and thirdly, in the sufferings of the Son of God, as the only possible way by which justice could be satisfied and mercy be granted to sinful man. Faith, as before stated, in any or either of these things, comes only through evidence. The three thousand sinners on the day of Pentecost never would have enquired so earnestly of the apostles to know what they should do, if they had not believed these three things.

After the apostles had, through evidence, established *faith* in the hearts of the sinners, they next taught them *repentance*, which we shall now proceed to explain. True and genuine repentance is, to cease to do evil and learn to do well, confessing past sins, with a fixed determination to sin no more. It would be of no use for a sinner to confess his sins to God, unless he were determined to forsake them; it would be of no benefit to him to feel sorry that he had done wrong, unless he intended to do wrong no more; it would be folly for him to confess before God that he had injured his fellow-man, unless he were determined to do all in his power to make restitution. Repentance, then, is not only a confession of sins, with a sorrowful, contrite heart, but a fixed, settled purpose to refrain from every evil way.

The next step to be taken by the believing, penitent sinner is to be baptized or immersed in water in the name of the Father, and of the Son, and of the Holy Ghost, FOR THE REMISSION OF SINS, by a man authorized of God to administer the ordinance. There are three very important items in connection with baptism which all persons should well understand before they suffer themselves to receive the ordinance. First, they should be well assured that the administrator has authority from God to baptize them. Second, they should satisfy themselves as to the correct mode of baptism. Third, they should understand the object for which baptism is administered.

It is evident that no one has a right to administer baptism unless he has been called of God, and authorized by NEW REVELATION to administer that ordinance, as we have very plainly shown in Chapter I., of this treatise. If the believing penitent sinner were to receive baptism at the hands of one who was not called and authorized, it would be a curse to him instead of a blessing—it would be a solemn mockery in the sight of God, bringing condemnation and darkness upon the mind.

Second: *Immersion* is the only mode of baptism sanctioned by the Lord. John, the forerunner of Christ, baptized numerous multitudes "in the river of Jordan" (*Mark* i. 5). After Jesus was baptized, "he went up straightway out of the water" (*Matthew* iii. 16). John also baptized "in Ænon, near to Salim, because there was MUCH WATER there" (*John* iii. 23). When Philip baptized the eunuch, "they went down both *into the water*, both Philip and the eunuch, and he baptized him. And when they were *come up out of the water*, the Spirit of the Lord caught away Philip" (*Acts* viii. 38, 39). If sprinkling and pouring were baptism, John must have been very foolish to have sought out places were there was "much water," and then put himself and the candidate to so much inconvenience by going down into the water, and getting their garments disagreeably wet. If a few drops, or a gill of water, sprinkled or poured upon them were sufficient, why did they go where there was much water? Why render their wearing apparel uncomfortable by going into the water? Why did the jailor and his household put themselves to the trouble of going out of their house in the darkness of night to be baptized? (*Acts xvi*). The jailor, about midnight, brought Paul and Silas out of the jail into his house, where they preached the word of the Lord to him, "and to all that were in his house. And he took them the same hour of the night, and washed their stripes; and was baptized, he, and all his, straightway. *And when he had brought them into his house*, he set meat before them, and rejoiced, believing in God with all his house." Here it will be perceived, that they went out of the house in the middle of the night to attend to baptism. If sprinkling or pouring were baptism, how much more convenient it would have been to have had it attended to in the house where he had a good light just previously procured, instead of going out at that late unseasonable hour. The Roman and Colossian Saints were BURIED *with Christ in baptism* (*Rom.* vi. 4 *Col.* ii. 12). Sprinkling or pouring is not *burial*, but immersion is. Jesus said to Nicodemus (*John* iii. 5) "Except a man be *born of water* and of the Spirit, he cannot enter into the kingdom of God." *Sprinkling* does not represent a *birth*, but *immersion* does. Coming out of the element of water into a new element is a fair representation of a birth. As in the natural birth, the tabernacle of the infant is filled, quickened, and animated by human spirit, so in the spiritual birth, the spirits of men are filled, quickened and animated by the Holy Spirit. As the blood of the infant, derived from the mother, is the medium of the natural life, or the means by which the union of the body and spirit is perpetuated, so the blood of Christ which was shed for us, is the medium of the spiritual life, or the means by which our union with the Holy Spirit is maintained. As the embryo is immersed in the fluid element in the womb, and by this means derives from its mother the blood so essential to the natural life, so a man must be immersed in the fluid element of water, in order to derive the benefit of Christ's blood so essential to spiritual life. As the embryo must *first* be immersed in water before it can receive the quickening of the human spirit, so a man must *first* be immersed in water before he has the promise of the quickening or life-giving power of the Holy Spirit. As the infant is born, or comes forth from the watery element into a new kingdom or world of existence, so a man in baptism comes forth from the liquid element of water into the kingdom of God's dear Son, which is a new state of existence. Jesus, in the above text, sets forth the birth of the water *first*, and *afterwards* the birth of the Spirit.

It is very evident from the whole tenor of scripture, that immersion is the only method of baptism. Several historians inform us, that the early Christians "immersed the whole body in water," and that sprinkling was not introduced into the church until the third or fourth century.

Every believing penitent sinner should make himself well acquainted with the *object* of baptism. This ordinance was instituted "for the remission of sins." John went "into all the country about Jordan, preaching the baptism of repentance *for the remission of sins*" (*Luke iii.* 3). After the ascension of Christ into heaven, the apostles commenced their great mission to all nations, by preaching to several thousand Jews, on the day of Pentecost, baptism "for the remission of sins" (*Acts ii.* 38). Ananias said to Paul, of Tarsus, "Arise, and be baptized, and wash away thy sins, calling on the name of the Lord" (*Acts xxii.* 16). Baptism is not, as many false teachers now affirm, "an outward sign of an inward grace," but it is an ordinance whereby a believing, penitent sinner obtains a forgiveness for all past sins. By being buried in the watery grave, the old man, as Paul says, is put off with all of his deeds; by rising from the liquid element, we put on the new man, become new creatures, and should henceforth walk in newness of life. Again, Paul says, "He that is dead is freed from sin." If sinners would be freed from sin, let them be "baptized into His (Christ's) death:" and thus, being dead with Him, they become free from sin, that is, all their former sins are remitted (*See Rom. vi*).

The great majority of religious people in modern times, consider baptism as non-essential to salvation. But we ask, is it essential that the repenting sinner should be forgiven? If so, then it is just in the same degree essential that he should be baptized, for that is the condition of forgiveness; hence baptism is essential to salvation, as much so as faith or repentance. He that neglects baptism, neglects one of the conditions of salvation. "He that believeth and is baptized, shall be saved. He that believeth not (and consequently is not baptized), shall be damned." Jesus never incorporated anything that was non-essential into the plan of salvation. But men should live by every word which proceedeth from His mouth. "He that saith, I know Him, and keepeth not His commandments, is a liar, and the truth is not in him" (*I. John ii.* 4). Again, Jesus says, "If a man love Me, he will keep My words. He that loveth Me not, keepeth not My sayings." The *commandments, words*, and *sayings* of Jesus, must be *kept* as well as *believed*, in order to obtain salvation. Unless baptism were essential to salvation, Jesus never would have commanded His apostles to "Go and teach all nations, baptizing them in the name of the Father, and of the Son, and of the Holy Ghost." A man may be a very good man, in many respects, yet if he rejects baptism, he rejects his salvation. As for instance, Cornelius was "a devout man, and one that feared God with all his house; he gave much alms to the people, and prayed to God always." An angel came in to him, and said, "Cornelius, thy prayers and thine alms are come up for a memorial before God. Send men to Joppa, and call for Simon, whose surname is Peter; who shall tell thee words whereby thou and all thy house shall be saved" (*Acts x. and xi*). When Peter had come, while he was speaking the word of the Lord to this man, and to his household, the Holy Ghost fell upon them, and they spake with tongues, and magnified God. And Peter "commanded them to be baptized in the name of the Lord."

What would have been the result if they had refused to obey this commandment, and had counted baptism non-essential, like many modern churches do? It is evident that not one of them could have been saved. Why? Because the angel said that Peter should "tell them words whereby they should be saved." If they had rejected baptism, they would have rejected the "words" of Peter, which the angel said should save them. No one can be saved who rejects baptism. It matters not how righteous he may have been; though he, like Cornelius, may have given "much alms," and prayed much, and feared God and worked righteousness for years; yea more, though he may have attained to greater blessings than the present sectarian churches now even believe, to say nothing of the enjoyment; though he may have seen a vision of angels, and spoken with tongues by the power of the Holy Ghost; yet, with all this righteousness and great power, he can in nowise be saved if he reject baptism. Hence, *faith, repentance,* and *baptism* are three essential conditions preceding remission of sins. Each is equally important. These are three of the rules of adoption by which strangers and aliens may become legal citizens in the church and kingdom of God.

Since the fourth century of the Christian era, infant sprinkling has been practised by a numerous multitude of false teachers. By age and long standing this great perversion of the apostolic doctrine has become exceedingly popular, until many millions at the present day are carried away with the wicked delusion. The apostles were commanded to *teach* first, and then baptize; but infants are incapable of being taught and therefore are not subjects of baptism. Jesus commanded the apostles to preach the gospel in all the world, and said, "He that *believeth* and is *baptized* shall be saved." Infants cannot believe the preaching of the apostles, therefore they should not be baptized. Peter commanded the thousands on the day of Pentecost to *repent* first, and then be baptized "for the remission of sins." But infants are incapable of repentance, and therefore it is a sin in the sight of God to baptize them. "Sin is the transgression of a law." Infants have transgressed no law, and therefore they are without sin. Baptism is FOR THE REMISSION OF SINS, but infants have no sins to be remitted, therefore they need no baptism. But even if infants had sins (as some false teachers assert), they could not be remitted by baptism alone. *Faith* and *repentance* would be equally as necessary for the infant as baptism. Either of these three conditions alone, or any two of them, would not bring remission: all must be voluntarily attended to by the candidate. But the infant cannot voluntarily attend to either, therefore the sprinkling or immersion of infants does not bring the blessings promised to the penitent believer, but it brings a curse both upon the parents and the administrator. It is a sin of which millions must repent if they ever enter into the kingdom of God.

Infant baptism is nowhere alluded to in the scriptures: some have supposed because whole households were baptized, that possibly there might have been some infants among them; but how many thousands of households there are that have no infants. The author of this treatise has himself baptized many whole households, but among them there were no infants, nor any persons incapable of believing and repenting. The scriptures inform us that the jailor and his household, and Cornelius and his household, *believed* and *rejoiced* in the Lord before they were baptized; hence there were no infants among them. Some again have supposed that the baptism of infants comes in lieu of circumcision; but this is only a wild, vague conjecture of impostors to deceive the ignorant; for there is not the least allusion to any such thing in the scriptures. Baptism has no more connection with circumcision than it has with the blowing of rams' horns for the demolishing of the walls of Jericho. There is no similarity between the two. Circumcision is a ceremony performed only on male infants at eight days old, whereas baptism is a burial in water of both male and female adults, who are capable of first believing and then repenting.

After the sinner has complied with the rules of adoption, so that all his former transgressions are forgiven, he should next seek after the gift of the Holy Ghost. God has ordained a certain ordinance through which he bestows this gift. He has authorized his servants to administer the Holy Spirit by the laying on of their hands in His name. For example: "Philip went down to the city of Samaria, and preached Christ unto them. And the people with one accord gave heed to those things which Philip spake. When they believed Philip, preaching the things concerning the kingdom of God, and the name of Jesus Christ, they were baptized both men and women. Now when the apostles, which were at Jerusalem, heard that Samaria had received the word of God, they sent unto them Peter and John: who, when they were come down, prayed for them, that they might receive the Holy Ghost: (for as yet he was fallen upon none of them: only they were baptized in the name of the Lord Jesus.) *Then laid they their hands on them; and they received the Holy Ghost.* And when Simon (the sorcerer) saw that *through laying on of the apostles' hands the Holy Ghost was given*, he offered them money, saying, Give me also this power, that on whomsoever I lay hands, he may receive the Holy Ghost" (*Acts viii*). Here we have the most positive evidence to establish the divine authority of this ordinance. That *laying on of hands* is an ordinance necessary to be attended to, is clearly seen from the fact, that no man or woman, among all the multitudes of baptized believers in Samaria, received the Holy Ghost until this institution was complied with. After Paul had rebaptized the Ephesians, "He laid his hands upon them, and the Holy Ghost came on them; and they spake with tongues, and prophesied" (*Acts xix*). Among the principles of the doctrine of Christ which the Hebrew church had received, Paul mentions faith, repentance, "the doctrine of baptisms, and of *laying on of hands*" (*Hebrew vi*).

That the Galatian church had received the Spirit by an administrator is evident from the following question put to them by Paul. "*He therefore that* MINISTERETH *to you the Spirit*, and worketh miracles among you, doeth he it by the works of the law, or by the hearing of faith?" (*Gal. iii.* 5).

Paul informs the Corinthian church, that both he and Timothy were made "able ministers, not of the letter," or word merely, "but of the Spirit."

Though Saul, of Tarsus, believed in Christ, and had been repenting, praying, and fasting for about three days, he could not obtain a forgiveness of his sins nor the gift of the Holy Ghost, without a servant of God sent to minister to him both the *water and the Spirit*. Hear what Ananias says to Saul: "The Lord, even Jesus, that appeared unto thee in the way as thou camest, hath sent me, that thou mightest receive thy sight, and *be filled with the Holy Ghost*" (*Acts ix*). Mark well the saying; Ananias was sent that Saul "might be filled with the Holy Ghost." Why not fill him with the Holy Ghost through his faith, repentance, prayers, and fasting? Because the Lord had authorized servants in His kingdom to minister, not the *word* and *water* merely, but also the *Spirit*.

We have now set forth the whole law of adoption, and the only law by which any man or woman can ever become a legal citizen of the Church or kingdom of God when established on the earth. By obedience to these rules mankind become the sons and daughters of God. By neglect of any or either of these rules they can never enter the kingdom. There is no other way or plan under the whole heavens that will save men. Many try to excuse themselves from obeying this plan by referring to the words of Jesus to the thief on the cross, "To-day shalt thou be with me in paradise." But we have no evidence to believe the thief was taken into heaven or into the celestial kingdom of God; for Jesus Himself said three days after, "Touch me not, for I have not yet ascended to my Father." Some have supposed that Jesus went directly into all the fullness of the Father's glory, and the thief with him.

But the scriptures expressly contradict this supposition. Peter says, in the third chapter of his first epistle, that "Christ also hath once suffered for sins, the just for the unjust, that he might bring us to God, being put to death in the flesh, but quickened by the Spirit: *by which also he went and preached unto the spirits in prison*, which sometime were disobedient, when once the long suffering of God waited in the days of Noah, while the ark was preparing, wherein few, that is, eight souls were saved by water." From this we learn that instead of Jesus going directly from the cross into His kingdom, he went to a certain "prison" where He found some "disobedient spirits" shut up, who had been there over two thousand years, or ever since Noah's flood. Jesus preached to them. Did the thief go with Him? "To-day shalt thou be with me in paradise." If Jesus went to preach in prison that day, the thief must have gone with Him; hence paradise must mean a place of departed spirits, without respect to its being either a good or a bad place.

Christ, speaking of His own mission by the mouth of Isaiah, says, "He hath sent me to bind up the broken hearted, to proclaim liberty to the captives, and the opening of the prison to them that are bound." This agrees with Peter, as already quoted. Forasmuch, therefore, as the thief had never, to our knowledge, been born of the water and the spirit, he could not, according to the words of the Savior, to Nicodemus, "enter into the kingdom of God;" but he in all probability went that day with Jesus to the old antediluvian prison among the disobedient spirits, where he had the privilege of being preached to: that he and all the rest of the prisoners "might be judged according to men in the flesh." (*1. Peter vi.*, 6.

If the third "article of religion," believed by the church of England, be true, then the thief must have gone down into hell. This article reads thus:

"III. Of the going down of Christ into hell.—As Christ died for us, and was buried, so also is it to be believed that He went down into hell."

If the thief went down into "prison," let every other unbaptized person beware lest he go there too.

Since the Apostles fell asleep, the simplicity and purity of the ancient gospel have been awfully perverted; its ordinances have been changed, especially the ordinance of baptism; while the ordinance of the laying on of hands for the gift of the Holy Ghost, has been almost universally done away. No churches, either among the Papists or Protestants, have taught all the first principles of the gospel in their proper order. By this we know they are not the church of God. God is not with them. Their sins are not forgiven them. The Holy Ghost is not given to them. And they cannot be saved in the fulness of the glory of the Father's kingdom— neither they nor their fathers for many generations past. All have gone astray—far astray, from the ancient gospel. The church of Christ never existed on the earth without inspired apostles and prophets in it, who administered all the laws and ordinances of the gospel without any variation from the true and perfect pattern. But the apostate churches now on the earth, have neither inspired apostles, nor prophets, nor any other inspired officers among them, neither do they consider them necessary; and yet without inspiration or revelation— without immersion for remission of sins, or the ordinance for the gift of the Spirit—they have the bold impudence to call themselves Christian churches. But they have nothing to do with Christ, neither has Christ anything to do with them, only to pour out upon them the plagues written. He has not spoken to any of them for many centuries, neither will He speak to them, only in His wrath, and in the fierceness of His anger, when He rises up to overthrow, to root up and to destroy them utterly from the earth.

## CHAPTER III.

#### THE NATURE AND CHARACTER OF THE LAWS GIVEN FOR THE GOVERNMENT OF ALL ADOPTED CITIZENS.

THREE important subjects relative to the kingdom of God have been already investigated in Chapters I. and II. We shall now proceed to the examination of the

Fourth—namely, *The nature and character of the laws given for the government of all adopted citizens.*

After having complied with the rules of adoption, mankind are considered the legal citizens of God's kingdom; and as such, they are required to obey strictly all the laws, ordinances, statutes, commands, counsels and words of the Great King; and in all things show themselves the faithful, honest and loyal subjects of His government. That the citizens of the kingdom may be able to render strict obedience to its laws, they should make themselves thoroughly acquainted with them, and thus obey understandingly. Persons ignorant of the laws of the kingdom are liable to be deceived. They may suppose themselves obeying the law, when, in fact, they are only complying with some vain and foolish tradition of men. They are in constant danger of transgressing laws of which they are ignorant, and of neglecting to observe others that are of importance.

Millions of modern Christians say they take the Bible as their "rule of faith and practice"—that the Bible is their law. But we ask, what part of the Bible is the law of God unto man in this age? Is the history of the creation a law unto any one? Is the history of the building of the ark, or of the tower of Babel, or of Solomon's temple, a law or "rule of faith and practice" for the saints now? Is the history of Abraham's travels—of the doings of Moses and Aaron—of Israel's wanderings in the wilderness—of the wars of Israel under the reign of their judges and kings—a law unto succeeding generations? Is the history of Jesus and the apostles a law binding upon the saints of latter days? Must we be baptized in Jordan because John baptized there? Must we ride upon an ass-colt into Jerusalem because Jesus did? Must we scourge the people out of the Jewish temple because Jesus thought it necessary to do so? Must we build up churches in Rome, in Corinth, in Galatia, or in any other place, because the New Testament gives the history of such events? Is the history of any of the events recorded in either the Old or the New Testament a law unto any man now living? No, it is not. The historical parts of the Bible, then, are not intended to govern the actions of modern Christians.

Let us now inquire if all the laws, ordinances, and commands in the Bible are intended as our rule of faith and practice—as a law now binding upon us? God commanded Adam that he should not eat of the tree in the midst of the Garden of Eden. Is this law unto modern Christians? No. God commanded Noah that he should build an ark of certain dimensions, and of a certain kind of wood: that he should take into the ark a certain number of beasts and fowls. Are these commands binding upon Christians *now?* Surely not. God commanded Abraham to leave the land of Chaldea and go into a land wherein he was a stranger. Must modern Christians obey this command? Abraham was commanded to offer up his son Isaac. Is this a law of God's kingdom *now?* God commanded the Israelites to leave Egypt—to walk through the Red sea—to pitch their tents in a certain way to travel in a certain order—to build a tabernacle after a certain pattern which he gave them—to offer various animals and fowls as sacrifices. Are these commands, laws or ordinances the saints' "rule of faith and practice" in these days? They are not. God commanded the tribes of Israel to slay both men, women and children—old and young. Must the saints in all ages be governed by that command? No. God commanded Israel to encompass the walls of Jericho a certain number of times, blowing upon rams' horns. Is this a law or command to be observed now? Verily no. Jesus commanded

Peter to go and catch a fish in order to pay taxes. Is this command in force yet? Jesus commanded the apostles to tarry in Jerusalem a certain time, until they were qualified to preach. Must all other saints wait in Jerusalem for a like qualification? An angel of the Lord commanded Philip to go into the south country; another angel commanded Cornelius to send for Peter; an angel commanded Joseph, the husband of Mary, to flee into Egypt, and, after tarrying there a certain time, an angel commanded him to return again to the land of Israel. Will any one pretend to say that any of these commands are to be observed now? There are many thousands of laws, commands, ordinances and sayings, like the foregoing, both in the Old and New Testaments, that modern Saints cannot obey; indeed, it would be the hight of delusion, and a great sin, to undertake to obey them now. Could any man remain guiltless and kill little infant children now, because such a command was given to Israel? No, he could not. The most of the commands and ordinances of the Bible were limited in their application, and were never intended to be binding upon future generations. Many were limited to single individuals, and they only were required to obey them; and when once obeyed, they were no longer binding upon those individuals nor any one else. Other laws in the Bible were given to govern all Israel for many generations; yet these also were limited to Israel, and were never intended to govern Gentile Christians. Most of the commands and laws in the Bible were given according to circumstances: as the circumstances were constantly changing, so the commands and laws were constantly changing to suit circumstances.

The moral law, however, never changes; it remains the same throughout all dispensations and ages. The Lord commanded Israel, saying, Thou shalt not kill, thou shalt not steal, thou shalt not commit adultery, etc. These laws, with many others, never were intended to be done away, but wherever the kingdom of God is established, these laws exist in full force as rules of faith and practice. Many of the laws of Moses and the prophets, and of Jesus and the apostles, were moral in their nature, and never were intended to cease. The moral law, or law of righteousness, has been revealed anew in different generations and to numerous individuals. Once revealing this law did not seem sufficient, hence it was revealed afresh, and over and over again, in successive generations. Each inspired writer received *new revelations* upon this great unchangeable law; and, in addition to this, each in his turn revealed thousands of commands, laws and ordinances suited to the conditions and circumstances of the people, which never were binding upon any but the individuals who received them, and to whom they were given.

Connected with the moral law, or the law which is intended to regulate the moral actions of men, there are certain ordinances which are intended as standing ordinances in the kingdom; such, for example, as the sacrament of the Lord's supper, the laying on of hands in the name of the Lord for the healing of the sick, and the anointing with oil for the same purpose. It might appear to some as superfluous for the Lord to reveal through successive prophets and inspired men the same things which He had previously revealed to former ages; but when we reflect upon the importance of being governed by righteous laws, and upon the frailty of man and his liability to forget God and His laws, we need not be surprised at this. It is certain that inspired men, in different ages, have revealed the same things anew, and have illustrated them in a great variety of ways, so as to impress the importance of them on the minds of men; as for example, how often mankind have been commanded through inspired men to worship no other god but the true and living God! How often have they been commanded through inspired men to keep the Sabbath day holy? Many of the laws given to Moses were often repeated again in the inspired writings of future prophets. Modern Christians suppose that the Bible contains sufficient revelation to save man. They argue "that the law of righteousness is clearly revealed in that book, and that more revelation would be superfluous." "If," say they, "the Bible contains the gospel, why should another revelation of the gospel be given?" It is said, "if another gospel be revealed it must be false; if the same gospel be revealed it is useless, for we already have it in ancent revelations." They further argue, "that if mankind in ancient days could be saved by what was revealed to them, the same revelations will save mankind in these days," hence they suppose there is no need of any more. This objection urged by modern divines against new revelation being given in these days, might have been urged with the same propriety five thousand years ago; as, for examples, the antediluvian world might have used this argument against Noah's new revelations. They might have said that Enoch, the seventh from Adam, had sufficient revelation to save not only his spirit but his body also, and that Enoch knew of Christ, and prophesied that He "should come with ten thousand of His saints to execute judgment,'' etc. and that if, through the vast numbers of revelations he had received, he could be translated, body and spirit, into the abodes of immortality, why not we be saved by the same revelations without any new ones? Why, they might have said, do you, Noah, pretend to give new revelations, when your great grandfather Enoch had revelations enough to translate him? Cannot we be saved, as well as he, if we take Enoch's revelations as our "rule of faith and practice?" "But," say the new-revelation-deniers of modern times, "Enoch's revelation said nothing about the flood and the ark, it was therefore necessary that more revelation should be given to warn the people of these events." Very well. May there not also be some judgments to escape, and important events to happen in our age, of which the ancient prophets have said nothing? And will not new revelation be equally as necessary to make known these unknown events that may happen in our day, as it was in Noah's day? After Matthew had been inspired to write the gospel, why was it necessary that Mark, Luke and John should be inspired to write the same gospel? According to the arguments of the false teachers of modern times, if the last three evangelists revealed a different gospel from Matthew, it would be false, and if they revealed the same it would be useless, there being no necessity for the same thing to be revealed over again. If the revelation of the gospel by Matthew were sufficient to save men, why, according to their logic, should any further revelation be given? Why should Mark, Luke, John, Paul, Peter, James and Jude give new revelation, after Matthew had given sufficient to save himself and others? But says the false teacher, it was necessary, that by the mouth of two or three witnesses every word should be established, and once being established, there was no further need of revelation. In reply, we say, if *two* or *three* witnesses were sufficient why did He give *eight* writers instead of two or three? We see no more impropriety in sending *eight hundred* inspired men, or *eight thousand* to write more revelation, than in sending *eight*.

Besides these eight inspired writers of the first century, vast numbers of others received revelations during that period, such as the Prophet Agabus, the four daughters of Philip, and the numerous prophets among the Corinthians and other churches. Surely the Lord was not very particular to confine the spirit of revelation to *two* or *three* witnesses, neither was He very careful not to have the same things incorporated in the revelations of different men.

The inspired writings of the first century, though given at different times, and through different men, reveal the same gospel, teach the same law of righteousness, and declare the same ordinances; yet no one pretends to deny the usefulness of either or any of these inspired writings, because the same gospel, law and ordinances had previously been revealed in some other writing. All of these inspired writings are considered valuable, because they contain, not a different gospel or law, but different items of revelation which were once adapted to the different circumstances of individuals and churches to whom they were given. These ever varying items of revelation are valuable, not as a law or rule for the church in these days, but as matters of history. The revelation to Saul of Tarsus to "arise and go into Damascus"—the revelation to Ananias to "arise and go into the street that is called Straight, and enquire in the house of Judas for one called Saul"—the revelation to the prophets in the church at Antioch to "set apart Barnabas and Saul to the work of the ministry"—the revelation to Saul to "make haste, and get quickly out of Jerusalem," for the Jews would not receive his testimony, and numerous other like revelations, are valuable as matters of history only; for no one will have the absurdity to say that such revelations are binding upon any one else excepting the persons that received them. The history of God's revelations, ever varying to suit circumstances, is an encouragement for the Saints in the ninteenth century to seek after new revelations, like the ancients, which shall be adapted to the ever-varying and innumerable circumstances with which they may be surrounded. It will do no good to read the history of the angel sending Philip into the south country to preach, unless ministers can be sent by revelation in these days into the right country or field of labor. It will be of no advantage to read the history of the revelations given through the prophets of Antioch, relating to the calling and ministry of Paul and Barnabas, unless there are prophets and revelations in these days to call men to the ministry in the same way. The history of other men's revelations, callings, and missions, would be of no more advantage to us than the history of a good dinner would be to a hungry man, or the history of the miraculous deliverance of the three Hebrew children from the fiery furnace would be to a man perishing in the flames. Callings and missions in the ninteenth century require new revelations as much as in the first century. The history of others' callings, missions and duties, under certain circumstances, gives no knowledge of our callings, missions and duties under different circumstances. As well might we say to a hungry man that he has no need to eat in these days, as to say to the Saints they have no need of new revelation in these days. If a hungry man be told to read the history of the loaves and fishes on which others feasted, and be satisfied therewith, his appetite would be greatly increased, and he would desire to eat for himself; so if the Saint who is hungering and thirsting after righteousness be told to read the history of the innumerable revelations given to the ancient Saints, varied to suit their circumstances, and be satisfied therewith, it will greatly increase his desire to receive revelation for himself suited to his own circumstances.

'Man shall not live by bread alone, but by *every word of God.*' This cannot mean every word which God has spoken in different ages; for it would be impossible to live by all the words of God spoken to Noah—to Abraham—to Moses—to the prophets and to the apostles. Thousands of words which God has given would be obeyed only by the very individuals to whom they were given. No other person could obey them. Man is to live by every word of God contained in those general laws which are given for the government of His kingdom in all ages; and he is also to live by every word which shall be given to him as an individual. In the latter case his circumstances may be such as to require vast numbers of new revelations suited to his condition. These revelations, no doubt, would greatly differ from any that were ever before given to man, or from any that would ever afterwards be given. No two individuals, churches, nations, or generations, are in the same condition; not even one individual is in the same circumstances in any two successive periods of his life. Consequently there is no period, nor year, nor generation, nor age wherein new revelations are not needed among the people of God. The nature and character of the laws given for the government of adopted citzens, then, are not only those which are binding on man in every age, but those new revelations which are given directly to the citizens from year to year during their own lives. When new revelations or laws are given for the benefit of a church or people, they are generally communicated through the prophets or other inspired officers of the Church. When they are given to suit the circumstances of an individual, they are sometimes communicated through an inspired officer, as in the cases of Samuel's revelation to Saul—of Nathan's to David, and numerous other instances that might be named; and sometimes they are given directly to the individual himself, as in the case of the revelation to Cornelius, to Philip, to the shepherds, to the wise men of the east, to Anna, to Simeon, and to great numbers of others mentioned in sacred history.

It may be thought by some that a doctrine of continued revelation is a dangerous doctrine, calculated to deceive and mislead weak-minded persons to believe in anything and everything pretending to be revelations. But let such persons reflect that God is the author of such doctrine; and it is not at all likely that He would establish continued revelation among His people if it were a dangerous doctrine. Can the wisest of our readers point out a people of God in any age of the world to whom He did not give continued revelations? Has God ever acknowledged any people or church as His own that did not receive new revelations for their own benefit? The danger, then, is all on the other side. The man who does not believe in *continued revelation* among the people of God, is already deceived and has not the religion of the Bible. By rejecting new revelation, he rejects one of the great fundamental principles by which the people of God in all ages are clearly distinguished from every other people. But the reader may ask, is there not danger of being deceived by false revelation? We reply, yes; but shall we reject the true coin, because there is danger of being deceived with the spurious? Shall we reject all vegetable food because some vegetables are poisonous? Shall we reject the gift of the Holy Spirit, because there are many false spirits abroad among men? Shall we reject the doctrine of salvation through Christ, because there have been many false christs? Shall we reject new revelation from God, because there have been many false ones?

Every faithful, upright person in the Church or kingdom of God enjoys the gift of the Holy Ghost, which is a sure preventative against all deception. The Holy Spirit knows all things, and never deceives any one. Jesus said (*see John xiv., xv., and xvi. chapters*), "The Comforter which is the Holy Ghost, whom the Father will send in my name, *He shall teach you all things*, and bring all things to your remembrance, whatsoever I have said unto you." "Howbeit, when He the Spirit of truth is come, *he will guide you into all truth:* for He shall not speak of Himself; but whatsoever He shall hear, that shall He speak; and *He will shew you things to come.* He shall glorify Me: for He shall receive of mine, and shall shew it unto you. All things that the Father hath are mine; therefore said I, that He shall take of mine, and *shall shew it unto you.*" Perhaps some may suppose that this Comforter which is called the Holy Ghost, was only to be given to the apostles; but Peter said to thousands on the day of Pentecost, that if they would repent and be baptized for the remission of sins, they should "receive the gift of the Holy Ghost;" and then to shew them that the promise of this gift was not limited to a few thousand persons, he says, in the next sentence, "For the promise is unto you, and to your children, and to all that are afar off, even as many as the Lord our God shall call." This passage evidently proves that the promise of the Holy Ghost, was a promise universal in its extent, embracing all mankind who would comply with the conditions of repentance and baptism. If, then, all mankind can receive the gift of the Holy Ghost, where is the danger of their being deceived by false revelations? Nowhere, if they are faithful enough to retain the Spirit. "He shall teach you all things." "He shall guide you into all truth." Oh! how easy it is with this Spirit to detect false revelations, and to be guided into the truth of all new ones! The Spirit knows its own revelations and can testify of them. Hence, says John, in one of his epistles directed to the saints generally, "The anointing which ye have received of Him abideth in you, and *ye need not that any man teach you, but as the same anointing teacheth you of all things, and is truth,* and is no lie; and even as it hath taught you, ye shall abide in Him" (*I. John ii. chap*). This "anointing" evidently means the promised Spirit which all the churches of the saints enjoyed. All the saints were taught by this Spirit in all things. By this Spirit they could detect false apostles, false prophets, false teachers, false spirits, false doctrines, and false revelations without the least difficulty

Paul said, that "eye hath not seen, nor ear heard, neither have entered into the heart of man, the things which God hath prepared for them that love Him. *But God hath revealed them unto us by His Spirit; for the Spirit searcheth all things, yea, the deep things of God.* Now we have received not the spirit of the world, but the Spirit which is of God? *that we might know the things that are freely given to us of God.*" "But the natural man receiveth not the things of the Spirit of God · for they are foolishness unto him : *neither can he know them,* because they are spiritually discerned. But he that is spiritual judgeth all things" (*I. Cor. ii. chap.*). Thus we perceive that the "natural man cannot know the things of the Spirit;" therefore he is liable to be deceived, and to embrace false revelations, and believe a lie and be damned, because without the Spirit he is unable to judge whether a revelation is from God or from some other source. Not so with the spiritual man; he *judgeth all things,* and decides by the Spirit between error and truth. Neither the eye, the ear, nor the heart of a natural man has perceived the things in reserve for the righteous; but the spiritual man has a knowledge of them by revelation. "God hath revealed them unto us by His Spirit." The Saints find out "the deep things of God" by the Spirit. The faithful Saints or the elect cannot be deceived, for the Holy Ghost dwells in them as a Spirit of constant revelation, teaching them all things; guiding them into all truth; shewing them things to come; taking of the things of the Father and shewing the same unto them by heavenly visions and dreams, and revealing the deep things of God such as no natural man could ever see, hear, think of, or know, for they are only spiritually discerned. Thus there is no possibility of a person's ever being deceived who follows the teachings and revelations of the Holy Ghost.

The revelations given by the Holy Ghost; by the voice of the Lord; by the ministry of angels; by visions and dreams, and by the inspired officers of the kingdom, are the kind of laws ordained for the government of the Saints. By such laws they have been governed in every age and dispensation. All churches who have not faith to obtain revelations and laws by the inspiration of the Holy Ghost, are not the churches of God. Though they may pretend to great piety; profess to be Christians; make long prayers; preach eloquent sermons, and meet together every Sabbath day under the pretence of worshipping God, yet if they have not faith to obtain new revelations, and visions, and the ministry of angels, they are not the church of God, and are deceiving themselves and others with a false and delusive religion; a religion by which they will perish, as the scripture saith, "Where there is no vision the people perish" (*Proverbs xxix.* 18).

In all human governments there is a necessity for new laws to be given, and sometimes in great abundance. No one will be so wild as to say that the laws given one thousand years ago to England, to France, and to the various nations of the earth, have been strictly applicable to the infinite variety of circumstances in which they have since been placed. Every one knows that all governments would soon fall into the most inextricable confusion should new laws cease to be given only for the short period of fifty years. Every town, city, and district, of any extent, pay out their thousands annually for the support of a law-making department. If new circumstances in all human governments are constantly calling for new laws, why not new circumstances in God's government also require new laws? It may, perhaps, be argued that human laws are imperfect, and therefore new ones are given; but that God's laws being perfect, no new ones are necessary. In reply to this we observe that in human governments new laws are not generally given because of the imperfections of the old ones, but because new conditions require it. New laws are not often give *instead* of the old ones, but in *addition* to them; both old and new remaining in full force. The want of new laws would be equally as necessary though human laws were ever so perfect. So in the kingdom of God, the perfection of the old laws does not in the least obviate the necessity of new ones as new circumstances arise.

In all human governments every law is made by the legal law-making department, or else it is of no force, and the people are not bound by it. So in the kingdom of God, all laws must come from the Great Law-Giver, or else they are of no force, and the people are under no obligations to obey them. If any body of unauthorized men on this land, were to write out a code of laws for the government of the United States, who would be so lost to all reason and common sense as to suppose such laws were legal and valid? Yet there are millions who consider themselves under obligations to believe and obey the uninspired writings in the "Thirty-nine Articles" of the church of England, and in the various creeds, catechisms, confessions of faith, and disciplines of other sects, as though they had actually come afresh from God. The vast variety of creeds and articles of faith now in the world, shows clearly that mankind consider that they have need of more rules and laws besides those given in ancient days. The necessity of more has appeared so obvious, that they have concluded to have more at all hazards. To obtain more, from the Great King, they suppose is entirely out of the question. The only way, in their estimation, is to usurp the place of God, and give laws to the people as He anciently did. To obtain laws from the legal Law-Giver in these days, they assert is the highest blasphemy, but to usurp authority and give laws and articles of faith in God's stead, they consider is all right. The archbishops, bishops, and whole clergy of the church of England, with the king at their head, thinking that the Lord had given all the rules, laws, and articles of faith in the Bible which He ever intented to give, and seeing the great necessity there was for more, concluded that wherein the Lord failed in supplying the present wants of their church they would make it up out of the superabundance of their own wisdom. The first rich display of their fruitful imaginations was to invent an entire new kind of god, which no former generation ever thought of. A description of this god they have given in their first article of religion. He is there represented to be "without *body, parts*, or *passions*." Such is the first effort of this great body of learned divines in helping the Lord make articles of faith. When the Lord made articles of religion in olden times, He had not the assistance of such learned men; perhaps that may be the reason that this *bodiless, passionless* god of modern times was not then discovered! Oh! what darkness the world would have been in relative to this god without "parts," if these modern divines had suffered the God of Israel to give articles of religion as He did in ancient days! Had it not been for this learned body, the world never would have known that the whole of any thing could exist without "parts!"—they never would have known the difference between this newly-invented god and the God of Israel, who said to Moses, "thou shalt see my back PARTS" (*Exodus xxxii*. 23). Let the church of England hush all their fears, for their god can neither see, hear, nor speak; they never need be afraid that he will give them new revelations, or laws, or articles of religion, or interfere in any way with their church matters. The God of Israel makes His own laws and articles of religion for His own church in all ages; but this modern god, having no tongue, nor mouth nor any other "parts," has left this work entirely to his Right Reverend Worshippers.

FIFTH.—*The character, disposition, and qualifications necessary for every citizen to possess.*

After being adopted into the kingdom of God it is necessary

that all citizens should cultivate such a character and disposition as shall be most pleasing to their King. Whenever the King shall give them advice or counsel upon any subject, they should, without any hesitation, adhere strictly to that advice or counsel. It is a great thing to find out the will of God, but it is still greater to do it. God requires the most perfect obedience on the part of His subjects. We may not always discern the end or result of doing as we are commanded; but this is no excuse for disobedience. Abraham did not know the useful result the Lord had in view in commanding him to offer up his son Isaac; if he had followed the dictates of his own natural feelings or affections, he never would have attempted to comply with this command; it was enough for him to understand that God required such a sacrifice, without waiting till He informed him of the reason why He required it. This should be the disposition and character of every child of God, to go with all his heart and do whatever the Lord requires, though he may be utterly in the dark as to the purpose which God may wish to accomplish by giving such commandment. Does a skillful general reveal to all his soldiers all his purposes and designs in regard to the enemy? No, he only reveals unto them what he wishes them to do, while the result of their obedience is oftentimes entirely hidden from their view. If soldiers were never to obey until they understood the useful results to be accomplished, they would not be very loyal to their officers. How many there are among mankind that would be delighted to obtain a revelation of God's will concerning themselves, if they could be persuaded that He would not reveal anything contrary to their wishes. They would be very sorry to get a revelation "to sell all that they had and give to the poor," as Jesus told the young man in ancient days. They would not like to hear "a voice from heaven" commanding them to come out of Babylon, or to leave their native land, their fine farms and splendid mansions, and go into a strange country as Abraham did: they would prefer to receive no revelations at all, rather than be directed to make such sacrifices. But not so with good, faithful citizens of the kingdom of God: they wish to be guided by new revelation day by day, and year by year: they delight to do every thing that the Lord reveals to them, believing that it will be for their future happiness and well-being.

It is not every one that crieth Lord, Lord, that shall enter into the kingdom of heaven, but it is he that doeth the will of the Father. Justification, sanctification, purification, and glorification, are all obtained through the atonement of Jesus Christ by doing the will of the Father, as made manifest by the revelation of His word. Jesus prays to the Father thus—"Sanctify them through Thy truth; Thy word is truth." Reader, do you desire to be justified from all your sins? if so, obey the law of justification as revealed from heaven, and your sins shall be blotted out. Do you desire to be sanctified and purified from all unrighteous and unholy desires? if so, seek to obtain the word of the Lord by new revelation, and after you have obtained it, either directly to yourself, or through others, be sure and obey it, and you shall be made pure and clean; but remember that after the word of the Lord has come unto you and His will is revealed, and you refuse to obey, your situation will be much worse than that of those to whom the Lord has never spoken. "He that *knoweth* his master's will," through the medium of new revelation, "and doeth it not, the same shall be beaten with many stripes; but he that knoweth it not," that is, has never been favored with a message or revelation from his master, "and doeth things worthy of stripes, shall only be beaten with few stripes."

When the children of the kingdom pray, let them be careful not to use vain repetitions as the church of England do in their "Litany," for they repeat the same thing over again on every Sunday, Wednesday, and Friday; the same things are asked for some fifty or sixty times on each of these days; so that in fifty years each member of that church repeats the same petition something like four hundred thousand times. The faithful Saints will avoid all such wicked mockery, for it is very displeasing to the true God to have such "vain repetitions" constantly sounding in His ears year after year. Where is there a sensible man in all the world that would not be disgusted with his own children, or with any other persons, who should constantly annoy him by asking for the same thing some fifty times a day, for three days every week, and follow it up year after year? Such persons would be counted as insane, or unfit for the society of rational beings. How much more, then, will the true God be disgusted, and abhor such nonsense? Any being, except a *bodiless, passionless nonentity*, would treat such worshippers with contempt, and consider them a nuisance in all civilized society.

When the Saints pray, they should endeavor to find out what they want most, and then calmly, simply, and honestly ask for it with an expectation of receiving it; for, says our Savior, "If my words abide in you, and ye abide in me, ye shall ask what ye will, and it shall be given unto you." Do not think that you will be heard for much speaking or for vain repetitions. If you fail in receiving any thing that would be for your benefit, or any that is promised, you may know that there is some cause for it: perhaps you may not have been as faithful as you ought; the fault, if any, must be in yourself; for God's promises are sure. Therefore seek to find out the reason why your prayer is not answered, and remove the cause, and then ask again, and if all is right on your part, you will receive an answer. Seek not to express your desires before the Lord in great swelling words, to be praised of men for your eloquence, neither convert your voice into some unnatural tone; but endeavor to speak to the Lord with the same degree of sincerity and confidence that a child has in asking its parents for food. When you desire any particular blessing, do not let your mind be wandering upon hundreds of other blessings which are foreign from the one which you more earnestly desire, lest your faith become divided, and you fail of receiving any answer. If a great multitude of things are asked for in the same prayer, the Saints are sometimes apt afterwards to forget some things which they have prayed for, and consequently do not look with earnest expectation for the answer, and because of this the blessing is withheld.

The great secret in obtaining favors from God, is to form, modify, and cultivate such characters and dispositions as will correspond in every respect with the teachings of the word and spirit of Christ. Condescend to men of low estate. Despise not the poor because of his poverty; and when you prepare a feast, invite in, "*the poor, the halt, the maimed and blind; for* they cannot recompense you again in this life, but you shall receive your recompense at the resurrection of the just." Feed the hungry—clothe the naked—administer to the widow and the fatherless in their afflictions—visit the sick. Let your love abound unto all men: endeavor to reclaim men from the error of their ways by telling them the plain, unvarnished truth in meekness and with sobriety, remembering that you yourselves were once in gross darkness, because of the traditions and false religions with which you were surrounded; therefore have compassion upon the millions of deluded beings who have deceived themselves with the pomp and vain show of modern Christianity. Be upright and honest before all men. Practice virtue and holiness continually. Such should be the disposition and character of all the children of God, in order to qualify themselves for usefulness in this world, and to inherit eternal life in the world to come.

## CHAPTER IV

### THE RIGHTS, PRIVILEGES AND BLESSINGS ENJOYED BY THE SUBJECTS IN THIS LIFE.

IN the preceding chapters of this treatise, we have already illustrated FIVE important subjects relative to the kingdom of God. The next to be considered in the order of our arrangement is the

Sixth—Namely, *The rights, privileges, and blessings enjoyed by the subjects in this life.*

The faithful subjects of the kingdom of God are entitled by promise to certain rights and privileges which are not granted to the citizens of any other kingdom. All the children of the kingdom have the right of offering up daily petitions to the King. This inestimable right or privilege is one with which the citizens of other governments are not favored. It is not only granted as a privilege, but it is also enjoined as a duty upon all the inhabitants of the kingdom, to plainly make known all their wants, and represent all their grievance or wrongs which they may have endured from the citizens of other governments. Those petitions offered in righteousness, are always favorably received; and the blessings asked for in faith, if calculated to benefit the petitioner, are never withheld.

The blessings promised to the children of the kingdom in this life, are wisdom, knowledge, joy, healings, miracles, tongues, interpretations, revelations, visions, dreams, the ministry of angels, prophesyings, power to cast out devils, power against deadly poisons, and in fine, all the other gifts of the Holy Ghost as recorded in the scriptures of truth.

Many thousands of sincere honest inquirers have been exceedingly anxious to know whether they were really in the kingdom of God or not. This is an inquiry of infinite importance, and one upon which none should rest satisfied short of a certain knowledge. For the benefit of such inquirers, we here give them an infallible sign by which they may always know the kingdom of God from all other kingdoms. Whereever the miraculous gifts of the Holy Ghost are enjoyed, there the kingdom of God exists: wherever these gifts are not enjoyed, there the kingdom does not exist.

That believers might be distinguished from unbelievers throughout all the world, Jesus promised certain signs to the former. He said unto them, "These *signs* shall follow them that believe: in my mame shall they cast out devils; they shall speak with new tongues; they shall take up serpents; and if they drink any deadly thing, it shall not hurt them; they shall lay hands on the sick, and they shall recover. (*Mark xvi.* 17, 18, 19.) This promise has been supposed by many to have been limited to the apostles or to the official members of the Church of Christ; but it will be perceived from the context, that Jesus made this promise to every creature throughout all the world who would believe the gospel. In the 15th verse, He commanded the apostles to "go into all the world and preach the gospel to every creature." In the 16th verse, He promised salvation to every baptized believer, and damnation to every unbeliever. In the three following verses, He promises miraculous signs to the believer. The promise of miraculous signs was as unlimited in its nature as the promise of salvation. Where the one ceases, the other ceases also. Miraculous signs are a part of the gospel plan, as much as the remission of sins or the gift of the Holy Ghost.

The gospel plan embraces certain commands or ordinances to be believed and obeyed, and certain blessings to be received. To limit the blessings of the gospel to the first age of Christianity, is to limit the gospel to that age; for all the blessings, including the signs, were to be received wherever the gospel was received.

Nothing can be more erroneous than to suppose that these signs were merely given to establish the truth of Christianity, and that when that was once established, they were no longer needed. The signs are as much included in the system of Christianity, as any other blessing that can be named. If the signs have ceased, true Christianity, of which the signs are a component part, has ceased. If signs have established the system of Christianity, why should they, as a part of the very system itself cease as unnecessary, while the other part of the system remains? Why not the *whole* system cease, as well as a *part?* Why tell the world that Christianity was established by miraculous signs, and then declare, that as soon as it was established, nearly all of its blessings ceased? If it be established, the whole system, signs and all, should continue in full force, as long as there is a soul on the earth to be saved.

If so great a portion of the gospel blessings were intended to cease as unnecessary, is it not exceedingly strange that no intimation should be given in the scriptures to that effect? When the commands, ordinances, and blessings of the system of Christianity have been once established in the earth, have we not every reason to believe, without the least shadow of a doubt, that they are intended to continue, unless something to the contrary is intimated in the word of God? After Jesus had promised miraculous signs to the believers in all the world, would He withhold the promised blessings from them in any part of the world, or in any age, without giving some reason for not fulfilling His promise? Every believer in all the world, and in every age, should seek after the miraculous signs with as much confidence and assurance as he would seek after any other promised blessing, until Jesus intimates in His word that He no longer intends bestowing them according to promise. Until our Lord declares that He will no longer bestow the promised signs upon believers, every church who are not in possession of these signs, may know that they are not true believers. If true believers fail in receiving the promised signs, they have no reason to suppose that they will receive the promised salvation. Modern Christians who do not enjoy the signs of believers, cannot expect to enjoy the salvation of believers.

One of two things is certainly true, either modern Christians who do not enjoy the miraculous signs, are not true believers, or else Jesus fails on His part to fulfill His promise. If they are not true believers, they will fail of salvation; if Jesus fails on His part to fulfill one promise, what confidence have they to suppose that He will fulfill the others? If true believers learn that Jesus withholds one promise without rendering any reason for so doing, what certainty have they that He will not also withhold every other promise? They can have no certainty at all. Nothing sure upon which to build their hopes of salvation. If one promise fails, all may fail. If the words of Jesus are not fulfilled in one thing, this is calculated to destroy all confidence in the rest of His sayings. Therefore, if they really are true believers, Jesus has refused to fulfill His promise, and give them the signs of true believers, and consequently they may expect that He will refuse to give them a glorious resurrection and an inheritance in His presence.

It may be argued that Jesus has nowhere in His word limited the promise of a glorious resurrection, and of salvation to the believers who should live in the first age of Christianity, and therefore, these promises may be claimed in all successive ages. So, likewise, it may be argued that, as Jesus has nowhere in His word limited the miraculous signs to the believers of the first age of Christianity, therefore they may be claimed by believers in all subsequent ages, as long as the earth should stand.

Jesus promised both the salvation and signs: both were promised to every creature in all the world who should believe the gospel: both, so far as we can discover from the word of God, were intended for believers of all future generations. Modern believers assert that they have not obtained the promised signs. Why, then, do they assert that they shall obtain the promised salvation? Why suppose that Jesus will fulfill one promise, when He fails to fulfill the other? To illustrate this subject, we offer the following parable:—

A certain king, great and powerful, reigned over a numerous and happy people. His territories were situated in the most beautiful and delightful portions of the earth. The land abounded with the most valuable treasures, such as were unknown in any other country. Nothing could exceed the order, peace, prosperity, and happiness diffused throughout all his dominions.

At a certain time, the king sent forth ambassadors among all nations, to invite them to become subjects of his government, and in due time to emigrate to his happy country. These ambassadors were invested with power to legally administer the oath of allegiance, and all other laws and ordinances which the king had established for the purpose of adopting citizens into his own government. And the king said unto them, "He that receiveth you and becomes an adopted citizen, shall, when he emigrates, receive an inheritance in my dominions: but he that is not adopted shall in no wise enter into my kingdom. These signs or tokens shall accompany the adopted citizens: in my name they shall carry a costly metal, enstamped with the great seal of my authority; they shall wear upon one of their fingers a choice jewel from my own dominions; they shall have a white stone upon which shall be engraved, in unknown characters, a new name known only to themselves. All these signs or tokens shall accompany them."

The ambassadors went forth as they were directed, and many thousands in all parts of the world received the ordinances of adoption; and the signs or tokens of their legal citizenship were abundantly manifested. When the adopted citizens received the promised signs, they were greatly confirmed, and believed with much assurance that they should, after emigration, receive the promised inheritance.

In process of time a great persecution arose. Many of these adopted citizens were put to death. Many others began, through carelessness, to lose the precious signs and tokens of their citizenship. At length persecution began to abate, and the proclamation of the king was received more favorably. Many, on account of its increasing popularity, assumed the authority to administer the oath of allegiance and the ordinances of adoption, without either seeing or hearing from the king. For fear the people would question their authority, they flattered them with the idea that the king would no longer call ambassadors by revealing any new commission, and that the whole work of commissioning and authorizing was left entirely to their own wisdom. But it was soon found that the signs and tokens of citizenship were no longer granted, although many petitioned the king very earnestly to send them, but their petitions were unheeded. The reason of this was, because no one was authorized from the king to administer the oath of allegiance and adopt citizens legally. Therefore the king would not give the tokens of citizenship. But these unauthorized usurpers, who had already made the people believe that it was unnecessary to receive a commission by any new revelation, next actually persuaded the people to believe that the signs and tokens of citizenship were also unnecessary. Popularity and age soon established these false traditions, insomuch that the people almost universally believed, in direct opposition to the promise of the king, that the signs of citizenship were unnecessary.

They continued to emigrate in great numbers as was supposed to the promised land, where it was expected they would receive the promised inheritance. But as it was absurd, according to their traditions, to expect any communication from that land, they could not tell whether the emigrants were permitted to enter into the kingdom and receive their inheritance or not. Now the king was very angry with those who had usurped authority, and had administered the laws of adoption without being sent. He was also very angry with the people who had suffered themselves to be so grossly imposed upon, as to suppose that any could be sent without some communication from him. He, therefore, withheld from them the promised signs and also the promised inheritance, for none of them had been legally adopted. Though they obtained none of the tokens or signs, yet they vainly flattered themselves that they should get the inheritance. But as many as were found who had been deceived, and had not the promised signs of citizenship, were taken and bound as enemies and aliens, and cast into their own place; and great misery prevailed among them—weeping, and wailing, and gnashing of teeth.

And after a long time had passed away, the king sent forth from his dominions one mighty and strong, clothed with great power; and many other messengers were called and sent even according to the first pattern. And they were commanded to go unto every nation, kindred, tongue and people, and call upon all men to come forth and be legally adopted, and take the oath of allegiance from such as were authorized to administer it, and from their hands to receive the ordinances of adoption. And the king again renewed his promise, and said that the signs and tokens of citizenship should again be enjoyed, and such should receive the promised inheritance.

Now these messengers went forth according to the commandments of the king, and those who received them were blessed with the signs, and had much assurance. Now these unauthorized usurpers who pretended to be the servants of the king, and those whom they had deceived, when they saw the signs and tokens of citizenship again made manifest, were exceedingly angry, and sent forth all manner of wicked accusations and lies against the king's messengers, and those who had received them; and by these wicked means the people were stirred up to greatly persecute them, destroying many, and driving others from place to place, and from city to city. At length they were driven forth a great distance from among the nations; and there they were nourished until they became exceedingly strong: the king himself greatly strengthened them by additional tokens of his goodness.

The king's messengers, notwithstanding the cruelties which they received from the people, continued to go from nation to nation, and the signs and tokens of citizenship began to shine forth with greater brilliancy, which enraged the pretended citizens who had not these tokens still more, and they gathered together in multitudes upon all the face of the earth to fight against those who had the signs of citizenship. In process of time, after passing through many tribulations, the lawful heirs went out from among the nations with power and great glory, and gathered themselves in one. And it came to pass that they built a great city unto the king, and he came with all the mighty ones of his dominions, and dwelt among them; and those who had fought against his messengers, perished; and all the earth came under the dominion of the great king.

Let us now examine the use or benefit of these miraculous signs. Jesus said, "*These signs shall follow them that believe.*" If they were to be of no particular use or benefit to the believer, it is not reasonable to suppose that Jesus would have promised them. Modern Christendom asserts that these signs were given, not so much for the benefit of believers, as for the convincing of unbelievers. The servants of God, it is said, wrought signs and wonders to establish the divine authenticity of their calling and message. Signs followed, they assert, that all people might know believers from unbelievers—the true Church from every other church.

If these signs, as modern divines suppose, were given for these purposes, then we ask, why should they be done away in succeeding ages, when there were millions of unbelievers upon the earth? How are people to determine at the present day which among the modern churches is the Church of Christ? How shall they know believers from unbelievers? or the ministers of Christ from deceivers or impostors? We can distinguish them now, says modern Christendom, by the word of God. But the word of God says, "signs shall follow them that believe." And as they deny signs in these days, the word of God would at once condemn them all as unbelievers.' Not any of the Papist or Protestant sects can prove, by the word of God, to the unbelieving world, that they are the true church—that their ministry is authorized of God, and that they are true believers in Christ. The word of God condemns them all, because they have not the signs which Jesus said should follow the believers.

The Protestants denounce the Catholics as the mother of harlots—the most wicked and corrupt power on earth. The Catholics denounce the Protestants as heretics and apostates from the true church. The word of God denounces them both as unbelievers, because they lack the signs. The infidel world denounces the word of God, because miraculous signs follow neither Catholics nor Protestants, who pretend to be believers. The sincere inquirer is almost distracted, because he is in greater doubt whether to believe in Catholics, Protestants, infidelity, or the word of God. If signs then were given to distinguish the ministers of Christ from impostors, surely the present generation need them if ever they were needed.

In the midst of all these conflicting opinions, the humble servant of God comes forth and boldly declares that no church can be the true church, unless they obey the words of Christ and enjoy the signs of believers. He testifies with authority that all the promises of Jesus will be fulfilled while there is one believer upon the face of the earth to be perfected and saved. He testifies that all who deny that signs will follow them that believe, are unbelievers, who, according to the words of Christ, must be damned.

It is very evident, however, that these signs were not given merely for the purpose of convincing unbelievers. "In my name," says Jesus, "*they shall cast out devils.*" although this power might, in certain cases convince the unbelieving world, yet it is by no means to be supposed that this was the principal design. Devils and unclean spirits frequently took possession of the human tabernacle, tormenting individuals in various ways. Jesus promised believers that they, in His name, should cast them out. Now one object which Jesus had in view in granting this power, was to benefit the one possessed. Another object was to confirm the believers, that they by having power over the devil in this life, might be more fully assured that they should obtain a complete victory and final triumph over him in the world to come. That person who cannot obtain power in the name of Jesus to cast out devils in this life, has great reason to fear lest the devil shall obtain power over him in the next life. What assurance has any one that he shall obtain a complete salvation from the power of the devil, when his spirit shall leave the body, if he cannot claim the promise of Jesus, and cast him out while his spirit dwells in the body? One of the purposes then which Jesus had in view in bestowing this blessing, was that believers might learn to prevail against the devil before they should enter the invisible world of spirits. And another purpose, as we have already named, was to deliver the unhappy demoniac from his miserable and wretched condition, and set him free from the grasp of this awful monster.

Now both of these purposes are just as essential for the good of mankind in this age as in the first age of Christianity. It would be equally as essential for a man who is possessed of devils in this age to be liberated, as it was in any former age. And it would also be equally as essential that a believer should learn to command the devil in the name of Jesus, that he might obtain a complete victory over him in all things, as it was for ancient believers. Therefore, as there is no scripture to do away this promise, nor any reason to prove it unnecessary, it must be intended for believers of all ages until the devil is bound.

"They shall speak in new tongues." The benefit of this miraculous sign is obvious to every one. If a servant of God were under the necessity of acquiring in the ordinary way a knowledge of languages, a large portion of his time would be unprofitably occupied. While he was spending years to learn the language of a people sufficiently accurate to preach the glad tidings of salvation unto them, thousands would be perishing for the want of the knowledge. If he could be endowed immediately by the power of the Holy Ghost to speak in any language necessary, how much laborious study would be avoided! how much time would be saved that could be occupied more usefully in the spread of the gospel! how much more accurately would principles be expressed, when, not only the ideas, but the lauguage itself is given by the Holy Ghost! How vastly superior is God's plan of qualifying His servants to preach in different languages and tongues, to the plans adopted by modern divines! The servant of God is qualified in a moment, as it were, to preach by the inspiration of the Holy Spirit in the language of any people to whom he may be sent; while modern divines will throw away years in acquiring the knowledge of a language; and when they have acquired it, they cannot preach in it by the inspiration of the Holy Ghost, but are still dependent upon their own learning and wisdom.

In one day the unlearned fishermen of Galilee acquired a more extensive qualification for preaching in the different languages of the earth, than all the various grades and ranks of clergymen who have disgraced the name of Christianity on the eastern hemisphere for the last seventeen centuries. The gift of tongues was not confined to the ministers of Christ alone, but it was bestowed liberally upon the private members of the Church. Indeed, it was one of the signs promised to believers throughout all the world. As soon as Paul baptized the Ephesians, he laid his hands upon them and they received the Holy Ghost, and immediately spake with tongues and prophesied (*See Acts xix.* 6.). When the household of Cornelius received the Holy Spirit, they also spake with tongues and glorified God (*Acts x.* 46). The Corinthian church were abundantly blessed with this gift(*See I. Cor. xii., xiii. and xvi. chapters*).

That the principle use of this gift was to preach the gospel to the people of different tongues and languages we presume no one will deny. And that there was another benefit derived through the medium of this gift is also evident The members of the church were confirmed and strengthened in their faith by the enjoyment of this gift. Jesus had promised this miraculous sign, among many others, to believers; if they had failed to receive the blessings, they would have had reason to doubt whether they were true believers; but when they received tongues, together with all other promised blessings, they were no longer in doubt, but were assured, not only of the truth of the doctrine, but that they themselves were accepted of God.

The benefits to be derived from this gift are as essential in this age, as in the first age of Christianity. It is as necessary that people of different languages should hear the gospel now, as in early ages. It is also as important that believers should be confirmed by this gift now, as it ever was. Therefore, as there is no scripture to limit this gift to the early Christians, and no reason why believers should not enjoy it now, we are compelled to admit that this promise of Jesus is in full force yet, and that whenever and wherever we find a church of true believers in Christ, there we shall also find the signs of believers. And as the gift of tongues is not among the apostate churches now on the earth, we are compelled by the word of God to consider them all unbelievers. Indeed, they cannot be believers; for if they were they could speak with new tongues, as Jesus promised.

"They shall take up serpents, or if they drink any deadly thing it shall not hurt them." This promise of our Great Redeemer was also made to every creature in all the world who should believe the gospel. The use of this miraculous gift was to preserve life, in case any believer should accidentally be bitten by a poisonous serpent as Paul was (see *Acts xxviii.*); or should unintentionally swallow a deadly poison, as the sons of the prophets did (see *II. Kings iv*). Jesus promised that it should not hurt them. When the Israelites were bitten by poisonous serpents, they were healed by simply looking at a brazen serpent which the Lord commanded Moses to raise up in the wilderness; so the believers in Christ can prevail against deadly poisons by simply looking to Him in faith; for Jesus cannot fail to fulfil His promise to the believer.

"They shall lay hands on the sick, and they shall recover." This also is one of the signs of believers. Sickness is a very prevalent calamity among the inhabitants of our fallen world. Any medical discoveries that will benefit the sick, are considered of inestimable value. Medicines are valued in proportion to their usefulness. Some medicines are useful in one disease, but, at the same time, will leave a lasting injury upon the human constitution. Others have a more salutary effect; and are beneficial in numerous diseases; such, when their beneficial tendencies are thoroughly understood, are generally prized in preference to those of inferior quality.

One of the most simple and harmless prescriptions for the sick, and one which is a certain cure for diseases and plagues of every description—is that prescribed by one of the most celebrated physicians that ever lived among men. The prescription is simply this—"THEY SHALL LAY HANDS UPON THE SICK, AND THEY SHALL RECOVER." There is no disease so violent in its nature—so deadly in its operations, but what this remedy, when properly attended to, will effect a complete cure, without in the least injuring the human system like many other prescriptions. This remedy is infinitely superior to all others, first because of its universal application to all diseases, plagues, and pestilences; secondly, because of the certainty with which it removes pain and every cause of disease; thirdly, because of the expeditious and immediate relief which it affords the patient; fourthly, because it does not prostrate the human system, and injure the constitution like many other powerful prescriptions, which frequently terminate in the worst of consequences; fifthly, because it can be obtained without money, or price, being within the reach of the poor as well as the rich; sixthly, because it does not require years of laborious study to acquire a knowledge of the nature of the disease or of the nature of its treatment like most other theories; and seventhly, because it can be obtained in all parts of the world where true believers are to be found.

Another prescription of equal value, and producing like effects is given by another celebrated author in these words: "Is any sick among you? let him call for the Elders of the Church, and let them pray over him, anointing him with oil in the name of the Lord; and the prayer of faith shall save the sick, and the Lord shall raise them up; and if he have committed sins, they shall be forgiven him" (*James v.* 14, 15). The prayer of faith accompanied by the ordinances is the most universal, powerful, and effective remedy of any that has ever yet been discovered.

The great Physician, who has unfolded to the nations this infinitely valuable and all powerful remedy, has been jealous of His own glory, and has so prepared it that it can never be administered with the least effect only in His name by one that is authorized, that is by a true believer. This is an effectual preventative against all quacks and impostors who may undertake in His name to counterfeit the genuine; for in all cases, such will fail like the seven sons of Sceva (*Acts xix.* 13, 14, 15, 16).

The apostate churches for many centuries past have been destitute of this promised blessing of our Savior. They have endeavored to blind the eyes of mankind, by telling them that this blessing was not needed after the first age of Christianity. This false tradition, invented by a set of wicked impostors to hide their own unbelief and want of authority, has been handed down by successive false teachers, until the present day; and what is still more strange, there are millions of poor, ignorant fanatics, who have been led away with the fatal delusion. It has been the study of the wicked impostors of modern times to persuade the people that the promised signs of the gospel are not needed now. In this thing there is great policy; for as they have so far apostatized as to be entirely destitute of the blessings themselves, if they could not succeed in deluding their followers to suppose that miraculous signs are not needed in these days, all people would at once discover that they were not believers, but impostors, acting without authority, having a form of godliness, but destitute of its promised powers, pretending to be believers without the signs of believers.

If their deluded followers should, by any means, get the scales of priestcraft off from their eyes sufficiently to believe the promise of Jesus in preference to the traditional impositions of their false, rotten-hearted, and corrupt ministers, away would go the popularity of long-established institutions, and down would tumble, with a tremendous crash, the long-loved salaries of a hireling priesthood, and they would stand forth as monuments of shame and disgrace before all men. To save themselves from this open disgrace, they have used all their cunning and ingenuity to deceive the people into the belief that the gift of healing, and the other promised signs of Jesus, are unnecessary now.

But are there any sick in these days? if so, would it not be just as beneficial for the sick to be relieved in these days as at any former time? Would it not confirm and establish believers to lay hands on the sick, and see them healed in these days, as much as it did ancient believers? If then, it would confirm believers and benefit the sick the same now as anciently, we have no reason to limit it to the early Christians. Hence, both scripture and reason show that the promised signs are as unlimited as the promised salvation.

The affliction of devils—the confusion of tongues—deadly poisons—and sickness, are all curses which have been introduced into the world by the wickedness of man. The blessings of the gospel are bestowed to counteract these curses. Therefore, as long as these curses exist, the promised signs are needed to counteract their evil consequences. If Jesus had not intended, that the blessings should be as extensive and unlimited in point of time as the curses, He would have intimated something to that effect in His word. But when He makes a universal promise of certain powers, to enable every believer in the gospel throughout the world to overcome certain curses, entailed upon man, because of wickedness, it would be the rankest kind of infidelity not to believe the promised blessings necessary, as long as the curses abound among men.

If these signs are necessary, why have they not existed among the churches for the last seventeen centuries? Because no true believers have existed among them during that time; for Jesus says, they shall follow the true believer; hence, if there had been any true believers, the signs would have been among them. But the very fact that the signs have ceased during that time, prove that true believers have ceased also. This is a sad picture of mankind, but it is none the less true. We say, let the promise of our blessed Redeemer be true, though it prove every man a liar or a hypocrite. The fault cannot be in Jesus, therefore it must be in man. The promises of Christ are as unchangeable as His own nature, and can never fail; but man is as changeable as the wind, and is very apt to fail in almost every respect.

Since the great apostasy, sincerity has characterized millions of professed Christians, but none of them have obeyed the ancient gospel, because no one was authorized to legally administer its ordinances to them; therefore, notwithstanding their sincerity, they could not obey the gospel for the want of a legal administrator; hence, they could have no legal claim on the gospel blessings. And, for this reason, they could not become legal or adopted believers; therefore, they could have no legal claim on the signs promised to believers; and this is one reason why the sincere, honest-hearted, professed Christians of modern times have not enjoyed these great blessings promised by our Savior. Neither can they enjoy the promised salvation in all its fullness, but must be rewarded according to their works, and the opportunities they have enjoyed, in some of the mansions or kingdoms inferior in glory to the kingdom possessed by the ancient saints, who obeyed the law and enjoyed the promised blessings. And all who will not now repent, as the authority is once more restored to the earth, and come forth out of the corrupted apostate churches, and be legally adopted into the Church of Christ, and earnestly seek after the blessings and miraculous gifts of the gospel, shall be thrust down to hell, saith the Lord God of Hosts; for now they have no excuse for their belief; therefore, if they will not now repent, they shall be damned. This is the word of the Lord to priests and people of all churches, and of all nations.

We will now give a few examples to show the principle upon which the sick were generally healed. This was accomplished through faith in Jesus Christ. If the sick were capable of exercising faith, then faith was required of them in order to obtain the blessing. The woman who had the issue of blood for twelve years said, 'If I may touch but His clothes, I shall be whole.' Jesus turned to her and said, "Daughter, thy faith hath made thee whole" (*Mark v.*) When Jesus went over into the land of Gennesareth, and passed through their villages, cities, and countries, so great was their faith in Him, that they brought their sick and laid them "in the streets, and besought Him that they might touch if it were but the border of His garment, and as many as touched Him were made whole" (*Mark vi.*) Blind Bartimæus cried unto the Lord for mercy. "And Jesus said unto him, go thy way; thy *faith* hath made thee whole" (*Mark x.*) When Jesus touched the eyes of two blind men that came into the house where He was, He said unto them, "according to your *faith* be it unto you" (*Matthew ix.* 29.) A certain cripple "heard Paul speak, who steadfastly beholding him, and perceiving that he had *faith* to be healed, said with a loud voice, Stand upright on thy feet. And he leaped and walked" (*Acts xiv.* 9. 10.)

Many other examples might be given to show that the power of healing was manifested through *faith*. Sometimes the faith of others was exercised in behalf of the sick, as examples: A woman of Canaan sought a blessing for her daughter, who was grievously vexed with a devil. "Jesus answered and said unto her, O woman, great is thy faith: be it unto thee, even as thou wilt" (*Matthew xv.*) A centurion exercised faith in behalf of his servant, who was sick of the palsy. "And Jesus said unto him, Go thy way; and as thou hast *believed*, so be it done unto thee. And his servant was healed in the self-same hour" (*Matthew viii.*) A certain man whose son had been tormented of the devil from a child, says to Jesus, "If thou canst do anything, have compassion on us and help us. Jesus said unto him, If thou canst believe, all things are possible to him that believeth. And straightway the father of the child cried out, and said with tears, Lord, I believe: help Thou mine unbelief" (*Mark ix.*) The devil was rebuked, and his son was liberated. Jairus, whose daughter lay at the point of death, came to Jesus, and fell down before Him, and requested Him to go and lay His hands upon her, that she might be healed. While on the way to his house, one met them, saying, "Thy daughter is dead: why troublest thou the Master any further? As soon as Jesus heard the word that was spoken, He said unto the ruler of the synagogue, Be not afraid, only believe" (*Mark v.*) And Jesus restored his daughter to life again. Many other instances are recorded where friends exercised faith in behalf of the afflicted.

Therefore, it may be considered as a general law that sick and afflicted were healed, either through their own faith, or the faith of some of their friends. There may be some rare instances where the blessing is bestowed through the faith alone of the administrator.

It is the general opinion of modern churches that the principal object of miracles was to do away unbelief. But when Jesus went into His own country, among His old acquaintances, He marveled because of their unbelief (*See Mark vi.* 5.) "And He did not many mighty works there because of their unbelief" (*Matthew xiii.*) But according to the ideas of the false techers of modern times, He should have performed greater works there, than anywhere else. As they consider signs to be for the convincing of the unbeliever; therefore the greater the unbelief, the greater should be the signs. When He found His own countrymen so very unbelieving, He should, according to modern notions concerning the object of signs, have performed far more splendid and magnificent miracles there, than He did in any other region where their unbelief was not so great. But the facts of the case were directly the reverse. The greater the wickedness and unbelief of a people, the less were the mighty works performed among them. So among the Christian churches, as their unbelief increased, the mighty works decreased. And when the people became hardened in apostasy and unbelief, all mighty works ceased, and the salvation ceased also.

Thus it will be seen, that the signs and blessings of the gospel are enjoyed only by faith. The greater the faith, the greater will be the manifestations of the miraculous power of God. The miracles will decrease as faith decreases; and cease when faith ceases. The miraculous signs bestowed upon believers in this life, are blessings far inferior to the blessings of a glorious resurrection and eternal life. But he that has not faith sufficient to obtain the miraculous signs, or smaller blessings, how can he obtain faith sufficient to receive the greater blessings? If the smaller blessings are withheld for the want of faith, will not the greater blessings be withheld for a like reason? If a person has not means enough to buy himself a coat, how can he expect to purchase a splendid habitation? So likewise, if a person has not faith enough to obtain the miraculous signs promised, how can he expect to obtain a glorious mansion in the kingdom of God? If his faith is so weak that it will not procure for him the smaller blessings, he may be much more assured that the same weak faith will not procure for him the greater blessings.

Jesus said, as we have already quoted, that "All things are possible to him that believeth." Jesus also said, "Have faith in God. For verily, I say unto you, that whosoever shall say unto this mountain, Be thou removed, and be thou cast into the sea; and shall not doubt in his heart, but shall believe that those things which he saith shall come to pass; he shall have whatsoever he saith. Therefore, I say unto you: What things soever ye desire, when ye pray, believe that ye receive them and ye shall have them" (*Mark xi.* 22, 23, 24). This promise was not confined to the apostles and early saints, for the term, "whosoever," embraces all mankind who shall have faith, in every age throughout the world. Who can read these precious promises of our Savior, without perceiving in the plainest light, the awful apostate condition of the churches? They are without faith—without any confidence in God. They despise those who are sincerely seeking after the ancient faith. Both from the pulpit and from the press they boldly avow their infidelity in the above promises, and say all manner of evil against those who do believe them. They will greatly praise up the faith of the ancient saints, and build synagogues and chapels to their memory; but for any person to teach that the same faith is necessary now, is, in their estimation, the highest blasphemy. O ye hypocrites! Why do you profess to be the followers of Christ, and yet deny His promises? O ye blind guides! Why do you deceive the people with a form of godliness, and yet deny the promised powers? Why do you make void the promises of Jesus through your unbelief and wicked traditions? Why do you, through great swelling words of man's wisdom, pervert the truth, and deny the inspiration of the Holy Ghost and the gift of revelation and prophecy? Why do you preach for hire, and through covetousness make merchandise of the people, while the poor and the needy are crying for bread? O ye wicked and corrupt teachers! Ye hirelings! Why do you, through your mock piety and cunning craftiness, not only close the gates of heaven upon yourselves, but hedge up the way of others who would know the truth and be saved? How can you escape the vengeance of eternal fire? How long will the Lord suffer you to practice your deceptions and wickedness? The hour of your judgment is nigh! Howl, ye apostate churches, for the miseries which shall come upon you! The day of fierce vengeance is at hand, and ye shall utterly perish from the earth!

The Church of Christ is called the body of Christ. "Now ye are the body of Christ, and members in particular" (*I. Cor. xii.* 27). We shall here give the names of the different members, composing the various parts of the body or Church of Christ. "God hath set some in the church, first, *apostles*; secondarily, *prophets*; thirdly, *teachers;* after that *miracles;* then gifts of *healing, helps, governments,* diversities of *tongues*" (*Verse* 28). These members of the body were joined together upon one common principle which I have already explained in Chapter II. of this treatise. They were all introduced into the church through faith, repentance and the ordinances. Paul says, "By one spirit are we all baptized into one body, whether we be Jews or Gentiles, whether we be bond or free; and have been all made to drink into one spirit" (*Verse* 13).

This one body into which all members are baptized, is quickened and animated in all its parts by one spirit. The operations of the Spirit in different parts of the body are various. "To one," says Paul, "is given by the Spirit the word of wisdom; to another, the word of knowledge by the same Spirit; to another, faith by the same Spirit; to another, the gifts of healing by the same Spirit; to another, the working of miracles; to another, prophecy; to another, discerning of spirits; to another, divers kinds of tongues; to another, the interpretation of tongues; but all these worketh that one and the selfsame Spirit dividing to every man severally as He will" (*Verses*, 8, 9, 10, 11). Paul has here so clearly described the Church of Christ, that none need be at a loss when they have found it. Every faithful member of the body of Christ possesses some gift of the Spirit. All the churches now on the earth can compare themselves with this scriptural pattern; if they do not resemble the pattern, they may know at once that they are not the body or Church of Christ. If they have no apostles nor prophets—no officers that can receive the word of wisdom, and the word of knowledge by the inspiration of the Spirit—if they have no member possessing the gift of healing —no worker of miracles—no beholder of visions or discerner of spirits—no speaker in tongues—if they have none of these members of the body of Christ, then they have nothing that resembles the pattern, and, therefore, they cannot possibly be the Church of Christ.

The body of Christ is wholly made of the above named members. To do away with the least member there mentioned would produce a schism in the body, and it would be imperfect like the human body, with one of its members lacking. The body, or church, like the human body, would become more and more imperfect and mutilated in proportion to the usefullness and number of the above members that are done away. And when all the members or parts of the body vanish, it ceases to exist on the earth. It is an admitted fact that the greater part, if not all of the members described by Paul are done away, and considered unnecessary at the present day. And as the body or church is *nothing*, separate and apart from its members; therefore, where they cease, the body must cease also.

There are many parts of the human body that are essential to its existence, and without which, the body must inevitably perish; such for examples, as the mouth—the heart—the lungs—the stomach—the liver—the bowels, and many others too numerous to mention. Deprive the body of either of these essential parts, and all other parts will perish also. Two of the most prominent parts or members of the body of Christ are, "First, *apostles;* secondly, *prophets.*" These may be considered the eyes and mouth-piece of the body. Take these away, and the body is left in total darkness without eyes to see with, or a mouth through which to receive the nourishment essential to its existence. If, therefore, only these two members were to cese, all the other members would speedily perish, and the Church of Christ would cease to exist among men. The apostate churches have had neither of these members for upwards of seventeen centuries, therefore, during that time, they have had no eyes nor mouth through which they could receive light and nourishment.

If the mouth and eyes of the human body were to be destroyed, the human spirit would take its flight, and the body would soon become a mass of putrid corruption, sending forth a most offensive stench, engendering pestilence and disease, and affecting the health of all who should come within its nauseous influence. Such would be the fatal consequeuces attending the church should they so far depart from God as to lose inspired apostles and prophets, the first two essential and most important members which God placed in the body. If these members were taken away, the Holy Spirit, which is the life of the church, would take its flight, even as the human spirit flees from the mortal body, when its essential parts are destroyed. When the Holy Spirit takes its departure, the body, or church, is left in a lifeless state; all the miraculous operations of the Spirit cease.

In ancient times, after apostles and prophets ceased, the other members of the body began immediately to die for want of nourishment; the member possessing the gift of healing—the worker of miracles—the speaker with tongues—the interpreter of tongues, and all other members, withered away and died, leaving a mass of putrid corruption whose nauseous stench and abominable filthiness have spread forth a deadly malaria among all nations.

It is in vain for the apostate churches to endeavor to prove themselves to be the body of Christ, by pretending that they have one or two of the members still in existence; for Paul enquires, "If they were all one member, where were the body?" (*Verse* 19). If every part of our bodies were destroyed, except hands and feet, they could in no wise constitute a living body; so, likewise, if every member of the church were done away, except professed teachers, and some two or three other pretended members of different functions, these could no more constitute a living church, than hands, and arms, and feet, and legs, could constitute a living man. The Holy Spirit would no more dwell in these pretended fragments of the church, which are falsely said to still remain, than the human spirit would dwell in the hands, feet, or legs, after the rest of the body was gone.

Reader, would it not be marvelously strange to behold hands, feet, and legs moving, acting and performing their accustomed functions after all the rest of the body was destroyed? Yet this would not be any more strange, than it is to see teachers and some few other pretended members, endeavoring to move, and act, and perform certain other functions, after nine-tenths of the most important and vital members of the church have been done away for centuries. As well might you undertake to retain life in an isolated human hand, as to retain life in teachers for centuries after apostles, prophets, workers of miracles, etc., have ceased.

Paul says, "The eye cannot say to the hand, I have no need of thee; nor again, the head to the feet, I have no need of you" (*Verse* 21). But in direct opposition to this instruction, the apostate teachers of modern times say to the worker of miracles, I have no need of thee. And their pastors say to the speaker with tongues, and the interpreter of tongues, we have no need of you in the body. It matters not how feeble, or how inferior in use some members are, when compared with others, yet none can be dispensed with. "Nay," says Paul, "much more, those members of the body, which seem to be more feeble, are necessary" (*Verse* 22). If the speaker with tongues, or the interpreter of tongues, is considered a more feeble member, and not as useful as the prophets or apostles; yet Paul says expressly, that such "are necessary." Therefore, for a teacher or pastor to say that they are not necessary, is to come out in direct opposition to the scriptures.

How superlatively ridiculous it would be for the hands and feet to rise up in rebellion to the eyes—the mouth—the heart —the lungs—the bowels—the breast—the neck, and say, we have no need of you: we can get along without your assistance; you are useless appendages to us, hands and feet: we can feel and walk without your help. And yet as a parallel to this, the teachers and pastors of our day have arisen up in rebellion to Paul's words, and have said to apostles—prophets —the healer of the sick—the worker of miracles—the beholder or discerner of spirits—the speaker with tongues—the interpreter of tongues—we have no need of you: we can get along without your assistance, you are all unnecessary parts of the body: you are perfectly useless to us pastors and teachers: we can perform all the functions of our office without your aid. Such has been the state of the apostate churches for the last seventeen hundred years. And such is the awful darkness that now reigns in their midst.

It is in and through the body or church of Christ that the Spirit manifests itself: "The manifestation of the Spirit is given to every man to profit withall" (*Verse* 7). It is, therefore, by these manifestations that every man in the church is profited. There is as much necessity for these various manifestations now as anciently. Paul mentions in this chapter nine different gifts or manifestations of the Spirit. All churches which have not these miraculous manifestations have not the Holy Spirit; and without the Spirit they are none of Christ's.

The distinguishing characteristics between true and false churches are so evident that none need be mistaken. The one enjoys the Holy Spirit with all its gifts, as set forth in the word of God; the others profess to enjoy the Spirit, but have none of the gifts and operations ascribed to it. The only way by which we discover that the human body is animated by the human spirit, is by its operations; so likewise, the method by which we determine that a church enjoys the Holy Spirit is by its diversity of operations or manifestations. If these cease, we have every reason to believe that the Holy Spirit has departed also.

Among all nations, and in all ages of the world, whenever the Holy Spirit has been given, it has exhibited itself in supernatural gifts. These gifts were given, not only for the benefit of the church in this life, but to prepare them for still greater blessings in the world to come. It is altogether a mistaken idea to suppose that these gifts were merely given for the convincing of unbelievers. Paul says expressly, that the gifts which were given by our Lord after His ascension were intended for other purposes. "When He (Christ) ascended up on high, He led captivity captive, and gave gifts unto men." (*Eph. iv.* 8.) "And he gave some apostles, and some prophets, and some evangelists, and some pastors and teachers." (*Verse* 11.) These, together with numerous other gifts, were given, not merely to establish the truth of Christianity, but as Paul says, "For the perfecting of the Saints, for the work of the ministry, for the edifying of the body of Christ: till we all come in the unity of the faith, and of the knowledge of the Son of God, unto a perfect man, unto the measure of the stature of the fullness of Christ: that we henceforth be no more children, tossed to and fro, and carried about with every wind of doctrine, by the sleight of men, and cunning craftiness, whereby they lie in wait to deceive; but speaking the truth in love, may grow up into Him all things, which is the head, even Christ: from whom the whole body fitly joined together and compacted by that which every joint supplieth, according to the effectual working in the measure of every part, maketh increase of the body, unto the edifying of itself in love." (*Verses* 12, 13, 14, 15, 16.)

By these declarations we discover the objects which the Lord has in view, by giving gifts unto men. One object is declared to be "*For the perfecting of the Saints.*" It is very evident from the whole tenor of the scripture, that unless the Saints are perfected they can never enjoy a perfect salvation. The only plan which Jesus has devised for the accomplishment of this great object, is through the medium of the spiritual gifts. When the supernatural gifts of the Spirit cease, the Saints cease to be perfected, therefore they can have no hopes of obtaining a perfect salvation. To do away from the Church, apostles, prophets, and other gifts, is to do away the great plan which heaven has devised for the perfection and final salvation of the righteous.

The author of the epistle to the Hebrews urges upon the Saints the necessity of "going on unto perfection," (*see chap. vi.* 1), but this would be impossible for those churches who have no apostles, prophets, and other gifts which Jesus gave after His ascension. Such churches could not "go on unto perfection," for they have lost, and continue to do away the very gifts which were intended to accomplish that object.

Has Jesus anywhere in His word told us that His plan of perfecting the Saints should cease, and that mankind would introduce a better one? If not, why then should we not prefer our Savior's plan in preference to all others? Why do away the powers and gifts of the Holy Ghost, which were intended, not merely for the convincing of unbelievers, but for the perfecting of believers? In every nation and age, where believers exist, there the gifts must exist to perfect them, otherwise they would be altogether unprepared for the reception of the still greater powers and glories of the eternal world. If there were no unbelievers on the earth, still there would be the same necessity for the miraculous gifts that there was among early Christians; for if the whole world were believers in Christ they could not possibly be perfected without these gifts, and hence they could not enter into the fullness of His glory.

It is, therefore, directly in opposition to the word of God for the apostate churches to declare that "the object of miraculous gifts was merely to establish the Christian religion, and that after that object was accomplished they were no longer necessary, and therefore ceased." The word of God declares they were "for the perfecting of the Saints;" and, therefore, wherever there are *Saints*, there the gifts are needed, not merely to establish the truth by supernatural evidence, but to *perfect* those who already believe.

Another great object which the Lord has in view, in sending gifts unto men, is "the work of the ministry." Without these gifts the "work of the ministry" never could be carried on; without inspired apostles and prophets the gifts of revelation and prophecy cease, and where these cease the work of the ministry ceases. The apostate churches have no more authority for taking away the gifts of apostles and prophets, than they have for taking away the gifts of pastors and teachers. There is precisely the same evidence for doing away the whole of the gifts, as there is for doing away a part and pretending to retain the others. "The work of the ministry" is clearly manifested in the scriptures. It is required to preach the gospel to all nations in the different tongues and languages of the earth. The ministry is required to receive revelations for the benefit of themselves and all the Saints, reproving by revelation those who need reproof; comforting those who need comfort; forewarning the Church of approaching judgments; pointing out by the spirit of revelation a way of escape; revealing doctrine and principle in relation to things both temporal and spiritual, and unfolding all things necessary for the perfection and eternal exaltation of the righteous. Besides this, the ministry are to lay on hands for the gift of the Holy Ghost, and for the healing of the sick, and administer all other ordinances of the Church. Therefore, without the supernatural powers and gifts of the Holy

Spirit the "work of the ministry" would cease, and when that ceases men cease to be saved.

Paul declares, as we have already quoted, that the gifts were given "for the edifying of the body of Christ." But the various bodies or apostate churches declare boldly, that the gifts are no longer necessary in this age of learning and refinement. Now, say they, we can be edified by learned divines who have become eminently qualified by a long course of study in our great theological institutions. Now, they exclaim, we have a glorious substitute in the stead of the inspiration of the Holy Spirit. In the first age of Christianity—in the days of ignorance and darkness, the gifts of the spirit were given to edify the Church; but now, we have become so learned and enlightened, we need some better plan than the one devised in that day of ignorance; then they knew no better than to be edified through the gifts of the Spirit, but now we have sought out a plan far superior; then they had nothing but knowledge and certainty, and were all of one mind, but now we are blessed with the opinions and commentaries of uninspired men, all differing and contradicting one another, dividing us in our sentiments and doctrines. Oh, how great is the wisdom of our modern divines! How immensely superior are opinion and guess-work to certainty and knowledge! Then they had nothing but direct revelation—the spirit of prophecy, visions, and the ministry of angels to guide them into the truth, but now we have advanced to the high and exalted privilege of being taught by men who despise new revelation and the gifts of the Spirit, and favor us with their superior opinions, and creeds and articles of religion. Great is the plan devised by human wisdom, for the edifying of the church; God's plan can be dispensed with now as unnecessary. This is the language of modern Christendom if we are to judge from their opposition to the gifts which Paul says, were given for the "edifying of the body of Christ."

That no one need be mistaken, and suppose the gifts in the future ages of the Church to be unnecessary, Paul says expressly, that they shall continue for the purposes which he specifies, "Till we all come in the unity of the faith, and of the knowledge of the Son of God, unto a perfect man, unto the measure of the stature of the fullness of Christ." This puts the subject beyond all doubt and controversy; all can see that the gifts were intended as long as there was a Church of the Saints that needed perfecting and edifying. If the modern churches of Christendom have not attained to the unity of the faith and knowledge—to all the perfection and fullness of Christ, they certainly need the gifts until they shall arrive at that state. The period when the Saints shall attain to the perfection and fullness of Christ is very clearly and definitely unfolded by the apostle in his first epistle to the Corinthians. "Charity never faileth: but whether there be prophecies, they shall fail; whether there be tongues, they shall cease; whether there be knowledge, it shall vanish away. For we know in part, and we prophesy in part. But when that which is perfect is come, then that which is in part shall be done away." ($xiii$, 8, 9, 10.) "For now we see through a glass darkly; but then face to face; now I know in part; but then I shall know even as also I am known." (*Verse* 12.)

Thus it will be seen that the gifts were not to cease until "that which is perfect is come"—until we see the Lord face to face—until we know as we are known. Then tongues will cease, and the heavenly glorified throng will all speak the same language. Then prophesying in part will be done away; for the knowledge of the future will be fully understood. Then knowledge in part shall vanish away and the Saints will know in full. Then the day of perfection will come, and all the Saints shall enjoy the fullness of Christ, and see Him no longer through a glass darkly, but face to face. Until that day of glory and perfection shall arrive, all the spiritual gifts will be indispensably necessary, without which the Saints can never attain to that great salvation promised.

Another object for which the miraculous gifts are given unto men, is to keep them from delusion. They are given that the saints "henceforth be no more children, tossed to and fro, and carried about with every wind of doctrine, by the sleight of men, and cunning craftiness, whereby they lie in wait to deceive." The very reason why the apostate churches have for the last seventeen centuries been carried about by the doctrines, creeds, and traditions of uninspired men who have craftily deceived them—is because they lacked the gifts which Paul says were given as an effectual perventative against such winds of doctrine. All churches which have not the gifts, are already deceived and deluded. If it were possible, these popular and learned impostors would deceive the very elect; but this is impossible, for the elect enjoy the gifts which will detect with the most unerring certainty every imposition, however plausible and popular it may be.

The Papist and Protestant churches of modern times, notwithstanding the greatness of their numbers and their exceedingly great popularity—are impositions, under the pious name of Christianity, of the most glaring and dangerous kind.

Their cunning, learned, arch-impostors, have multiplied their followers to millions, and flooded all Europe and America with their pernicious doctrines. Thousands of the honest and unwary are annually led away by these fatal delusions under the false and vain suppositions that they are embracing Christianity. Instead, however, of embracing the Christian religion of the New Testament, they have only embraced some traditional forms that bear but a faint resemblance to it, while its miraculous powers, gifts and blessings are entirely unknown among them, and indeed, are considered as altogether unnecessary. Oh, apostate Christianity! Oh, modern Christendom! Thou, that corruptest all nations with thine abominations, and makest merchandise of the souls of men! Oh! that thou didst but know the day of thy visitation—the hour of God's judgments—and wouldst awake from the awful slumber of ages! But alas! Thine eyes are closed no more to be opened, until they are lifted up in torment, in the midst of lamentations, and woes, and miseries, and hopeless despair!

Seventh.—*The rights, privileges and blessings, promised to the faithful obedient subjects in a future life.*

Eternal life is the greatest of all the gifts of God. It is a blessing promised to all the faithful subjects of His kingdom. The hopes of a future life of happiness that will never end, serve to comfort and cheer them through all the sorrows and tribulations of the present life. We shall endeavor to point out the nature of that eternal life, promised to the children of the kingdom. "This is life eternal, that they might know thee, the only true God, and Jesus Christ, whom thou hast sent." (*John xvii.* 3.) It is not enough merely to have a knowledge of the existence of the Father and Son; but to know them aright is to understand their character—their attributes—their glory—and the nature of the laws which they have ordained for the government of all happy, glorified, and intelligent beings. Such knowledge, when once obtained, is eternal life. Eternal life is not merely to *believe* on the testimony of others in the existence and attributes of God, but it is to obtain something more than a *belief*; it is to obtain a certain *knowledge*. Such knowledge can only be obtained by direct and immediate revelation. "No man knoweth the Son, but the Father; neither knoweth any man the Father, save the Son, and he to whomsoever the Son will REVEAL him." (*Matt. xi.* 27.) All men can *believe* in the existence of God on the testimony of others; but no man can *know* God only by revelation.

Hear this, ye that deny new revelation, and fear and tremble for yourselves; for you can in nowise inherit eternal life, without *knowing* "the only true God, and Jesus Christ whom He hath sent;" and you can in nowise know them without you receive a new revelation. Peter did not obtain his knowledge that Jesus was the Christ, only by a new revelation. Jesus said to Peter, "Blessed art thou, Simon Barjona; for flesh and blood hath not revealed it unto thee, but my Father which is in heaven." (*Matt. xvi.* 17.) No man can know God unless "the Son REVEAL Him. Hence we can perceive, that eternal life can only be enjoyed by a people who believe in, and receive new revelation. All others are in uncertainty and doubt, like the apostate churches, who do not believe in any later revelations than the New Testament, which plainly proves, that they have not attained to the *knowledge* of God, and therefore, eternal life is not among them.

But the children of the kingdom have a knowledge of both the Father and the Son through the medium of new revelation; therefore, eternal life is with them. Their happiness and joy in eternal life will increase as their knowledge of the glory, power, wisdom, and goodness of God increases; and this knowledge will increase only through the medium of new revelation. Hence the whole system of salvation and eternal life, and the increase of knowledge and happiness, are founded upon continued revelation to the children of the kingdom throughout all ages in this world, and in all worlds to come.

---

We have in this treatise briefly touched upon some of the most important subjects connected with the kingdom of God. We shall now proceed to give a summary statement of some of the leading arguments contained in the foregoing.

1.—We have endeavored to point out the nature and character of the great Supreme governing Power of the universe, consisting of the Father, the Son, and the Holy Ghost. The person of the Father consisting of a most glorious substance, called Spirit, which we have shown must have extension and parts, and consequently must be material. Without these qualities no substance could exist.

The Son is in the express image of the Father, and is also a material being. The same material body that was crucified and laid in the tomb, arose again. The same flesh—the same bones were reanimated by the same material spirit. This glorious compound of flesh, and bones, and spirit—all material, ascended into heaven to dwell in the presence of the glorious personage of the Father, of whose express image and likeness He was the most perfect pattern. Therefore, from the description given of Jesus we are irresistibly led to the conclusion, that both He and the Father must appear, so far as it relates to form and size, very much like man. If then, both of these glorious personages are about the size of man, they must, like man occupy a finite space of but a few cubic feet in dimension; and, according to the admitted truths of philosophy, no substance can be in two or more places at the same time, therefore neither the Father nor Son can, consistently with those truths, be in two places at once. Revealed truths never will contradict any other truths. The revealed truths contained in the Bible, inform us that God is everywhere, sustaining and upholding all things, and that in Him we live, and move and have our being. How can these important truths of divine revelation be reconciled with other admitted truths of philosophy which are equally certain? They can be reconciled in no way only by admitting the omnipresence of the Holy Spirit. This all-powerful substance extends throughout the material universe, uniting and mingling with all other matter in a greater or less degree, not absolutely filling all space, for then there would be no room for other matter, but like the rays of light or heat, existing in different degrees of density in different parts of space. By it all things are governed in the most perfect order and wisdom, according to the will of the Father and the Son. This view of the subject does not necessarily do away a personal Spirit, acting in conjunction with the other two persons of the Godhead; for myriads of personal spirits could be organized out of the inexhaustible quantities which exist, and still an abundance would be left to govern and control the various departments of the universe where those personages could not always be present.

2.—We have clearly shown that apostles, prophets, and all other officers of the kingdom of God, must be called and ordained by the inspiration of the Holy Ghost; and that without new revelation these officers never could be qualified to perform the various duties of their calling. We have also proved that the officers of the kingdom have the authority to administer the word, the water, and the Spirit, according to certain conditions, and through certain ordinances in the name of Jesus.

3.—We have pointed out the great scriptural plan of salvation, and the conditions to be complied with on the part of man. These conditions are, faith, a humble repentance, an immersion in water for the remission of sins, the gift of the Holy Spirit through the laying on of hands, and a strict observance of every other requirement of heaven, even unto the end.

4.—We have proved from the dealings of God with His people in all ages, that continued revelation is absolutely necessary for the well-being of the Church, and for its existence among men—that new circumstances are constantly requiring new information from heaven, adapted to these circumstances; and that the Church in one age never could learn its whole duty from revelations given to the Church in a former age.

5.—We have urged the Saints to cultivate such a disposition and character as would best correspond with the word and spirit of Christ.

6.—We have clearly shown from the word of God that all the supernatural gifts of the Spirit, the miraculous signs promised to believers, and every blessing promised under the gospel dispensation, are all necessary in the Church *now*, and should be earnestly sought after by all the faithful Saints—and that no church have any reason or scripture by which they can suppose themselves to be the Church of Christ, unless they believe in and enjoy those miraculous powers.

7.—The word of God, promises to all who faithfully adhere to the laws and ordinances of the kingdom—a paradise of rest—a glorious resurrection—an eternal life of happiness—and an everlasting inheritance upon the new earth, where they shall reign as kings and priests for ever and ever. These are the subjects which we have endeavored to elucidate in this small treatise. They are subjects with which every man throughout the world should be well acquainted, however imperfect they may have been set forth in the foregoing pages, they are none the less important.

The Almighty has decreed to rend and break in pieces all earthly governments—to cast down their thrones—to turn and overturn, and break up the nations—to send forth His messengers, and make a way for the establishment of the everlasting kingdom to which all others must yield, or be prostrated never more to rise. Awake then, O ye nations, for with you, the Lord hath a controversy! His kingdom is now for the last time organized upon the earth—all nations are invited to become citizens—it is the only government of safety or refuge upon all the earth—it hath its seat in the everlasting mountains—its dreadful majesty shall strike terror to the hearts of kings in the day of His power! Awake, for troublous times are at hand! Nations shall no longer sit at ease! The troubled elements shall foment, and rage, and dash with tremendous fury! A voice is heard unto the ends of the earth! A sound of terror and dismay! A sound of nations rushing to battle—fierce and dreadful is the contest—mighty kingdoms and empires melt away! The destroyer has gone forth—the pestilence that waketh in darkness. The plagues of the last days are at hand, and who shall be able to escape? None but the righteous—none but the upright in heart—none but the children of the kingdom. They shall be gathered out from among the nations—they shall stand in holy places, and not be moved! But among the wicked, men shall lift up their voices, and curse God because of His sore judgments, and die. And there shall be a voice of mourning and lamentation unto the ends of the earth; for the cup of the indignation of the Almighty shall be poured out without mixture of mercy, because they would not receive His messengers, but hardened their hearts against the warning proclamation—against the gospel of the kingdom—and against the great preparatory work for the universal reign of the King of kings and Lords of lords.

# DIVINE AUTHENTICITY

### OF THE

# BOOK OF MORMON.

BY ORSON PRATT.

INTRODUCTION—TO EXPECT MORE REVELATION IS NOT UNSRIPTURAL.—TO EXPECT MORE REVELATION IS NOT UNREASONABLE.

## CHAPTER I

THE Book of Mormon claims to be a divinely inspired record, written by a succession of prophets who inhabited ancient America. It professes to be revealed to the present generation for the salvation of all who will receive it, and for the overthrow and damnation of all nations who reject it.

This book must be either *true* or *false*. If true, it is one of the most important messages ever sent from God to man, affecting both the temporal and eternal interests of every people under heaven to the same extent and in the same degree that the message of Noah affected the inhabitants of the old world. If false, it is one of the most cunning, wicked, bold, deep-laid impositions ever palmed upon the world, calculated to deceive and ruin millions who will sincerely receive it as the word of God, and will suppose themselves securely built upon the rock of truth until they are plunged with their families into hopeless despair.

The nature of the message in the Book of Mormon is such, that if true, no one can possibly be saved and reject it; if false, no one can possibly be saved and receive it. Therefore, every soul in all the world is equally interested in ascertaining its truth or falsity. In a matter of such infinite importance no person should rest satisfied with the conjectures or opinions of others: he should use every exertion himself to become acquainted with the nature of the message: he should carefully examine the evidences of which it is offered to the world: he should, with all patience and perseverance, seek to acquire a certain knowledge whether it be of God or not. Without such an investigation in the most careful, candid, and impartial manner, he cannot safely judge without greatly hazarding his future and eternal welfare.

If, after a rigid examination, it be found an imposition, it should be extensively published to the world as such; the evidences and arguments upon which the imposture was detected, should be clearly and logically stated, that those who have been sincerely yet unfortunately deceived, may perceive the nature of the deception, and be reclaimed, and that those who continue to publish the delusion, may be exposed and silenced, not by physical force, neither by persecutions, bare assertions, nor ridicule, but by strong and powerful arguments—by evidences adduced from scripture and reason. Such, and such only, should be the weapons employed to detect and overthrow false doctrines—to reclaim mankind from their errors—to expose religious enthusiasm—and put to silence base and wicked impostors.

But on the other hand, if investigation should prove the Book of Mormon true and of divine origin, then the importance of the message is so great, and the consequences of receiving or rejecting it so overwhelming, that the various nations—to whom it is now sent, and in whose languages it is now published, should speedily repent of all their sins, and renounce all the wicked traditions of their fathers, as they are imperatively commanded to do in the message: they should utterly reject both the Popish and Protestant ministry, together with all the churches which have been built up by them or that have sprung from them, as being entirely destitute of authority; they should turn away from all the priestcrafts and abominations practiced by these apostate churches (falsely called Christian), and bring forth fruits meet for repentance in all things: they should be immersed in water by one having authority, and receive a remission of their sins, and be filled with the Holy Spirit. After thus being baptized into the kingdom of God, they should seek to translate the Book of Mormon into every written language of the earth, and send it forth by millions of copies to every nation, and not cease their exertions until all people have heard the glad tidings. Every synagogue, church, and place of public worship should be thrown open to the servants of God. Presidents, governors, and rulers—kings, lords, and nobles, and all in authority, should set the example before the mass of the people, by receiving with all meekness and humility this great revelation of modern times. Every periodical throughout their dominions should devote its columns to disseminating, far and near, among all classes, the evidences, arguments, and reasons, which establish the divine authenticity of so great and important a work. These are some of the present duties of both the American and European nations if this message be true.

The great majority of the world, however, reject the Book of Mormon without the least examination as to its claims. They have heard there was such a book, but they know nothing of its contents, only that it claims to be a divine revelation. They at once reject it as an imposture. Is this method of judging justifiable? Has God ever authorized His creatures to judge, without an investigation, a matter that professes to involve their eternal salvation? Has He ever informed the world that they have enough revelation, or that He will never give them any more? All who have read the Bible know that He has given no intimations of the kind. He has given no grounds whatever for supposing that there is to be no more revelation. Why, then, should the world be so presumptuous as to reject a professed revelation as false without investigation? This method of judging is not only unjustifiable, but fearful in its consequences. As long as there is a possibility that man may receive more, he is in danger of losing his salvation, by rejecting indiscriminately all that comes. By this rash and unjustifiable method of judging, he is not only in danger, but he is sure to lose his salvation if God should condescend to give more.

The conduct of millions in relation to the Book of Mormon goes to show that they would reject all true revelations as well as false ones: they are determined to reject at all hazards, without the least inquiry, every thing under the name of new revelation. They seem to be absolutely certain, as their conduct abundantly indicates, that God will never favor men with another communication of His will concerning them.

To expose this popular, though fatal error, invented by priestcraft in the early ages of the apostasy, and transferred to succeeding generations, will be the object of the following chapters. In the first, it will be shown that *to expect more revelation is neither* UNSCRIPTURAL *nor* UNREASONABLE, and in those which follow, it will be further shown, that the doctrine of *continued* revelation in the Church of God, is one that rests upon the most *infallible testimony*, being necessary for the salvation of man, connected with which, the THE DIVINE AUTHENTICITY OF THE BOOK OF MORMON WILL BE DEMONSTRATED.

TO EXPECT MORE REVELATION IS NOT UNSCRIPTURAL.

1.—If it could be proven from scripture that God had revealed to man all that He ever intended to reveal, then a professed revelation would not require investigation; for it would be known at once, that every thing of the kind was an imposition. It would be folly in the extreme to enquire whether a professed new revelation were true or false; for if God had declared in His word that no more was to be given, all writings or books purporting to be a new revelation could not be otherwise than false.

2.—If the books in the English translations of the Old and New Testaments are the only ones which are to be received as divine revelation, then why do we not find some intimations in those books to that effect? If God saw that man had enough, why did He not tell him so? His mind would then have been relieved from all dubiety on the subject. Then, all nations and generations would have known that the canon of scripture was complete and full: then, there would not have been the least possible chance of palming upon the world any more: then, it would have been known that all possible communications between God and man were, from thenceforth, cut off—that the heavens were to be sealed up, and the mouth of the Deity to be closed in a deep, profound and perpetual silence throughout all future generations.

3.—If God never intended to speak to man after the first century of the Christian era, it certainly would have been a great blessing to the human family, and saved many millions of them from delusion to have told them of so important a matter. But as God has failed to give any such notice, learned divines have concluded to give the notice themselves: hence they have invented "Articles of Faith," in which their followers are required to reject, under the penalty of excommunication, all books professing to be of divine origin, except those named in their "Articles," or those few which human wisdom has selected and compiled into a Bible. This is as much as to say, that the Bible contains all that God ever has given or ever will give unto man, and you must not receive any more; and thus the whole Protestant world are circumscribed and limited, and bound down by their "Articles of Faith"—their "Creeds"—and their "Disciplines." It matters not how important a message may be sent, nor how great its accompanying evidences, they are positively forbidden to receive it, because it does not happen to be bound up with the rest of the books of the Bible.

4.—The learned and popular false teachers of modern times who have so presumptuously rejected all revelation except the few books of the Bible named in their "Articles," have endeavoured to make their deluded followers believe that it was contrary to scripture for any more books to be added to the Bible, or for God to give any additional revelation to man. As their strongest proof upon the subject they quote the following text, spoken to John on the isle of Patmos, when in the act of finishing his manuscript: "For I testify unto every man that heareth the words of the prophecy of this book, if any man shall add unto these things, God shall add unto him the plagues that are written in this book; and if any man shall take away from the words of the book of this prophecy, God shall take away his part out of the book of life, and out of the holy city, and from the things which are written in this book" (*Rev. xxii.* 18, 19). Here, it is supposed, is proof that the Bible is forever closed, and that the addition of any other revelation is forbidden under the penalty of great plagues. But every man who has read this text, knows that there is not the least intimation given in it about the Bible's being closed. Such a book as the Bible did not then exist in its compiled state. The gathering together of the few scattered manuscripts which compose what is now termed the Bible, was the work of uninspired man which took place centuries after John had finished his manuscript. Among the vast number of professedly inspired manuscripts, scattered through the world, man, poor, weak, ignorant man, assumed the authority to select a few, which, according to his frail judgment, he believed or conjectured were of God, but the balance not agreeing, perhaps, with his peculiar notion of divine inspiration, were rejected as spurious. The few, selected from the abundance, were finally arranged into one volume, divided into chapter and verse, and named the Bible. Afterwards a set of cunning, wicked impostors, under the name of Protestant ministers, make their appearance, who finding themselves entirely destitute of the spirit of prophecy, of visions, of revelations, and of every other power and gift which always characterized the ministers of Christ, have endeavored to invent some cunning, crafty arguments, to hide from the people their powerless, apostate condition, and make their deluded followers think that they are really genuine ministers of Christ. The best scheme to carry out their corrupt purposes and deceive the people, is, in their estimation, to tell them that God did not intend to reveal anything more—that the Bible contains all— that the caution not to add to the words of John's prophecy, means not to add to the Bible. Thus the consciences of the common people become quieted, and they sincerely begin to think that the Bible contains all the sacred books ever given to man, and they at length become willing to subscribe to a set of cunningly-devised "Articles of Faith," requiring them to renounce all others as spurious.

5.—How do the Protestant world know that the compilers of the Bible, in hunting up the sacred manuscripts which were widely scattered over the world, one in one place and another in another, found all that were of divine origin? How do they know that the compilers of the Bible found even the one-hundreth part of the manuscripts that were sacred? And as the compilers rejected many that they did find how do they know but what some of the rejected books were equally sacred with those received into the collection? Would not the prophecy of Enoch with which the Apostle Jude was familiar, and from which he makes a quotation relative to the second coming of Christ, be as sacred as any other prophecy of the Bible? Would not the book of Iddo, the seer—the book of Nathan the prophet—together with some twelve or fifteen other books and epistles, written by inspired prophets, seers, and apostles, and referred to in scripture, be as worthy of a place in the Bible as any that human wisdom has already compiled? Would it have been any more a violation of the caution not to add to the words of John's prophecy, for the compilers to have added the book of Gad, the seer, with the collection called the Bible, than it was for them to add to the volume the book of Ezekiel—the book of Solomon's Song—the book of Matthew—the book of James, or any other book of the collection? If the book of John's prophecy means the Bible, as these false teachers assert, and if the Bible means a collection of all the sacred books written by inspired men, and if the adding and diminishing to the words of John's prophecy mean adding and diminishing to the Bible, then the whole Protestant world are under the curse for diminishing many sacred books from the Bible which are certainly referred to as being written by inspired men, but which they in their "Articles of Faith" absolutely exclude and diminish from the Bible by prohibiting their deluded followers from receiving only such as happens to be compiled. Should any of these sacred manuscripts hereafter be found, the "Articles" and "Creeds" of men prohibit their reception. If they had happened to be found by the compilers of the Bible, they would have been sacred, but to be found afterwards renders them false. For men a few centuries ago to hunt up a few scattered manuscripts, and compile them into a Bible, was considered a very laudable undertaking, but for any man to find a sacred book since that time is considered the highest blasphemy!

6.—If the caution about adding and diminishing means that there is to be no more revelation after the caution is given, then all books purporting to be a revelation, and given after such caution, must be false. Now such caution was given as early as the days of Moses. "Ye shall not add unto the word which I command you, neither shall ye diminish ought from it" (*Deut. iv.* 2). The caution in John's book must mean the same thing as the caution in the book of Moses; if the one means that there is to be no more revelation, the other means the same. Therefore, according to the arguments of modern divines, all the Old and New Testaments which have been added since Moses gave the caution must be false, and consequently, they and all their followers must be under the curse for believing in and advocating sixty-two other books as divine revelation, which they know were all given after the caution by Moses. Thus it will be seen, that if their application of these texts be correct, they are under a double curse; first, they are cursed in John's revelations for diminishing some fifteen or twenty books from the compilation of the Bible; and, secondly, they are cursed in Deuteronomy for receiving sixty-two books which were added after the caution was given by Moses. If modern divines, rather than subject themselves to a double curse should be willing to give up their perverted applications of these texts, then what becomes of their scriptural arguments against receiving more revelation? There is certainly no other application of these passages that forbids additional revelation.

7.—To add to the words of the book of John's prophecy, means nothing more nor less than to add words or sentences of our own to his book, so as to alter the meaning, and to publish such additions as the words of John. For Isaiah to have added to the words of the books of Moses, so as to alter their meaning, and to have represented Moses as the author of these altered writings, would have subjected him to a curse. But to receive, as he did, a separate and independent revelation was no more adding to the words of Moses, than a deed conveying an estate in America would be adding to the laws of England. If ten thousand new revelations were to be given, it would be no more adding to the words of John's book than a message of the president of the United States would be adding to the words of a proclamation by Queen Victoria. No revelation given from God needs any alterations, additions, or diminutions, by the wisdom of man. If they need altering, God alone has the right to alter them, or to add to them, as He did in the case of a revelation which He gave to Jeremiah, which was burned by the king of Judah, but afterwards Jeremiah was commanded to write all the words again, "and there were added besides unto them many like words" (*Jer. xxxvi.* 32). God has never prohibited Himself from giving revelation as often as He pleases, neither has He prohibited Himself from adding or diminishing words in case He sees it necessary. But woe unto that man who pretends to give a revelation, and is a deceiver; who adds, or diminishes, or alters a revelation which God has given; such cannot escape the threatened judgments of the Almighty.

8.—We have now shown by the most conclusive arguments that the passages concerning adding and diminishing, so often referred to by the new-revelation denier, does not contain the most distant intimation that the day of revelation is gone by. They never would have resorted to such a perverted application of these passages if they had any better evidence in the scriptures to sustain themselves. The very fact that they so often pervert these passages from their evident meaning, shows most conclusively the weakness of their position. No other passages are susceptible of being so grossly misapplied. It is under this shallow covering that they endeavor to hide their apostasy and deceive mankind.

9.—In their zeal to oppose every thing under the name of new revelation, some of the more ignorant have assumed that when Christ was lifted upon the cross, and cried, "It is finished," it put an end to all further revelation. If this assumption be correct, then all the books of the New Testament, written years after, must be false. If Christ finished the work of revelation, when He exclaimed, "It is finished, then the apostles must have been base impostors for pretending to receive revelation scores of years after this exclamation. All, therefore, who reject new revelation upon these grounds, are required by their own application of this saying, to reject all the writings of the New Testament: thus, in their heated zeal to oppose new revelation, they not unfrequently destroy the very books which they profess to believe.

10.—A saying of Paul to Timothy is sometimes referred to by the enemies of new revelation, and applied in the most deceptive manner, in order to strengthen the world in the fatal delusion that God will no more speak with man: it reads as follows: "From a child thou hast known the holy scriptures, which are able to make thee wise unto salvation" (*II. Timothy iii.* 15). The objector to new revelation argues, from this passage, that the scriptures with which Timothy was acquainted in his childhood, were abundantly sufficient to make him wise unto salvation, and consequently *there was no need of any more.* If this conclusion be correct, it would do away with all the scriptures of the New Testament; for Timothy when a child was only acquainted with the scriptures of the Old Testament, the scriptures of the New Testament not being yet written. Thus, again, the enemy of new revelation in his fanatical zeal to close up the volume of inspiration, has done away the very scriptures which he pretends so firmly to believe.

11.—Modern false teachers, in order to sustain their impositions, sometimes quote the following. "All scripture is given by inspiration of God, and is profitable for doctrine, for reproof, for correction, for instruction in righteousness, that the man of God may be perfect, thoroughly furnished unto all good works" (*II. Tim. iii.* 16, 17). They assert that this passage means that "enough" scripture has been given to perfect the man of God—that "enough" has been given to thoroughly furnish him unto all good works; but the word ENOUGH is not found in the passage: it reads, "ALL SCRIPTURE is given, etc." The righteous man has no authority from this passage to assume that he has enough, but he should continue to seek for "line upon line, precept upon precept, here a little, and there a little;" and if he gives heed unto "all scripture" which God may condescend to reveal, it will perfect him, and thoroughly furnish him unto all good works. This passage, therefore, leaves the man of God to be perfected by *"all* scripture" which God has given by inspiration, in early ages, or which He may give in latter times. He is not limited to any particular number of books which uninspired man has happened to find and compile into a Bible. Indeed, if the assertions of these false teachers be true, then there are several books of the New Testament which must be rejected; for if the man of God had *enough* scripture at the time Paul wrote his epistle to Timothy, then the book of Revelations given on Patmos some years after, together with the book of John's gospel, and several of the epistles, must be excluded from the Bible.

12.—Well-educated and learned divines have been so utterly at a loss to find any scripture to sustain them in denying immediate revelation, that they have not hesitated to pervert, in the most glaring manner, not only the foregoing passages, but some few others of a similar nature which they have culled from the Bible, and which they, and all persons with the least reflection, know have the most distant bearing upon the subject. They tell their flocks that no more revelation is to be expected, because St. Paul, in addressing the elders of the church at Ephesus, says, "I kept back nothing that was profitable unto you. I have not shunned to declare unto you all the counsel of God" (*Acts xx.* 20, 27.) "All the counsel of God" having been imparted by St. Paul to the Ephesians, it is presumed that all further revelation was unnecessary. If this presumption be correct, it would like the former presumptions, not only cut off from the Bible several of the epistles, but the book of John's gospel, and the great revelation given on Patmos, all of which were certainly written years after Paul declared "all the counsel of God" to the elders of Ephesus. Paul, no doubt, had previously declared all the counsels which God had manifested to him in relation to their welfare, but this did not prohibit the Lord from revealing afterwards other counsels as the future circumstances of the Ephesians might require. Indeed, notwithstanding this saying of Paul, the Lord did, a long time after, give further revelations and counsels to this same church, through His servant John, on Patmos (*see Rev.* ii. 1-8.)

13.—It has been furthermore presumed that revelation would cease when the "seventy weeks" mentioned by Daniel had passed away  The angel, Gabriel, said to Daniel, "Understand the matter, and consider the vision. Seventy weeks are determined upon thy people and upon the Holy City, to finish the transgression, and to make an end of sins, and to make reconciliation for iniquity, and to bring in everlasting righteousness, and to seal up the vision and prophecy, and to anoint the Most Holy" (*Daniel ix* 23, 24.)  Here the enemies of new revelation assert, that as soon as the Messiah came, and was annointed, and the seventy weeks had elapsed, "the vision and prophecy were sealed up."  But we ask, what vision and prophecy were sealed up?  They reply, that all new revelation by vision and prophecy was then come to an end.  If this wild conjecture be correct, then all the visions and prophecies, and revelations, and books of the New Testament, given from fifty to a hundred years after the seventy weeks had ended, must be false.  The vision and prophecy which God had given to Daniel, and which the angel commanded him to consider, no doubt were the ones which were to be sealed up, or to have their fulfillment at the time therein specified.  But to suppose that God was to give no more visions and prophecies after that time is contradicted by the fact that abundance of heavenly manifestations were given during the whole of the first century of the Christian era, all of which new-revelation deniers must exclude from the Bible, or give up their perverted application of this text.

14.—Another passage is often quoted by objectors to new revelation—namely, the declaration of Paul in relation to the cessation of some of the spiritual gifts.  He says, "Charity never faileth; *but whether there be prophecies, they shall fail*; whether there be tongues they shall cease; whether there be knowledge it shall vanish away" (*I. Corinthians xiii* 8.)  Modern ministers will read to their followers this passage, and very gravely tell them that the time when prophecies were to fail arrived upwards of seventeen centuries ago; but they are very careful not to read the two following verses, lest their hearers should find out the true meaning of the passage, and learn the very time when this event should happen.  Paul, as if fearful that false teachers would take the advantage of his saying, and undertake to do away prophesying and tongues from the church, says, in the next sentence, "For we know in part, and we prophesy in part; but when that which is perfect is come, then that which is in part shall be done away." These gifts, then, which were only given in part, were to cease and be done away as unnecessary, not seventeen centuries ago, as false teachers assert, but "when that which is perfect is come." In the 12th verse he describes the condition of the church, when that time shall come. He says, "Now, we see through a glass darkly; but then, face to face: now, I know in part; but then shall I know even as also I am known." Here we learn that the time when these gifts are to cease is not to be here in this world, but in the next state of existence, where the Church shall no longer "see through a glass darkly, but see the Lord face to face," and "know as they are known:" then "that which is perfect" will have come; then "tongues will cease;" then "prophecy in part," and "knowledge in part" will be done away, till then, all these gifts are necessary. Therefore these sayings of the apostle, instead of favoring the groundless deceptions of new-revelation deniers, are evidences of the most positive kind in favor of continued revelation.

15.—The church in its militant and imperfect state, compared with its triumphant, immortal and perfect state, is, in the 11th verse, represented by the two very different states of childhood and manhood. "When," says St. Paul, "I was a child, I spake as a child; understood as a child, I thought as a child; but when I became a man, I put away childish things." In the various stages of education from childhood to manhood, certain indispensible rules, and diagrams, and scientific instruments are employed for the use and benefit of the pupil, that he may acquire a correct knowledge of the sciences, and be perfected in his studies. When the principles have been once acquired, and the student has been perfected in every branch of education, he can dispense with many of his maps, charts, globes, books, diagrams, etc., as being, like childish things, no longer necessary; they were useful before his education was perfected in imparting the desired knowledge; but, having fulfilled their purposes, he no longer needs their assistance. For instance, the chemist, before sufficient experiments have been made, cannot predict in full the result of the union of several different elements. It is true, that from former imperfect experiments he may know in part, and prophesy in part, what will be the nature and properties of the resulting compound. But when he has, through the medium of a good chemical apparatus, determined by a perfect experiment, all the results, laws, and proportions of the combination of the elements under consideration, knowledge in part, in relation to the results, is done away, and he knows in full; he no longer prophesies in part how these elements will act, and what will be the nature and properties of the compound, for his knowledge is perfect concerning it; he no longer needs to give an imperfect prediction concerning that which he has fully seen, and known, and comprehended; he no longer looks through a glass darkly, as he formerly did, but he sees the principle as he is seen, having learned it through an experiment; he can now do away with the apparatus, and still retain the knowledge that he formerly gained by it. So it is with the Church in relation to spiritual gifts. While in this state of existence it is represented as a child; prophecy, revelations, tongues, and other spiritual gifts, are the instruments of education. The child or Church can no more be perfected in its education without the aid of these gifts as instruments, than the chemist could in his researches if he were deprived of the necessary apparatus for experiments. As the chemist needs his laboratory for experiments, as long as there remains any undiscovered truths in relation to the elements and compounds of our globes; so does the Church need the great laboratory of spiritual knowledge—namely, revelation and prophecy, as long as it knows only in part. Without this heavenly treasure, the child can never progress to perfection—can never become "a perfect man in Christ Jesus"—can never "see as it is seen," and "know as it is known"—can never attain "to the measure of the stature of the fullness of Christ"—can never dwell in that perfect state of society where they see the Lord face to face—where fullness of knowledge, glory, and happiness pervades every soul. As a human being, when a child, speaks as a child, understands as a child, and thinks as a child; so does the Church in this state of existence know only in part: but as the child, when it becomes a man, puts away childish things; so will the Church put away such childish things as "prophecy in part," "knowledge in part," and seeing in part, when it grows up, through the aid of these things, to a perfect man in Christ Jesus: that which is in part will be done away or merged into the greater fullness of knowledge which there reigns. Perfection will then swallow up imperfection; the healing power will then be done away, for no sickness will be there; tongues and interpretations will then cease, for one pure language alone will be spoken; the casting out of devils and power against deadly poisons will not then be needed, for in heaven circumstances will render them unnecessary.

16.—But charity, which is the pure love of God, never faileth; it will sit enthroned in the midst of the glorified throng, clothed in all the glory and splendor of its native heaven. As charity, then, never fails, we can say, with the Apostle Paul, "Follow after charity, and desire spiritual gifts, but rather that you may prophesy;" for all these things, with faith and hope, should be the companions of charity in this world, though circumstances will require some of them to part, "when that which is perfect is come;" but while traveling in this world of imperfection, let them be friends. And as God has joined them together in happy wedlock during this state of existence, let no man put them asunder. That habitation that will not admit them all as occupants, cannot retain either singly. Faith, Hope and Charity, will not abide where their dear friend Immediate Revelation is rejected. Though Christendom may pass bills of divorcement, and try to separate them, yet they will not be separated. Wherever they are unitedly received, they impart salvation and eternal life; wherever either is rejected, death—eternal death—is sure to be the result.

17.—New-revelation deniers, to sustain their false position, sometimes refer to the saying of our Savior, "For all the prophets and the law prophesied until John" (*Matthew xi. 13.*) From this they draw the conclusion that John was to be the last prophet of the human race with which our world were to be favored; and to strengthen this conclusion they connect this saying with the following prediction of Zechariah: "And it shall come to pass in that day, saith the Lord of hosts, that I will cut off the names of the idols out of the land, and they shall no more be remembered, and also I will cause the prophets and the unclean spirit to pass out of the land. And it shall come to pass, that when any shall yet prophesy, then his father and his mother that begat him shall say unto him Thou shalt not live; for thou speakest lies in the name of the Lord; and his father and his mother that begat him shall thrust him through when he prophesieth. And it shall come to pass in that day, that the prophets shall be ashamed every one of his vision when he hath prophesied; neither shall they wear a rough garment to deceive" (*Zechariah xiii.* 2, 3, 4.) It is said that the prophets were until John, after which the Lord caused the prophets to pass out of the land, as no longer necessary. If this conclusion be correct, then the "book of John's prophecy," revealed some sixty-five years after John the Baptist's death, must be false. If there were to be no more prophets after John, then Paul must have been entirely mistaken when he says to the Ephesians, that God, "by revelation, made known unto me the mystery which in other ages was not made known unto the sons of men, as it is now revealed unto His holy apostles and PROPHETS" (*Eph. iii.* 3. 5.) If Paul's word be credited, instead of the words of the false teachers of latter times, then there must have been *prophets* connected with the apostles after the days of John, and prophets, too, who received greater mysteries by revelation than the prophets of other ages. This agrees with another saying of Paul, that "God hath set some in the Church—first, apostles; secondarily, PROPHETS, thirdly, teachers," etc. (*I. Corinthians xii.* 28.) In accordance with this, we read of certain *prophets* in the Christian church at Antioch, to whom the Holy Ghost spake and gave directions concerning the calling and missions of Paul and Barnabas (*see Acts xiii.*) After the days of John the Baptist, we read of Agabus, the prophet, who prophesied of a great famine which came to pass in the days of Claudius Cæsar, and also the four daughters of Philip the Evangelist, who prophesied of the persecution which awaited Paul at

Jerusalem (*see Acts*). To reject prophets from the Christian church would be one of the greatest perversions of God's word.

18.—The prediction of Zechariah to which we have referred has not yet had its fulfillment; for "the idols" and the "unclean spirit" there spoken of have not yet passed away out of the land; they are not yet "no more remembered," as is said in this prediction. That the prophets which the Lord should cause to pass away were to be *false* prophets, and not *true* ones, is evident from their being connected with the idols and unclean spirit which were all to pass away together. These prophets, are no doubt, the same characters which are spoken of in another place of his prophecy, "For, lo, I will raise up a shepherd in the land, which shall not visit those that be cut off, neither shall seek the young one, nor heal that that is broken, nor feed that that standeth still: but he shall eat the flesh of the fat, and tear their claws in pieces. Woe to the idol shepherd that leaveth the flock! the sword shall be upon his arm, and upon his right eye: his arm shall be clean dried up, and his right eye shall be utterly darkened" (*Zechariah xi.* 16, 17.) When the Lord cuts off the names of the idols out of the land, he will then cause the sword to be upon "the arm" and upon "the right eye" of the "idol shepherd;" or, in other words, the prophets and the unclean spirit, who tear, and devour, and destroy the flock, and eat the fat thereof, he will, in very deed, cause them "to pass away out of the land." This destruction of idol shepherds, false prophets, etc., will take place at the time, or a little after, the Savior's second coming: "In that day," says Zechariah, "the Lord shall be king over all the earth," and "there shall be one Lord and His name one," the names of the idols having passed away, being no more remembered. This will be after He comes with all His Saints and stands upon the Mount of Olives, as is predicted in this same connection. Therefore these passages have not the most distant allusion to the doing away of prophets from the Christian church, as many reverend false teachers assert. None but the most ignorant and unreflecting could ever be deceived by such barefaced and glaring perversions of those passages by modern divines. Were it not to cover up their apostasy, ministers of modern Christendom never would have resorted to such wilful and awfully wicked perversions of God's word—perversions, too, which, if admitted, would destroy many of the very books of the Bible which they pretend to believe.

19.—As the foregoing are the only passages referred to by those who reject new revelation, we conclude that there are no others that, in their estimation, have any bearing upon the subject; and we have clearly shown that these passages contain not the slightest intimation that God has revealed all that He ever intended to give to man. Therefore, the proposition containing the subject matter of these paragraphs is fully established, and it can be asserted, with the greatest assurance, and without fear of contradiction, that *it is not unscriptural to expect more revelation.*

TO EXPECT MORE REVELATION IS NOT UNREASONABLE.

1.—In the foregoing we have shown that in so far as the enemies of new revelation have undertaken to prove their position by scripture, they have utterly failed. We shall now proceed to examine the *reasons* offered by the world for rejecting new revelation. If it can be demonstrated that the giving of more revelation would be unreasonable, then all professed revelation should be rejected at once without investigation, for it could not be otherwise than false.

2.—It is said that God revealed enough to save man in ancient days, and it is concluded that the revelations which saved the ancients, will save men in all future generations, and, therefore, it is argued that it is unreasonable to expect any more. Now we must freely admit that God revealed enough to save man in ancient times, but that these were sufficient for future generations, we deny. No one will for a moment dispute but that the revelations given to Abel were sufficient to save him; but to argue that Abel's revelations were sufficient for all future generations, would be the very hight of absurdity. The revealed will of God to Abel, though sufficient to save him, was altogether insufficient to guide Noah and his family; nothing short of a new revelation could unfold to him the awful judgment that awaited the world by a universal deluge:

nothing short of a new revelation could point out to him the way of escape. But new revelation was as unpopular to the antediluvians as it is now to the apostate churches of the ninteenth century. They, without doubt considered Noah an impostor for offering to them a new revelation, when Abel and Enoch had enough to save them. In vain did Noah urge upon them the necessity of believing in his message; in vain did he portray the awful consequences of rejecting it; they considered the revelations of their forefathers all sufficient without any additional ones; and thus the whole world, except eight persons, were carried away with the fatal delusion that new revelation was unnecessary, and the whole mass of deluded fanatics perished together as a fearful warning to all the enemies of new revelation who should live after them.

3.—Lot, though a righteous man, could not have been saved from the shower of fire and brimstone about to be poured upon the cities of the plain, had he not believed in new revelation, pointing out to him his only course of safety. In vain did he plead with his kindred to believe in new revelation, and depart out of Sodom to escape the threatened judgment; he seemed to them as one that mocked. They doubtless thought, like modern divines, that the old revelations that saved their fathers would also save them; they persisted in their strong delusions until overwhelmed by a shower of fire; and as it was with the cities of the plain, so shall it also be with the multitude of all nations who are enemies to new revelation in the days of the coming of the Son of man: they shall become as stubble in the midst of the devouring flame, and shall, like Sodom and Gomorrah, be punished with the vengeance of eternal fire.

4.—When Jesus offered to the Jews a new revelation they immediately appealed to the old ones, saying, "We have Moses and the prophets, but as for this man Christ Jesus, we know not whence He is." The devil had put it into their hearts to suppose that the revelations of their forefathers were sufficient, and for any person to offer them a new one was considered an imposition; they continued to reject every thing of the kind, until they brought upon themselves and their beloved city swift destruction.

5.—The apostate Gentile churches of the present century are following in the same dangerous path. The cunning arch impostors of modern times, under the name of Popish and Protestant ministers, have persuaded millions of their deluded votaries to reject every thing under the name of new revelation, and to receive only such ancient books as they have named in their "Articles of Religion." If this wicked imposition had only deceived here and there a few, there would be some hopes of mankind, but alas! the delusion is as popular as it was in the days of Noah. Learned and unlearned—rulers and ruled—philosophers and the ignorant—the great and the small—the high and the low, and in fine, all nations and people, have fallen into this whirlpool of delusion—this vortex of destruction, that has swallowed up nations and generations of ancient times, and left a sad but fearful warning to those who should live in after ages.

6.—Nothing can be more erroneous than to suppose that the revelations given to one individual, people, or generation, are sufficient to fully develop the duties of another individual, people, or generation. That there are many duties which are common to all mankind in every generation, is a truth that no one can dispute. It is equally clear that there are many duties which are limited in their nature, and only required of such as God may name or designate under existing circumstances. Those *general laws* which are universal in their application, though revealed ever so often, are always the same; they are as unchangeable as the great Law Giver in whom they originated, while those individual or circumstantial laws which are limited to the individuals for whom they are given, are changeable in their nature. New circumstances require new laws which must continue to change in order to suit the condition of the people. No man, either in ancient or modern times, has ever yet learned his whole duty from the general laws which God has revealed. Without new revelation adapted to the peculiar condition of himself as an individual, and varied at sundry times, according to the change of circumstances, he will forever remain ignorant of a part of his duty.

7.—As the present generation are so universally in error, in supposing that the ancient revelations are sufficient for all present purposes, we shall point out still further the absurdity of this supposition by showing the distinction between general and circumstantial laws, as revealed to govern the actions of men, and by pointing out the absolute necessity of continued revelation, growing out of the nature of the varied circumstances in which man is placed. *General laws*, given to regulate the actions of all men, are those which prohibit them from doing that which in its very nature is evil; and which enjoin upon them to do that which in its very nature is good. *Circumstantial laws* are those which prohibit man from doing that which in its nature is not evil, but which, if done, circumstances would render evil; and which enjoin upon him to do that which in its nature is neither good nor evil, but which if done, circumstances would render good.

8.—The first class of laws are termed general because of their universal adaptation to the conditions of all men in all generations and ages, and under every dispensation of God to man. There are many things which are naturally evil, and no change of circumstances can render them otherwise than evil: they are recognized as evil by all men, whether in a civilized or savage state: there is but one law of conscience in regard to them, independent of all revealed law. That which tends to unjustly injure another in his person or character is naturally an evil: the law of conscience tells all men that it is evil: the revealed law of God coincides with that of conscience, and proclaims it an evil, and forbids mankind under a heavy penalty to unjustly injure one another. To bear false witness against a neighbor is an evil in its very nature. It is not the revealed law of God which makes it an evil, but it is clearly perceived to be an evil where the revealed law is unknown. To take the advantage of a good man and cheat him out of his property—to rob, or steal, or wantonly waste, or destroy it—is an evil, recognized by the consciences of all men: it is not necessary for the revealed law to proclaim these things as evil in order that man may perceive them as such; for the savage, as well as the sage, readily perceives, by the aid of his conscience alone, that the inherent nature of these things is vicious. To murder or shed innocent blood is distinguished by all men to be a great evil: there is something in the nature of the act that proclaims loudly that it is one of the greatest of evils. If God had never revealed it an evil in written words, yet mankind would be none the less assured of its evil nature. The object of the revealed law is not merely to show that these acts are evil and vicious, but to show the penalty and consequences of such acts—to show that judgment and misery must necessarily result from a vicious course of life. We have now given a few items of evil that are in their nature evil, and against which God has enacted *general laws* to govern men in all ages.

9.—We shall next point out some things which in their very nature are good, and which the consciences of all men, at once perceive to be good. To show pity to the poor—to feed the hungry and clothe the naked—to administer relief to the sick and afflicted—to do unto our neighbors that which we, in like circumstances, would consider they ought to do for us—and in fine, to love them, and seek to benefit them, and make them happy, are things which are inherently good: it is not a command to do these things which renders them good: they were good before any revealed law enjoined mankind to do them; they were good independent of all revealed law; they were good from the beginning in their very nature; and man is so constituted that he cannot look upon them otherwise than as being inherently good. These are the virtuous acts which the revealed law has enjoined upon men to perform. It is not the object of the revealed law, merely to point out that these acts are good and virtuous, for this was already understood, but the object was to enjoin upon man the importance of doing good—to make known to him the reward which should be received for every virtuous act, and the happy results which should follow a virtuous course of life. We have now given a few items of good that are in and of themselves naturally good, concerning which God has enacted general laws to govern man in every age and dispensation.

10.—These items of good and evil, together with all others of like nature, are the principal items embodied in a code of laws which are intended to be general in their application.

Those who violate them, though they are not acquainted with the revealed law concerning them, yet they will be judged by the law of their consciences so far as they were able to perceive the nature of right and wrong, but not being acquainted with the penalty annexed to these laws, they will only be punished with a few stripes; while those who have, not only the law of conscience, but also the revealed law, and shall violate its sacred commands, will be beaten with many stripes.

11.—There are many things which are not naturally evil, but which become evil circumstantially; for instance, God having finished this creation in six days, rested on the seventh, and from this circumstance, he ordained the Sabbath as a day of rest, and commanded that man should not labor on that day. Now a man unacquainted with this revealed law, would be as likely to labor on the Sabbath as on any other day; there would be nothing in the nature of this act, nor in the nature of anything connected with it, that would indicate to him that he was doing an evil. Those things which are naturally evil are the only ones which are perceptible to the conscience as such, without the light of revelation; and consequently, God will neither judge, condemn, nor punish a man who has ignorantly transgressed and done an evil which his conscience could not possibly detect as such, and unto whom he has never sent the revealed law. To labor on the Sabbath day, therefore, is only an evil *because it is forbidden;* there is nothing in the nature of it that is evil: not so with stealing, bearing false witness, committing adultery, murdering, and such like crimes; they are all evils by nature, though they were not forbidden; for the conscience of the savage, as well as the civilized man, regards them as such.

12.—Incorporated in the code of general laws, concerning good and evil, are many other laws of a circumstantial nature which are also binding upon all people to whom they are sent with proper authority; such, for instance, as the law of baptism--the laying on of hands in confirmation, in ordination, and in healing the sick—anointing of the sick with oil in the name of the Lord with prayer—the Lord's supper, and the keeping of the Sabbath day holy. These are duties revealed in ancient times to be perpetuated among all people to whom they should be sent with divine authority. But these general laws of good and evil, including all the annexed ordinances and institutions, intended to be perpetuated, unfold but a very small portion of the individual duties of man, arising from the circumstances with which he is surrounded. Indeed, no code of laws which were intended to be generally applicable could, from their nature, possibly unfold the vast variety of constantly changing duties required even of one man. Much more impossible would it be for such a code to make manifest the multifarious duties of some fifteen thousand millions of the human race who have lived since the days of the apostles.

13.—We shall now point out a few specimens of revelation which were not intended to be perpetuated, being confined to a very limited period of time, and only intended for the benefit of those for whom they were given; these may be termed *peculiar* or *circumstantial* revelations, and are as necessary to fulfill the purposes of God for the well being of man, as those of a higher order or of a more general nature. Circumstances required a peculiar revelation to be given to Noah in relation to building an ark. The peculiarity of this revelation will be seen from the fact, that Noah was required to do a work altogether different from what had been required of any man anterior to his day. If the objector should say, that this revelation to Noah, having reference to temporal salvation, was of minor importance, compared with those great revelations on moral subjects, and should conclude that it was not a matter of much consequence whether such a revelation was given or not, we reply, that the all-wise Creator who knows what is for the good of man, does not give revelation upon subjects of no importance: but every thing connected with revelation, is of great importance, and intended not only for the temporal, but for the eternal good of man. For man to reject a command of God in relation to temporal things, or temporal salvation, would have a serious bearing upon his future state, and deprive him of future salvation. Therefore all things which God commands a person to do, however unimportant they may appear to finite creatures, are nevertheless of infinite importance, and will most assuredly influence his eternal destiny.

14.—Peculiar revelations were given to Abraham: he was commanded to depart out of Chaldea, his native country, and go to a land wherein he was a stranger. This command was not general, but individual, in its application. Abraham and his household seem to be the only persons required to obey it. Here, then, was a duty which they never could have learned from any general laws: new revelation alone could make it manifest. If we read the short history of Abraham's life, we find a great variety of duties made known to him of which he must forever have remained in ignorance, had it not been for new revelation. At one time he was commanded to circumcise all the males of his household; at another, to walk through the land of Canaan, in the length of it and in the breadth of it; at another, to lift up his eyes eastward, westward, northward and southward; with a promise that all the land over which he traveled, and which his eyes beheld, should be given to him and his posterity for an everlasting possession, at another time he was commanded to offer as a sacrifice different kinds of animals and fowls; at another, to offer his only son Isaac as a burnt offering upon a mountain; at another, to stay his hand, and not destroy the child. Now, all these were duties which could not be learned from ancient revelation, from the fact that no other people had been previously commanded to do these things. They were duties that could not be incorporated in a system of lws that were intended to be general in their application, and for this very reason Abraham considered new revelation indispensably necessary; it was the only possible way to learn the whole of his duty. O! how different were the feelings and views of this good old patriarch from those entertained by modern enemies to new revelation! The one saw the impossibility of learning the whole will of God from previous revelation; the others consider that a few ancient books called the Bible reveal the whole will of God to all nations and generations for the last seventeen centuries. O! the impenetrable darkness of apostate Christianity! It is heart-sickening to every man of God! Who among the saints of ancient times could have supposed, that a race of people would arise professing to believe in the revelations of old time, but considering that all new ones were entirely unnecessary? The worshipers of Baal were far more consistent than apostate Christendom; for they had a faint hope that Baal would hear and answer them; but modern divines have no expectation that their God will say anything to them or to their followers. Baal's followers cried from morning until evening for him to give unto them a miraculous manifestation, in the presence of Elijah; but to even expect a supernatural manifestation or revelation now is considered, by modern religionists, as the greatest absurdity. Baal's worshipers, therefore, with all their absurdities, approached nearer the religion of heaven, in some of their expectations, than those who falsely call themselves Christians.

15.—The history of the people of God, from the earliest ages, shows that *continued revelation* was the only way that they could possibly learn all their duties, or God's will concerning themselves. They never once thought that the revelations given to previous generations were sufficient to guide them into every duty. A doctrine which rejects new revelation is a new doctrine, invented by the devil and his agents during the second century after Christ; it is a doctrine in direct opposition to the one believed in and enjoyed by the saints in all ages. Now, to subvert and do away a doctrine four thousand years old, and introduce a new one in its stead, can only be done by *divine authority*. But have the propagators of this new doctrine, at any period since its invention, established its authority either by scripture, reason, miracles or any other way? If not, how dare they to break in upon the long-established order of God, and invent a new doctrine, excluding all further revelation? How dare they to promulgate a doctrine so entirely different from what the ancient saints ever believed or thought of? How dare they assume and teach that God will no more speak with man, when He never had failed, in any instance, to converse with His saints in every previous generation? How dare they call themselves the people of God, and yet reject the great, fundamental, and infinitely important doctrine of *continued revelation*, which always distinguished the people of God from every other people? None but the most blind and determined enemies to new revelation could for a moment believe the Bible, and at the same time believe that the ancient saints and the apostate churches of Christendom were both the people of God—the one class believed in a doctrine of continued revelation, established not only by several thousand years' experience, but by a continued series of miracles during that long period of time; while the other class have entirely excluded this heavenly doctrine from their midst, and, as a substitute, have invented, through the aid of uninspired men, "Articles of Religion," "Creeds," "Disciplines," "Commentaries," etc. Who, then, with a knowledge of these two systems of religion, so widely different and opposed to each other, would have the hardihood or wicked presumption to call the latter Christians or the Church of God?

16.—As the doctrine, then, of continued revelation is one that was always believed by the saints, it ought not to be required of any man to prove the necessity of the continuation of such a doctrine. If it were a new doctrine never before introduced into the world, it would become necessary to establish its divine origin; but, inasmuch as it is only a continuation of an old doctrine, established thousands of years ago, and which has never ceased to be believed and enjoyed by the saints, it would be the greatest presumption to call it in question at this late period; and hence it would seem almost superfluous to undertake to prove the necessity of its continuance. Instead of being required to do this, all people have the right to call upon the new-revelation deniers of the last seventeen centuries to bring forward their strong reasonings and testimonies for breaking in upon the long-established order of heaven, and introducing a new doctrine so entirely different from the old. If they wish their new doctrine to be believed, let them demonstrate it to be of divine origin, or else all people will be justified in rejecting it, and in still cleaving to the old. When Jesus came and did away the old law of Moses, and introduced a new system of religion, he established the divine origin of the new by the most incontrovertible testimony; the most splendid miracles were wrought both by Himself and His followers. Now, if the new-revelation deniers will bring as much testimony as Jesus and His followers did to establish their new doctrine, then they may, with some little propriety, call upon mankind to believe in it; but as yet they have given the world no evidence whatever only their own conjectures. We are called upon to reject a doctrine much older than the law of Moses, and of far greater importance, and to receive in its stead the doctrines of uninspired men, excluding all new communications from heaven; and as yet not one testimony has been offered the world in confirmation of this newly-invented religion. How strange that any one should ever have been deceived with such absurdities! How incomprehensibly more strange that millions should still cling to the awful delusion!

17.—When a doctrine has been originated by divine authority, and has been believed and enjoyed by the people of God, without an exception, in all ages, it is not unreasonable to expect the continuance of such doctrine among the Saints in all future ages, unless some cause can be shown for its discontinuance: for instance, the doctrine of *Faith, Repentance* and *Remission of Sins,* was originated and taught by divine authority immediately after the fall, and, like the doctrine of continued revelation, was embraced and enjoyed by every people of God until the apostles fell asleep. Now, if a people had arisen in the second century of the Christian era who excluded from their religion any of these principles, would not such a newly-invented religion have been considered as a gross imposition, and all its originators as the basest of impostors? At least, would not the inventors of such a religion have been required to show some authority or cause for thus discontinuing a doctrine which even they themselves continued to admit was necessary in all previous ages? If faith, repentance, remission of sins and continued revelation, were necessary for four thousand years, what reason can be shown that any one of these heavenly principles should ever afterwards become unnecessary? If the second century were chosen as the memorable period for the discontinuance of an essential and long-established principle of religion, and for the introduction of a new religion diverse from what the people of God ever before enjoyed, then, indeed, it must be a period of great importance in the history of man. But the great and infinitely important question is, how shall mankind know that this sudden and unexpected change in the religion of heaven was produced by divine authority? Have its propagators ever established its divine authenticity in any way? If not, then they must be 'the vilest and most dangerous impostors that ever disgraced our earth, deceiving, not a few only, but their thousands of millions, and corrupting all nations with their abominable and soul-destroying apostasy.

18.—A doctrine or principle established by divine authority will require divine authority to do it away. That which is established by a superior being cannot be abolished by an inferior power. This may be beautifully illustrated by the kingdoms, governments and powers of the earth. Each has its law-making department: this power is sometimes invested in a legislative body and sometimes in the king, queen or emperor. Whenever any of these departments enact laws for the welfare of the people, they are considered to be in force and binding upon all citizens until the law-making department shall repeal them, and notify the people of such repeal. Private citizens or inferior councils could never repeal that which was enacted and ordained by higher powers. If the king ordained the law, then none but the king can repeal it. If the people should undertake to abrogate or do away the law, it would be considered an act of rebellion against the government. So if the king should ordain certain rights or privileges to be enjoyed by his subjects, no inferior power would have a right to disannul such legal grants—none would have a right to say that the privileges, ordained by the king in behalf of his subjects, were done away. The power that ordains rights and privileges, can alone disannul them. The subjects have no right to suppose that any law or privilege is done away, unless the law-making department has notified the people to that effect. So it is with the kingdom of God. God is the King; He is the legal Law-Giver to all the children of the kingdom; He has ordained certain rights and privileges to be enjoyed by them all; He has given to them all the right of petition, with a sure and certain promise that He will hear and answer. These rights and privileges were enjoyed for about four thousand years by all the subjects of

His government; they petitioned the King, to show them by revelation many great and glorious things, which He, according to His promise, granted. Among the promised rights and blessings, granted by the great and unchangeable Law-Giver, may be enumerated, the privilege of conversing with Him and with His angels, and to receive knowledge by visions, by dreams, by the revelations of the Holy Spirit, and by prophecy. After having enjoyed those chartered rights for many thousand years, the people all at once assumed the authority to disannul them, and thus came out in open rebellion against the government of the Almighty. Oh, what a fearful responsibility rests upon those who have thus dared to repeal and disannul that which God had established!

19.—What would be the consequences, if a portion of the inhabitants of Great Britain were to rise up against some of the dearest and most precious rights which had been granted by the law-making department, and which had been enjoyed by the subjects for many generations? Would they not be considered in a state of rebellion? Would they not be taken and tried before the proper tribunals, and condemned and punished, as guilty of treason? How much sorer punishment, then, must the world of Christendom receive! For their crime is of much greater magnitude. They have not rebelled against the governments of the earth, but against the government of heaven; they have repealed, disannuled, and rebelled against some of the most sacred rights granted by the Kings of kings. If such a rebellion against the laws of earthly governments will subject the person to death, what must be the punishment of those who rebel against heavenly governments! Oh, Christendom! what hast thou done? Thou hast closed the door of heaven upon thyself, and upon the nations of the earth! Thou hast made the windows of heaven as brass that cannot easily be penetrated! Thou hast rejected the key of revelation, and thus cut off all communications from the heavenly worlds! Thou hast repealed and made void the chartered privileges, and most sacred rights, ordained of God, for the comforting, teaching and perfecting of His Saints! Thou hast veiled the heavens in darkness, and shrouded the earth with a black mantle of error!

Oh, Christendom, what wilt thou do! And whither wilt thou hide thyself in the day of thy visitation—in the day of the fierce anger of the Almighty! The mountains and rocks will not cover thy shame, nor hide thy guilt from the eye of Him who searcheth all things! Repent, then, of thy great wickedness, oh, thou destroyer of souls! no longer lift thy voice against the glorious gift of revelation; no longer deny the chartered rights of the people of God; no longer rebel against the ministry of angels, and the enjoyments of the gifts of vision and prophecy; no longer seek to repeal that which heaven has ordained, and which the children of God enjoyed for four thousand years. Remember that divine gifts and divine laws can only be repealed by divine authority.

20.—We are told by the ministers of Christendom, that God has repealed the gift of revelation, as no longer necessary. But they have utterly failed up to this day to point out the revelation that contains this repeal. The Old Testament does not contain it—the New Testament does not contain it. As the repeal act is not found in the Bible, where shall it be found? This is a question of great importance! If there be such an *act of repeal*, it must be somewhere, or how could these ministers have known it? We call upon Christendom to bring forward out of their sacred archives the REPEAL LAW. Let us search it—let us see what God has said about the world's having revelation enough. Let us see what time the repeal was passed, when it came in force—how long it is to continue in force—and whether there is any probability of a restoration of the former privileges? None can consider this call for the repeal law unreasonable. If God has ordained such a law it is reasonable that we should know it. The ministers say they know it. Why not let the people see the law that they may know it also? Why keep them in the dark— if such a law exists bring it forward. You cannot say that it is a law of not much importance; for surely, if God has passed a law repealing the gift of revelation, the gift of prophecy, the gift of visions and dreams by the spirit, the ministry of angels and all other miraculous gifts, which had been enjoyed by every people of God among all nations, and in all generations for four thousand years—if He has swept away all these long-established and most glorious privileges from the Church by a repealed law, then it must be one of the most important laws that has ever been communicated to man; it is a law that every one should be familiar with; and none should be prohibited from reading or perusing it.

21.—When God repealed the law of Moses He did not keep it to Himself, but He told the people plainly, not only of the *repeal act*, but also of the *new acts* which were introduced in its stead. The law of Moses required a man to give a writing of divorcement if he wished to put away his wife; but Jesus repealed that law, and gave a new one in its stead. The law of Moses required the people to "perform unto the Lord their oaths;" but Jesus repealed this law, and commanded the people to "swear not at all." The law of Moses required "an eye for an eye, a tooth for a tooth;" but Jesus repealed this law also, and commanded the people "not to resist evil." Here, then, we have the repeal law, abolishing that of Moses, and the new law introduced in its stead; both are revealed in perfect plainness: there is no dubiety or uncertainty as to what is repealed or as to what takes its place. If it be considered necessary to reveal to mankind that certain privileges, granted by the law of Moses, were repealed; how much more necessary is it, that mankind should know of the repeal of blessings and privileges far greater and vastly superior to those of the law of Moses! Would God take such particular care to notify man of the repeal of Moses' law, and yet leave him in entire ignorance with regard to the repeal of the gift of revelation, visions, prophecy, etc.? The law of Moses "was added because of transgression," and given "because of the hardness of their hearts;" Paul calls it a "law of carnal commandments;" therefore mankind could, with propriety, look for its repeal. But no one for a moment could have supposed that the Lord would repeal and do away such great and glorious gifts as ministers now declare to be unnecessary. But what seems still more strange, is, that He should repeal privileges granted, not only in the Mosaic dispensation, and in the ages preceding it, but also in the gospel dispensation, even down to the close of the first century, and yet give us no information of such repeal.

22.—But the ministers of apostate Christendom assert that God has repealed those precious gifts, and we now call upon them to tell us how they know it. Has God revealed it to them? No, say they; God reveals nothing in this age. Did you learn it from ancient revelation? If so, we call upon you in the name of the Lord, as you value your own soul's salvation, and that of others, to show us the revelation, that we may know it also. If you do not do this, it will be considered that you do not know any such thing, but that you have come to the people, like the prophets of Ahab, with a lie in your mouths to deceive, devour and destroy. O ye ministers of modern Christendom—ye enemies of new revelation! how can ye escape the damnation of hell! How many millions of good, honest-hearted people you have deceived by your cunning craftiness, and lying hypocraises! How many millions would have called upon God, in faith, for revelations, prophecies, visions and the ministry of angels, and received these precious blessings, had it not been for the wicked, most abominable and soul-destroying lies, which you have instilled into their ears by telling them that these things were repealed and done away! Repent, therefore, of this great wickedness, and be baptized for the remission of your sins, and you shall receive the Holy Ghost, which shall give you visions and revelations, and shall show you things to come; and except you do this, the wrath and indignation of that Being against whom you have lied, shall speedily overtake you, and you shall perish out of the earth. REPENT, THEREFORE, QUICKLY, THAT YOU MAY FIND MERCY.

## CHAPTER II.

#### MORE REVELATION IS INDISPENSABLY NECESSARY.

1.—In the former chapter it has been shown, that to expect more revelation is neither unscriptural nor unreasonable; hence, there is as great a probability that more will be given in our day, as in any former age. The object of this chapter is to show that more revelation is indispensably necessary,

#### FIRST, FOR THE CALLING OF OFFICERS IN THE CHURCH.

2.—Whenever God has called and authorized men to perform a work in any age or dispensation, it has been done by revelations, and not by mere impressions. or some undefinable, internal feelings, which leave the mind in uncertainty and doubt. Noah was called by the word of the Lord to be a preacher of righteousness, and to build an ark. Abraham, Lot, Isaac, Jacob and Joseph, were called by revelation to perform a great variety of duties. Moses and Aaron were called to the priest's office by the word of the great Jehovah. Seventy elders of Israel were called by revelation to assist Moses. Joshua was appointed by the word of the Lord through Moses to be his successor in leading Israel. The successors of Aaron were appointed to the priesthood by revelation. The Judges of Israel were called by visions, by angels and by the inspiration of the Spirit. Samuel was called by the voice of the Lord. And finally, all their officers, wise men and prophets, down to the days of Malachi, were called by new revelation.

3.—The calling of officers under the Christian dispensation continued the same. John, the forerunner of Christ, was called by the spirit of prophecy, as manifested through the angel Gabriel and his father Zacharias. Jesus was called by His Father, and appointed a priest forever after the order of Melchisedec: He is termed by St. Paul, "the Apostle and

High Priest of our profession." Jesus, being an Apostle, called others to the same office, and said unto them, "ye have not chosen Me but I have chosen you, and ordained you, that ye should go and bring forth fruit" (*John xv.*) When Judas fell through transgression, the apostles did not appoint another to take his bishopric through a mere impression, but they called upon the Lord to show whom He had chosen; and "the lot fell upon Matthias"(*Acts i.* 15-26). The seventy disciples were called by the word of the Lord. Paul and Barnabas were both Apostles (*see Acts xiv.* 14), and were set apart to the work of the ministry by new revelation through the inspired prophets and teachers, which were in the church at Antioch (*Acts xiii.* 1-4.) That the elders of the church at Ephesus were called by revelation, is evident by the following language of Paul to them, "Take heed therefore unto yourselves, and to all the flock over which *the Holy Ghost hath made you overseers*, to feed the Church of God which He hath purchased with His own blood" (*Acts xx.* 28). Timothy, the first bishop of Ephesus, was appointed by prophecy and by the laying on of hands (*I. Tim. iv.* 14.) Titus, the first bishop of the Cretians, was appointed by the Apostle Paul "to ordain elders in every city;" these elders were to be ordained after the manner, and in the way that Paul had appointed Titus (*Titus i.* 5.) And we have already seen that a spirit of prophecy was necessary to ordain a bishop; and as Bishop Titus was to ordain elders in every city after the *pattern* he himself had been ordained, he must, to have carried out his instructions, have enjoyed the spirit of prophecy. If the elders of Ephesus were made overseers of the Church by the revelation of the Holy Ghost, it is reasonable to infer, that revelation was necessary to the appointment of elders in all other cities. Paul says, "As God hath distributed to every man, as the Lord hath called every one, so let him walk, and so ordain I in all churches" (*I. Cor. vii.* 17.) Paul did not presume to ordain in all churches, only such as were called of the Lord, and he ordained them according to that calling; and such callings could only be made known by revelation.

4.—When mankind through their apostasy lost the spirit of prophecy and revelation, they also lost the other supernatural gifts of the Spirit, such as healing, miracles, tongues, interpretations of tongues, etc. These gifts ceased, not all at once, but by degrees, until the spirit had entirely withdrawn, leaving only a powerless form. The necessity of revelations, visions, prophesyings, ministry of angels and miraculous gifts, was never denied until mankind found themselves destitute of these promised blessings; when it was pretended that they were only designed for the first Christians; the people began by degrees to believe this wicked pretension, until, at length, they boldly denied the necessity of every miraculous power. Millions in every succeeding generation have continued to walk in the footsteps of the early apostates, fulfilling in every respect the prediction of Paul, that "in the last days perilous times should come; for men should be lovers of their own selves, covetous, etc." "having a form of godliness but denying the power thereof" (*II. Tim. iii.* 1-5.) Notwithstanding the universality of this apostasy, yet the numerous religious bodies which enter into its composition, have had the daring presumption to still call themselves Christians, or the church of Christ. But if they were the church of Christ, then the miraculous powers and gifts of Christ would be shown forth among them, and their ministers, as formerly, would be called by revelation. The Church of Christ cannot exist on the earth without an authorized ministry. This ministry cannot be called and authorized without new revelation. "No man taketh this honor unto himself," (that is the honor of the ministry), but he that is called of God as was Aaron" (*Heb. v.* 4).

5.—Without new revelation every office in the Church would necessarily become vacant. It is true, that those who held office at the time revelation ceased, would still, during their natural life, continue to retain it, unless through transgression they should be legally deprived of it. If revelation ceased at the close of the first century, it is not at all likely that any of the officers, then holding the authority, would be alive a century afterwards; and as they would have no authority to ordain others without new revelation, when they died, the authority upon the earth would necessarily become extinct. How overwhelming the thought! Yet there is no conclusion more certain. If all offices became vacant there could be no additions to the church by baptism; for it would be a great sin for private members to assume the authority to baptize; hence, as soon as those who had been baptized by authority were dead, the world would be entirely destitute of both the officers and private members of the Church of Christ. But when officers and members both cease, what is left? nothing at all. Hence, without continued revelation, the Church could no more continue in its existence on the earth, than a body could live without the spirit. Therefore, if revelation ceased with the Apostles, as the "Articles" and "Creeds" of men declare, every vestige of authority, as well as the Church itself, must have become extinct from the earth, as early at least as the third century; since which time the earth has been cursed with priestcraft and apostasy, and with every species of wickedness.

6.—Since the Church with its authority and power has been caught away from the earth, the great "mother of harlots" with all her "descendants has blasphemously assumed the authority of administering some of the sacred ordinances of the gospel. They have blasphemed the name of the Father, Son and Holy Ghost, by using it without authority in their ministrations. They have dishonored the name of Christ, by calling their powerless, apostate, filthy and most abominable churches, the Church of Christ. The whole Romish, Greek and Protestant ministry, from the pope down through every grade of office, are as destitute of authority from God, as the devil and his angels. The Almighty abhors all their wicked pretensions, as He does the very gates of hell.

7.—The great apostasy of the Christian church commenced in the first century, while there were yet inspired apostles and prophets in their midst;. hence Paul, just previous to his martyrdom, enumerates a great number who had "made shipwreck of their faith," and "turned aside unto vain jangling;" teaching "that the resurrection was already past," giving "heed to fables and endless genealogies," "doting about questions and strifes of words, whereof came envyings, railings, and evil surmisings, perverse disputings of men of corrupt minds, and destitute of the truth, supposing that gain is godliness." This apostasy had become so general that Paul declares to Timothy, "that all they which are in Asia be turned away from me;" and again he says, "At my first answer, no man stood with me, but all men forsook me;" he further states, that "there are many unruly and vain talkers and deceivers," "teaching things which they ought not, for filthy lucre's sake." These apostates, no doubt, pretended to be very righteous; for, says the apostle, "they profess that they know God; but in works they deny Him, being abominable and disobedient, and unto every good work reprobate." Near the close of the first century, the apostasy had become so universal that only seven churches throughout all Asia, Africa, and Europe, were considered worthy of being either reproved or blessed by the voice of revelation; and even these seven were so corrupted by the doctrine of the Nicolaitanes, and of Balaam, by the fornications and adulteries of Jezebel, and by losing their "first love," and becoming "neither cold nor hot," that the Almighty considered them, with a very few exceptions, as "dead," and threatened to "spue them out of His mouth," to cast them "into great tribulation," and "kill their children with death," to "fight against them with the sword of His mouth," and to "remove the candlestick," or church, "out of its place."

8.—That this apostasy, which had become so formidable, while yet inspired apostles were in their midst, was to greatly increase, instead of decreasing, is evident from the predictions of scripture. Paul prophesies that "the day of Christ shall not come, except there come a falling away first;" that "evil men and seducers shall wax worse and worse, deceiving and being deceived." As a reason for the strict charge which he gave to Timothy, he predicts, that "the time will come when they will not endure sound doctrine; but after their own lusts *they shall heap to themselves teachers*, having itching ears; and they shall turn away their ears from the truth, and shall be turned unto fables." The predictions concerning the apostasy were not expressed in a vague uncertain form of language, but in the clearest and most forcible terms. "Now the Spirit speaketh expressly," says Paul, "that in the latter times some shall depart from the faith, giving heed to seducing spirits and doctrines of devils, speaking lies in hypocrisy, having their conscience seared with a hot iron." Peter prophesies that "there shall be false teachers among you, who privily shall bring in damnable heresies, even denying the Lord that bought them, and bring upon themselves swift destruction; and many shall follow their pernicious ways; by reason of whom the way of truth shall be evil spoken of; and through covetuousness shall they with feigned words make merchandise of you" (*II. Peter ii.* 1, 2, 3.) These "fables," "doctrines of devils," and "damnable heresies" which false teachers should introduce into the world, were to constitute the religion of future ages, rendering the state of society fearful in the extreme. Paul gives a prophetic description of the religion of latter times as follows: "This know also, that in the last days perilous times shall come; for men shall be lovers of their own selves, covetous, boasters, proud, blasphemers, disobedient to parents, unthankful, unholy, without natural affection, truce breakers, false accusers, incontinent, fierce, despisers of those that are good, traitors, heady, high-minded, lovers of pleasure more than lovers of God; *having a form of godliness, but denying the power thereof*, from such turn away. For of this sort are they which creep into houses, and lead captive silly women laden with sins, led away with divers lusts; ever learning, and never able to come to a knowledge of the truth. Now as Jannes and Jambres withstood Moses, so do these also resist the truth: men of corrupt minds, reprobate concerning the faith. But they shall proceed no further; for their folly shall be made manifest unto all men, as their's also was" (*II. Tim. iii.* 1-9.).

9.—It seems from the foregoing predictions, that the religion of the latter-days was to be most awfully corrupt; that its teachers, instead of being sent by revelation from God, were to be heaped together by the people. These man-made teachers were to turn away the ears of the people from the truth, or from sound doctrine, and in its stead were to teach "fables," "doctrines of devils," "damnable heresies," "speaking lies in hypocrisy;" they were to come "with feigned words," or, "with great swelling words of vanity," to "make merchandise of the people;" they were to have a "*form* of godliness," but "the power" they were to deny; they were to meet with great success in deceiving mankind; for "many were to follow their pernicious ways." The people were to delight in these power-less, devilish, hypocritical, lying, damnable heresies, while the way of truth was to be evil spoken of; and "because they received not the love of the truth," God was to "send them strong delusions, that they should believe a lie, that they all might be damned who believed not the truth, but had pleasure in unrighteousness." Such was to be the religion of the latter ages, as prophetically described by the ancient apostles; and such is the religion of the Papal, Greek and Protestant churches of the ninteenth century. The predictions were uttered eighteen centuries ago, and modern Christendom exhibits a most perfect fulfillment. Instead of having apostles, prophets, and other inspired men in the church now, receiving visions, dreams, revelations, ministry of angels and prophesies for the calling of officers, and for the government of the church—they have a wicked, corrupt, uninspired pope, or uninspired archbishops, bishops, clergymen, etc., who have a great variety of corrupt forms of godliness, but utterly deny the gift of revelation, and every other miraculous power which always characterized Christ's Church. These man-made, powerless, hypocritical, false teachers, "make merchandise of the people," by preaching for large salaries, amounting in many instances to tens of thousands of dollars annually. They and their deluded followers are reprobate concerning the faith once delivered to the Saints. The faith which once quenched the violence of fire, stopped the mouths of lions, divided waters, and controlled the powers of nature, is discarded as unnecessary. The faith that inspired men with the gift of revelation—that opened the heavens and laid hold on mysteries that were not lawful to be uttered—that unfolded the visions of the past and future—and that called down the angels of heaven to eat and drink with men on earth—is denied as being attainable in this age. The sound doctrine taught by the apostles which put mankind in the possession of these glorious gifts and powers cannot now be endured. The doctrines, commands, fables, traditions and creeds, of uninspired men, are now substituted in the place of direct inspiration from God. "They are ever learning, but are never able to come to a knowledge of the truth." Guess work, conjecture, opinion, and, perhaps, in some instances, a belief in regard to the truth, are all that they attain to, while a knowledge they do not obtain, because they deny new revelation the only means of obtaining it. This great multitude of false teachers who have found their way into all nations, deceiving millions, "resist the truth," contend against the miraculous powers of the gospel, and reject inspired men, as "Jannes and Jambres," the magicians, did Moses; but "their folly shall be made manifest unto all men, as theirs also was;" yea, all nations shall see the righteous judgments which shall speedily be poured out upon them, for they shall, like Pharaoh's host, perish quickly from the earth.

10.—If the revelations contained in the sixty-six books of the Old and New Testaments, are the only ones to be received, it would be impossible for any man since the apostasy, to prove from those books that he was called of God. The Bible contains the record of the callings and commissions of many who lived during the first four thousand years; but it says not one word about the callings and commissions of those who have lived during the last seventeen centuries. Some who have seen the dilemma in which they are placed by rejecting new revelation, have endeavoured to extricate themselves from it, by pretending that the old commissions given to the apostles are sufficient for all present purposes. But this places them in another dilemma equally as great; for how can any man learn whether the commission given to the apostles is applicable to himself or not? Without new revelation he could never know. Surely the apostolic commission does not authorize *all* mankind who should live in future ages; and if it authorizes *a part* only, then it certainly would require new revelation to specify which part. Therefore, if we were to admit so absurd an idea, there still would be an equal necessity for new revelation. But commissions or callings given to one man never did, nor never can, authorize another. Mankind have no more authority to preach, baptize, and administer the ordinances of the gospel, by virtue of the apostolic commission, than they have to ascend the throne of Great Britain by virtue of the commission given to King David.

11 —As the church of England and other Protestants do not profess to have received any new commission by revelation, but

on the contrary, require their followers to reject everything of the kind, it may be asked, how did they get their authority? It will be replied, that they received it from Wickliffe, Cranmer, Luther, Calvin, and various other dissenters from the Papal church. But where did those dissenters get theirs from? They answer from the Roman Catholics. But the Catholics excommunicated them as heretics; and surely if they had power to impart authority, they had power to take it away. Therefore, if the Romish church had any authority, the Protestants, being excommunicated, can hold none from that source. But if the Catholics hold authority, they must be the true church, and consequently the Protestants must be apostates; but on the other hand, if the Catholics are not the true church, they can have no authority themselves, and therefore could not impart any to others.

12.—Now the church of England states in one of her homilies, "that laity and clergy, learned and unlearned, men and women, and children of all ages, sects and degrees, of WHOLE CHRISTENDOM, have been at once buried in THE MOST ABOMINABLE IDOLATRY (a most dreadful thing to think), and that for the SPACE OF EIGHT HUNDRED YEARS OR MORE!"\* Wesley in his 94th sermon states the same in substance; he says, "The real cause why the extraordinary gifts of the Holy Ghost were no longer to be found in the Christian church, was, *because the Christians were turned heathens again, and had only a dead form left.*" If, then, the "whole of Christendom," without one exception, have been "buried in the most abominable idolatry for upwards of eight hundred years," as the church of England declares, and if they, because they are destitute of the gifts, are not even now Christians, but heathens as Wesley asserts, we ask where the authority was during this eight hundred years, and where is it now? Surely God would not recognize "the most abominable idolators," as holding authority; if so, the authority of the worshipers of Juggernaut must be as valid as that of idolatrous Christendom. But the idolatry of "whole Christendom" must have been more corrupt, according to the church of England,

---

\*——Homily on the Perils of Idolatry.

than that of other idolators; for they call it "the most abominable idolatry," and most positively declare that there was no exception of either clergy or laity—of either man, woman or child—all were buried in it. This being the case (and we feel no disposition to dispute it), there could have been no possible channel on the whole earth through which authority could have been transferred from the apostles to our day. Therefore, as Wesley says, all Christendom are, sure enough, "heathens," having no more authority nor powers than the idolatrous pagans. If, then, the "whole of Christendom" have been without authority and power "for eight hundred years and upwards," we ask, when was the authority restored? It could not have been restored to the Papal churches, for they do not profess that any such restoration has been made to them; it could not have been restored to the church of England and other Protestants, for they do not admit of any later revelation than the New Testament; consequently their own admissions prove most clearly that the whole of Christendom are without an authorized ministry; therefore it is indispensably necessary that more revelation should be given to restore the authority to the earth and call men to the ministry again, as in ancient days.

13.—More revelation is not only necessary to restore an authorized ministry, that the church may again have place on the earth, but it is indispensably necessary,

SECONDLY, TO POINT OUT THE DUTIES OF THE OFFICERS OF THE CHURCH.

To call men to the ministry would be of very little use, unless the persons called could have a perfect knowledge of the duties of their calling. Noah was called to preach repentance and righteousness to the antediluvians, but without further revelations, he never could have learned the will of God relative to the preservation of himself and family, and the different kinds of beasts, fowls and creeping things, both clean and unclean, of all flesh; he never could have learned what amount of food of different kinds, and fresh water would be sufficient to sustain such a congregated host of living beings for the space of one hundred and fifty days, during which time the flood was to prevail. Jacob, though called of God, without further revelation, never could have learned what should befall the posterity of his sons in the last days, so as to have delivered a prophetic blessing upon the head of each according to the mind of God. Moses, though called by the voice of Jehovah, without further revelation, never could have delivered Israel from bondage, and led them forty years in the wilderness. Aaron, though called of God to the priestly office, and in possession of the written law, never could have sat upon the judgment-seat, and decided between man and man, according to the mind of God, without the "breastplate of judgment," containing the "Urim and Thummim," through which he could enquire of God and receive correct information relative to every case which should come before him. All the servants of God, down to the days of Malachi, were not only called by the Almighty, but directed in all their multifarious duties to the end of their days by immediate revelation.

14.—In the Christian dispensation it was the same. Every officer, after having been called, was instructed and guided by continued revelation in the various duties of his calling. John, the forerunner of Christ, was first called, and then was enabled through the inspiration of the Spirit, to tell the Scribes, Pharisees, Sadducees, soldiers and all the people, what they should do, as they came enquiring of him. Even Jesus Himself, though He was sent by His Father, and came forth from God, did not presume to teach of Himself, or perform anything pertaining to the work of the ministry, without first obtaining a revelation from the Father to direct Him. He says, "I have not spoken of myself; but the Father which sent me, He gave me a commandment what I should say, and what I should speak." "Whatsoever I speak therefore, even as the Father said unto me, so I speak (*John xii.* 49, 50). Again, He says, "The words that I speak unto you, I speak not of myself, but the Father that dwelleth in me, He doeth the work," "and as the Father gave me commandment, even so I do" (*John xiv.* 10-31.). He further states, "I can of my own self do nothing; as I hear I judge, and my judgment is just, because I speak not mine own will, but the will of the Father which hath sent me" (*John v.* 30.) Now if the great and glorious Redeemer of the world could not do anything of Himself pertaining to the ministry, but was dependent altogether upon the Father to give Him revelation and commandment what to do, and what to speak, how much more necessary it is for poor, weak and fallible man, after having been called of God, to be directed in all things pertaining to the duties of his calling by continued revelation. And yet, strange to say, the whole of Christendom have been without this essential qualification for centuries, and have still dared to act as ministers in the name of the Lord. Oh, the wickedness of apostate Christendom! Truly did the apostle behold her "full of names of blasphemy," making all nations drunk with her wickedness!

15.—The example that Jesus set, not to act nor speak in the duties of His calling, unless by new revelation, was followed by the apostles. All the teachings which they had heard from the mouth of the Savior while He was present with them, were not sufficient to qualify them for their duties in His absence. As soon as He left them, He began to give them commandments and revelations through the Holy Ghost (*see Acts i.* 2.) And without continued revelations, they, like their Lord and Master, could do nothing. It mattered not how much human wisdom or learning they might have acquired, nor how many revelations had previously been given; such things would in no wise qualify them for the ministry; it required constant revelation. St. Paul says, "The things of God knoweth no man, but the Spirit of God; now we have received not the spirit of the world, but the Spirit which is of God, that we might know the things that are freely given to us of God; which things also we speak, not in the words which man's wisdom teacheth, but which the Holy Ghost teacheth" (*I. Cor. ii.* 11, 12, 13.) From these passages we learn, first, that no man can know the things of God only by revelation, and secondly, that no man can teach them acceptably only in the words "which the Holy Ghost teacheth." Revelation, then, is necessary to call and authorize the ministry, to reveal their duties, to manifest the things of God to them and to give them utterance, "not in the words which man's wisdom teacheth," but in the words inspired and taught by the Holy Ghost.

16.—If human wisdom and learning could qualify any one for the ministry, Paul certainly could have claimed a higher qualification than the rest of the apostles; he was learned; he was eloquent; he was eminently prepared so far as the wisdom of man was available to move in the higher spheres of life, and to speak with honor and dignity in the presence of vast assemblies; he could, through human wisdom alone, have pathetically portrayed the death and sufferings of Christ, reasoned upon the benefits to be derived from the atonement, urged the importance of obeying the requirements of the gospel, and with all the thunders of his eloquence described the misery and wretchedness of the disobedient—yet he informs us, that he did not declare the things of God in the "words which man's wisdom teacheth." The words of man's wisdom are foolishness in the sight of God—they are inadequate to convey properly the things revealed by the Spirit. The Spirit not only gives the ideas, but in a measure clothes them in suitable and proper words. This is the spirit of revelation, so abundantly enjoyed by the Saints in all ages, that so enriched their minds with heavenly knowledge, and qualified them to speak as the oracles of God, uttering words taught by the Holy Ghost. This is the spirit of revelation, rejected and done away in the "Articles" and "Creeds" of modern Christendom, and in its place are substituted "the words which man's wisdom teacheth." This is the spirit of revelation, so necessary to unfold to the minister of Christ, those duties which he never could learn from ancient revelation, nor from the wisdom and writings of uninspired men.

17.—Without this spirit of revelation Joshua never could have known the mind of the Lord in relation to taking the city of Jericho; he never could have known that it was the will of God that all Israel should march around its walls for seven days, blowing upon rams' horns. If Israel had been left to their own wisdom, it never would have entered their heart to subdue a city by such simple expedients. Indeed, it was only necessary on that one occasion; and that one occasion required a new revelation to manifest the mind and will of

God. In subduing another city or nation, the Lord might have altogether a different plan, so that the rule followed in one instance, might never be applicable in another; hence the necessity of continued revelation; for no servant of God or leader in Israel could possibly learn the mind of God without it. "God's ways are not as our ways, nor His thoughts as our thoughts." Therefore, the wisdom of man, unaided by immediate revelation, cannot perform acceptably before God any work, either in directing the movements of an army, or in preaching the gospel of peace, or in ruling his own household, or in managing the affairs of a nation. When Israel went to battle, they first enquired of God, and then proceeded according to His direction; when they anointed kings to sit upon the throne, they did it by revelation; when a city was to be warned of approaching judgment, a Lot, or a Jonah, or some inspired man was sent by revelation to do it: when Israel turned aside from the law of God, multitudes of prophets were not only sent by revelation to reprove them, but the message which they were to deliver, was given by revelation also: when the Lord saw that Philip had warned the people of Samaria sufficiently, He did not leave him to the vague conjectures of his own mind where he should go next, but sent an angel who spake to him, saying, "Arise, and go towards the south unto the way that goeth down from Jerusalem unto Gaza, which is desert." (*Acts viii.* 26.) If Philip had been left to his own wisdom, he never could have learned whether his mission was done in Samaria or not; and even if he had learned this, the desert country off to the south, would have been the last place that human wisdom would have guided him. But after Philip had reached this lonely solitary desert, he still needed revelation to direct him in regard to further duties. The next thing which we find revealed to him was by the Spirit, which said unto him, "Go near, and join thyself to this chariot." He obeyed, and succeeded in convincing a man of great authority—a eunuch, of the truths of the gospel; and after having baptized him, "the Spirit of the Lord caught away Philip, that the eunuch saw him no more."

18.—In Damascus, there was another servant of God, called Ananias; he was not a Protestant clergyman, for he believed in visions and revelations; "and to him said the Lord in a vision, Ananias. And he said, Behold, I am here, Lord. And the Lord said unto him, Arise, and go into the street which is called Straight, and enquire in the house of Judas for one called Saul, of Tarsus: for, behold, he prayeth, and hath seen in a vision a man named Ananias coming in, and putting his hand on him, that he might receive his sight." (*Acts ix.* 10, 11, 12.) Here are two visionary characters, Ananias and Saul; if they had lived in our day, they would have been considered, by new revelation deniers, as appropriate subjects for the insane hospital. It is so natural for mankind to think that their own judgment is sufficient to guide them in the way of duty, that even Ananias himself was rather inclined to question the propriety of revelation, and follow his own wisdom; for he answered "Lord, I have heard by many of this man, how much evil he hath done to thy saints at Jerusalem; and here he hath authority from the chief priests to bind all that call upon Thy name." (*Verses* 13, 14.) But the Lord not feeling disposed to be governed by the weak judgment of Ananias, commanded him again, saying, "Go thy way; for he is a chosen vessel unto me, to bear my name before the Gentiles, and kings, and the children of Israel for I will show him how great things he must suffer for my name's sake." (*Verses* 15, 16.)

19.—Peter was another of these visionary characters so much despised by modern religionists. One of the first revelations he obtained, was about Jesus being the Christ. It seems that there was a great diversity of opinions among those who did not seek for new revelation, relative to whom Jesus was; some thought he was one of the old prophets, some thought he was John the Baptist, having risen from the dead, the wisdom of man had imagined a variety of opinions respecting Him. Peter, not being satisfied with the conjectures of men about it, was just simple enough to ask the Father whom Jesus was. The Father told him, that Jesus was "the Christ, the Son of the living God." Here then was certainty—conjecture and opinion had fled away. When the Savior enquired of His disciples what their views were in relation to Him, Peter could answer the question without any doubt or hesitation; and because of this knowledge Jesus blessed him, and said unto him, "flesh and blood hath not revealed it unto thee, but my Father which is in heaven." (*Matt. xvi.* 17.) The great mass of the Jews were destitute of this knowledge; they did not seek of the Father a revelation on the subject, but depended, like this generation, on former revelation and their own wisdom, and therefore not knowing by new revelation the Savior, they crucified Him. Peter, having had faith sufficient to get one revelation, the Savior, counted him worthy to receive more, therefore He took him up into a mountain with James and John, "and was transfigured before them; and His face did shine as the sun, and His raiment was white as the light; and behold there appeared unto them Moses and Elias talking with Him." (*Matt. xvii.* 1, 2, 3.) These visionary persons could now testify to the nations what they had seen, and heard and known about Jesus, about God and about angels. But such testimonies to be given by any persons in these days, would be counted the highest blasphemy. But we ask, what do modern Christendom know about God? they have not heard His voice, nor received a revelation from Him. What do they know about Jesus? nothing, only what they have read of the knowledge of others. What do they know about angels? they have never beheld them, nor heard their voice. What do they know about visions? nothing at all, for they despise all those that profess to have seen visions since the apostles' days. And finally, what do they know about the Holy Ghost? It has never spoken to them nor to any one else, in their estimation, for the last seventeen centuries. They have not heard, seen, handled nor known anything for themselves by revelation; consequently, they are entirely unqualified to be witnesses of any spiritual or heavenly knowledge: they know nothing, only what they know naturally "as brute beasts, made to be taken and destroyed." (*See Jude* 10.) Without new revelation, they are entirely unqualified to judge of the things of God: they would be as apt to call good evil and evil good, and put light for darkness and darkness for light, as ancient revelation deniers were. Their preaching would not justify nor condemn any one, because they know nothing, only what others have written, and therefore cannot testify. This is the sad, and awful, and most wretched condition of modern Christendom.

20.—Peter had another vision while he was praying upon a house top: he saw heaven opened, and all manner of beasts let down, and drawn up thrice; and "While Peter thought on the vision, the spirit said unto him, Behold three men seek thee, Arise, therefore, and get thee down, and go with them. doubting nothing: for I have sent them." (*Acts* x. 19, 20.) Peter, through this vision, and the sayings of the spirit, learned duties pertaining to his calling that never could have been learned naturally. Peter had had a vast amount of knowledge previously revealed to him, but that would not manifest to him his present duties. Present duties require present revelation; and without it, no servant of God ever did, or ever can do the work of God. Without it, he does not know where to go, or what to preach. But says the objector, it does not matter where he preaches, for he cannot go amiss; all must have the privilege of hearing. We reply, that though all must hear, yet the Lord designed some to hear before others, as is evident from the fact that Paul and Timothy "were forbidden of the Holy Ghost to preach the word in Asia;" and again, "after they were come to Mysia, they assayed to go into Bithynia; but the Spirit suffered them not." (*Acts xvi.* 6, 7.) Hence we learn, that the Lord has a choice where His servants shall go; and that in some places where their own judgment would dictate them to go, the Lord desires they should not go, and actually forbids them to go. Now, how, without new revelation, is the servant of God to know the mind of the Lord as to where he shall or shall not go? Would any former revelation communicate the desired intelligence unto him? Certainly not; former revelation contains the history of the revealed will of God to others, but it does not specify in all things the revealed will of God to us. To read of others learning the will of God in relation to their callings and mission, and enjoying manifestations of the Spirit by visions, dreams, angels, etc., would be of no more advantage to us, than to read of the history of a good dinner when we were hungry. It is the present enjoyment of blessings which we want, and not merely the history of others' blessings.

21.—How could Paul have known the mind of the Lord about going to Macedonia without being told? Therefore, "a vision appeared to Paul in the night: There stood a man of Macedonia, and prayed him, saying, Come over into Macedonia and help us." (*Acts, xvi.* 9.) And again, how did Paul know it was his duty to tarry in Corinth about a year and a half? He found it out by a vision. "Then spake the Lord to Paul in the night by a vision, Be not afraid, but speak, and hold not thy peace: For I am with thee, and no man shall set on thee, to hurt thee: for I have much people in this city." (*Acts, xviii.* 9, 10.) How did Paul learn that it was necessary for him to depart quickly out of Jerusalem, and go to other nations? He learned it by a vision in the temple. He says, "And it came to pass that when I was come again to Jerusalem, even while I prayed in the temple, I was in a trance; and saw Him saying unto me, Make haste, and get thee quickly out of Jerusalem; for they will not receive thy testimony concerning me." (*Acts, xxii.* 17, 18.) And when Paul reasoned with the Lord upon the subject, as if he thought that from their acquaintance with his former course of life, they would receive his testimony, the Lord again commanded him, saying, "Depart: for I will send thee far hence unto the Gentiles." Thus we see how impossible it is for a minister of the gospel to learn what to do, or where to go, or what to say, unless he is taught by new revelation. Without this heavenly principle, his own judgment would constantly lead him astray.

22.—New revelation is not only highly necessary to call men to the ministry, and afterwards to instruct them in the various duties of their calling, but it is indispensably necessary,

THIRDLY TO COMFORT, REPROVE AND TEACH THE CHURCH.

Jesus, before his ascension, promised the Holy Ghost to His disciples, which He calls "the Comforter." They had previously been comforted by the words of Jesus: He had unfolded to them His parables; He had instructed them for three years and a half; He had given them a vast amount of information upon a great variety of subjects; and now, as he was about to be taken from them in person, he promised to send unto them another comforter. He says, "If ye love me, keep my commandments; and I will pray the Father, and He shall give you another Comforter, that he may abide with you forever; even the spirit of truth, whom the world cannot receive, because it seeth him not, neither knoweth him; but ye know him; for he dwelleth with you, and shall be in you." (*John xiv.* 15, 16, 17.) The reason why the Holy Ghost is called the Comforter is, because of the office which he was to perform; he was to comfort the disciples, by revealing to them still further knowledge of the things of God. The mind of man is too weak to receive at once, all the knowledge which God is willing that he should know: hence Jesus says, "I have yet many things to say unto you, but ye cannot bear them now. Howbeit, when he, the Spirit of truth is come, he will guide you into all truth; for he shall not speak of himself, but whatsoever he shall hear, that shall he speak; and he will shew you things to come. He shall glorify me: for he shall receive of mine, and shall shew it unto you. All things that the Father hath, are mine; therefore, said I that he shall take of mine, and shew it unto you." (*John xvi.* 12, 13, 14, 15.) Here we find how the disciples, after Jesus ceased speaking unto them in person, were to be continually guided by revelation. Many things which they could not then bear on account of the weakness of their minds, were afterwards to be revealed to them through the Comforter: he was to guide them into all truth. But even the Holy Ghost was not to teach without first getting a revelation as to what he should teach, for, says Jesus, "he shall not speak of himself, but whatsoever he shall hear, that shall he speak." It is strange, indeed, that the ministers of modern Christendom dare speak of themselves, without getting any new revelation, when even Jesus and the Holy Ghost would neither of them presume to do such a thing The Comforter was to be the guide of the disciples, not only in this short life, but forever. Again, Jesus says, "the Comforter, which is the Holy Ghost, whom the Father will send in my name, he shall teach you all things and bring all things to your remembrance, whatsoever I have said unto you." (*John xiv.* 26.)

23.—This same Comforter which was to be a constant revelator to the disciples, was promised on the day of Pentecost, to *all* who would obey the gospel. After he had descended upon one hundred and twenty, on the morning of that day, revealing to them, not only other tongues, but also "the wonderful works of God, it excited the attention of thousands, who, after learning that it was the Holy Ghost that operated so powerfully, felt extremely anxious to obtain the same gift, and they were told the conditions on which they all might receive it. "Repent," says Peter, "and be baptized, every one of you, in the name of Jesus Christ, for the remission of your sins, and ye shall receive the gift of the Holy Ghost." (*Acts ii.* 38.) Thus, we perceive, that thousands had the promise made to them on certain conditions, even the promise of the Holy Ghost, which "promise" says Peter, "is unto you, and to your children, and to all that are afar off, even as many as the Lord our God shall call." (*Verse* 39.) Consequently, all persons, in all generations and ages, who will perform these requirements, have the promise of the Holy Ghost; the same Holy Spirit that Jesus promised, and the same that was given on the day of Pentecost—all could receive the spirit of revelation, and be guided into all truth. To show still further that the Holy Ghost was to be a revelator to the Church, as well as to the apostles, we will quote the words of John, written to the Church generally: "Ye have an unction from the Holy One, and ye know all things." And again, "the anointing which ye have received of him, abideth in you, and ye need not that any man teach you: but as the same anointing teacheth you of all things, and is truth, no lie, and even as it hath taught you, ye shall abide in him." (*I. John ii.* 20-27.) Nothing is more certain than that the Church, as well as the apostles, were to receive the promised Comforter, and that he was to teach all things to the Church, as well as to its officers; therefore, the revelations of the Holy Ghost, are indispensably necessary to comfort and teach the Church.

24.—When certain men began to teach heresy, and introduce false doctrines into the Church, commanding the Gentiles to be circumcised, the Holy Ghost immediately gave a revelation on the subject, and corrected the error; thus preventing endless controversies and strifes. (*See Acts xv.*) If this great guide and revelator of the Church be rejected as unnecessary, how quickly the body falls to ruin! New revelation is the only principle which will preserve the unity of the Church. The wisdom of man, taken individually, or the wisdom of councils, taken collectively, is fallible, unless directed by immediate revelation, and therefore liable to err; hence all doctrines, or principles, or matters of controversy which are not clearly revealed in ancient revelation, will be continually the subjects of dispute; and if any man or council without the aid of immediate revelation, shall undertake to decide upon such subjects and prescribe "Articles of Faith," or "Creeds," to govern the belief, or views of others, there will be thousands of well-meaning people who will not have confidence in the productions of these fallible men, and therefore, will frame creeds of their own, which they suppose, are more consistent. In this way, contentions arise, divisions multiply, sects are formed, the Church becomes rent into ten thousand fragments, and the whole world becomes a *babylon of confusion.* As an effectual preventative against all false doctrine, against all strifes and divisions, against all contentions and controversies in the Church, God has placed within it a great and infallible teacher or revelator, called the Comforter, who cannot err, whose decision is an end of controversy, whose counsel is perfect, and whose judgment upon all points of doctrine cannot be otherwise than correct. Differences of opinion cannot exist in the Church for any length of time; for the Holy Ghost will decide all matters of controversy, and thus preserve the unity of the Church: while all who rebel against his decisions, will be excommunicated as heretics or apostates, and will form no part of the Church of Christ, any more than the Chinese form a part of the English government. Hence, in the Church of Christ, there is a unity of faith—a oneness of spirit, such as characterizes no other people. In the Church of Christ, there can be no differences of opinion, in regard to baptism, or any other ordinance; for the Holy Ghost will guide into all truth, and teach the Church all things pertaining to doctrine or ordinances, things present, or things to come. The great variety of opinions which have torn asunder modern Christendom, and bewildered the minds of millions, can have no existence in the Church of Christ; for there, all matters of importance are decided by revelation, and not by creeds invented by human wisdom; there, the deep and hidden things of God are revealed by the Spirit of truth; there, rich treasures of wisdom and knowledge are brought to light; there, they have no need of uninspired councils to invent "Articles of Religion" to fetter the mind of man; there, the Holy Ghost takes the things of the Father and shows them by revelation unto the Church, and there, infallibility is indelibly and unchangeably stamped upon every doctrine, principle, ordinance and law of the Church. With such a revelator, certainty and knowledge abound in every heart; parables, mysteries and intricate subjects are unravelled; guess work, conjectures and opinions, flee away. With such a guide, there is no danger of being deceived. The elect, cannot be deceived; for they have an infallible detector of all delusions, however cunningly devised: they have a test by which they can try all things, prove all things, judge all things and overcome all things not ordained of God; they can soar aloft to the third heavens and gaze upon the mansions of the blessed, where the highest order of intelligence reigns: or they can descend in the visions of the spirit, and behold the kingdoms, dominions, principalities and powers, in worlds of an inferior order, in the great scale of universal existence.

-25.—When the Church falls into sin, or turns aside from her duties, new revelation is necessary to reprove and chasten her, that she may repent and be forgiven. We have frequent examples of the people of God being reproved by the revelations of the Holy Ghost. The Corinthians were severely reproved by the Spirit of inspiration, because they had suffered contentions and divisions to get in among them and disturb the harmony and peace of the Church. Although the divisions which existed there were not in relation to doctrine, but only in relation to the talents or abilities of Paul, Apollos and Cephas, yet even for this they were called carnal. (*See I. Corinthians, iii. 1-7.*) If the Corinthians were worthy of reproof because they were divided in relation to the talents or qualifications of the ministers of Christ, how much more worthy of censure would they have been if they had been divided in relation to doctrine, like modern Christendom? All divisions in the Church, of every kind, are utterly condemned by the apostle, and he pleads with them to banish all such things from their midst, and cultivate a perfect unity in all things. He says, "Now I beseech you, brethren, by the name of our Lord Jesus Christ, that ye all speak the same thing, and that there be no divisions among you, but that ye be perfectly joined together in the same mind and in the same judgment." (*I. Corinthians*, i. 10.) Are modern religionists "perfectly joined together in the same mind and in the same judgment?" Do they all "speak the same thing?" No; they are far from it: they declare doctrines diametrically opposite to one another; yet they have the presumption to acknowledge each other as Christians, enjoying the Holy Spirit. But it is an insult to the Holy Spirit to say that two churches, who are divided in doctrine, both enjoy his teachings. Where the Holy Spirit is he guides into all truth; and where two churches believe in doctrines directly opposite, one, if not both, must be destitute of the Spirit. The Holy Ghost must be a very uncertain guide, if he would teach one church to sprinkle infants, teach another to immerse none but adults, give the privilege to another to immerse, pour or sprinkle the candidates just as they choose; tell the fourth to baptize for the remission of sins and forbid a fifth to baptize any until they gave evidence that their sins were remitted; and teach a sixth that it is not necessary for them to be baptized at all. If all these churches, who teach and practice doctrines so very different, are in possession of the Holy Spirit, then the Holy Spirit must be divided against himself, and must come to nought. But the Holy Spirit is the Spirit of truth, and teaches the same doctrine in all places; and wherever we find differences of opinion in doctrine, we may know most assuredly that the Spirit-guide is not there; at least, all churches must be destitute of the Spirit but one, and even that one does not enjoy it unless she receives immediate revelation for her instruction and edification.

26.—Some have supposed these divisions to be unavoidable, being the necessary results of the fallible judgments of men. That the judgments of men are fallible, and that division is the necessary result of fallibility, we by no means deny; but to say that they are unavoidable throws contempt and insult upon the Holy Ghost and represents him as unable to guide the Church into all truth. While division is the result of fallibility, union is the result of infallibility. The Savior prayed for the most perfect union to be in His Church. He uses the following language—"Neither pray I for these alone, (meaning the apostles,) but for them also which shall believe on me through their word, (meaning the whole Church,) that they all may be one; as thou, Father, art in me, and I in thee, that they also may be one in us; that the world may believe that thou hast sent me. And the glory which thou gavest me I have given them; that they may be one even as we are one: I in them, and thou in me, that they may be made perfect in one, and that the world may know that thou hast sent me, and hast loved them, as thou hast loved me. (*John xvii.* 20, 21, 22, 23.) The oneness here prayed for was to be of the most perfect kind: there were to be no more jars—no more differences in sentiment than there is between the Father and the Son. Now there is no possible way to bring about this perfect oneness and union in a church composed of imperfect beings, only through the medium of immediate revelation. This, and this alone, can accomplish the work, and perfect the Saints in knowledge, wisdom and power. All other substitutions will be found totally inadequate to the task; for unless truth is revealed and known, too, after it is revealed, the frail judgments of men will clash together; discordant notes will be sounded, and disunion will make its appearance. And herein is the religion of heaven distinguished from all other religions. *Continued revelation* always was, and is now, its motto, and *Union, perfect Union*, the necessary result; while all other religions are destitute of this binding uniting principle and will ere long vanish away and perish with all who follow them.

27.—Some of the Corinthians had fallen into another heinous sin, namely, that of fornication in its most aggravated form—"such fornication," says Paul, "as is not so much as named among the Gentiles, that one should have his father's wife." (*I. Cor.* v. 1.) Without further revelation the Church would have been ignorant how to proceed in relation to such a case. Some might have supposed that the individual committing this great crime could, if he made confession, be forgiven, and be retained in the Church. But the apostle knowing the great magnitude of the crime, decided by the spirit of inspiration quite otherwise; therefore he commanded them, saying, "In the name of our Lord Jesus Christ, when ye are gathered together, and my spirit, with the power of our Lord Jesus Christ, to deliver such an one unto Satan for the destruction of the flesh, that the spirit may be saved in the day of the Lord Jesus." (*Verses* 4, 5.) Here, then, we perceive the penalty to be inflicted for this particular transgression: first, a deliverance unto Satan; second, a destruction of the flesh; and third, no salvation for the spirit until the day of the Lord Jesus. The wisdom of man would have been entirely at a loss how to have rendered a correct judgment concerning this matter, therefore it required the wisdom of God by revelation. The Corinthians themselves seem to have been ignorant of their duty on this subject; for Paul says to them, "Ye are puffed up, and have not rather mourned, that he that hath done this deed might be taken away from among you." (*Verse* 2.) Oh! how different are the decisions of the Spirit from the decisions of fallible man!

28.—It was necessary that the Corinthians should be reproved by the voice of inspiration for going to law before unbelievers. They were informed that both men and angels were to be judged by the Saints and therefore they ought to judge among themselves the smaller matters of the Church pertaining to this life. It was necessary that they should be reproved for partaking of the Lord's supper unworthily, some using the wine to excess and becoming intoxicated, "not discerning the Lord's body." Sickness and death prevailed among many of that church, the cause of which was revealed to them by the apostle; he informs them that they had not properly examined themselves previous to receiving this solemn ordinance, and "for this cause," says Paul, "many are weak and sickly among you and many sleep." (*1. Cor. xi.*) If sickness and death prevail to a great extent among modern religionists, instead of getting a revelation to know the cause, they fancy up a great variety of causes, one imagines one thing and another supposes another, and the imaginary causes are nearly as numerous as the individuals. Oh! what a blessing it would be to modern Christendom had they an inspired man among them who, like Paul, could point out to them the very causes of the cholera and such like plagues with which they are so frequently visited! Knowing the cause, they could, by a thorough reformation, have the judgment removed from them; but so long as they are ignorant of the cause, and depend upon their own conjectures upon it, they will not be likely to repent acceptably before God so as to have these judgments removed.

29.—The seven churches of Asia were reproved by revelation for their sins, threatened with various judgments if they did not repent, and promised on certain conditions great and inestimable blessings. These threatenings and promises were not the same to all churches, but each had its peculiar promises and threatenings according to its works. But for centuries past the Lord has not had a church on the whole earth whom He considered worthy of being reproved by revelation, or of receiving any promises. None knew anything about God, or heaven, or the future state, only what others have told them in the sacred scriptures. Eternal life does not abide in them; for, says Jesus, "This is life eternal, that they might know Thee the only true God and Jesus Christ whom Thou hast sent." (*John xvii.* 3.) The only possible way to know God is by new revelation; for Jesus says again, "No man knoweth the Son, but the Father; neither knoweth any man the Father, save the Son, and he to whomsoever the Son will REVEAL Him." (*Matthew xi.* 27.) Here is the most positive testimony that no man can know God without he obtains a revelation, and that no one can have eternal life without such revealed knowledge. Think of these sayings of our Savior, all you enemies of new revelation, and tremble at your awful, benighted and sinful condition. Remember that the only way to obtain eternal life is *to know God*, and the only way to know Him is by NEW REVELATION.

30.—Further revelation is indispensably necessary.

FOURTHLY, TO UNFOLD TO THE CHURCH THE FUTURE.

In every age of the world God has considered a knowledge of the future of the utmost importance to His people. To impart this knowledge He has invariably appointed a certain office among His people, called the prophetic office. Persons holding this office were filled with the Holy Ghost who taught them, not only of doctrine and principles, but of the future. One of the earliest prophets, of whom scripture gives an account, was Abel. The Savior ranks Abel among the prophets, when he says to the wicked Jews, that the blood of all the prophets, from that of righteous Abel to that of Zacharias, who was slain between the porch and the alter, should be required of that generation. Enoch, the seventh from Adam, predicted things which have not yet come to pass. (*See Jude xiv.*) Noah predicted events of the utmost importance to the generation in which he lived. All the patriarchs called of God, from Noah to Moses, were endowed with the spirit of prophecy. Moses was peculiarly blessed with a knowledge of future events. The Lord did not confine the spirit of prophecy to Moses alone, but poured out His spirit upon the seventy Elders of Israel, and they all prophesied. Eldad and Medad, two that remained in the camp, prophesied as well as those who were assembled together; and Joshua, hearing of this, and feeling somewhat contracted in his views of this glorious gift, exclaimed, "My Lord Moses, forbid them." And Moses said unto him, enviest thou for my sake? would God that all the Lord's people were prophets, and that the Lord would put His spirit upon them. (*Num. xi 28, 29.*) We have no account of the predictions uttered by these seventy prophets being written, and therefore it is not likely that they could be of any benefit to after generations: but it is very probable that the things predicted were intended to benefit more particularly that generation of Israel. Moses had hitherto the whole burden upon himself, but now it was divided among others, and in order to be qualified to take part in the teaching and leading of Israel, it was necessary that they should understand future events, that all might be prepared to act in relation to such events and thus, by foreseeing things, escape thousands of difficulties. All prophets do not enjoy an equal degree or measure of fore-knowledge, for the Lord said to Israel, "Hear now my words: If there be a prophet among you, I the Lord will make myself known unto him in a vision and will speak unto him in a dream. My servant Moses is not so, who is faithful in all mine house. With him will I speak mouth to mouth, even apparently, and not in dark speeches; and the similitude of the Lord shall he behold." (*Num. xii.* 6, 7, 8.) To some prophets the Lord speaks in visions, dreams and dark speeches; to others, He reveals in great plainness. Some prophecies are written: others only uttered verbally.

31.—Great companies of prophets existed among Israel at different times. When Saul after his first interview with Samuel the Seer, met one of these companies, "the Spirit of God came upon him and he prophesied among them." (*I Sam. x.* 10.) When he afterwards sent messengers to take David that he might slay him, they met one of these companies of prophets with Samuel over them, and the Spirit of God came upon the messengers and they prophesied also: Saul then sent a second company, and they all turned prophets, and he sent a third and the same thing happened to them; and despairing of success by his messengers, he concluded to go himself, and while on his way "the Spirit of God was upon him also, and he went on and prophesied, until he came to Naioth in Ramah. And he stripped off his clothes also and prophesied before Samuel in like manner and lay down naked all that day and all that night. Wherefore they say, is Saul also among the prophets?" (*I. Sam. xix.* 20-24.) In the days of Elijah and Elisha, there was an abundance of prophets these prophets seemed to have a knowledge of almost every thing before it came to pass; when Elijah was about to be translated, he could not keep it a secret, though he sought diligently to do so; Elisha was too much of a prophet to be ignorant of what was about to happen, therefore he followed Elijah wherever he went; and also fifty other "prophets went and stood to view afar off." (*II. Kings ii.* 7.) These prophets lived in various cities and generally had masters or chief prophets over them. One company dwelt at Ramah, over whom Samuel was appointed to preside, as just mentioned; another company dwelt at Bethel: another at Jericho. (*See II. Kings ii.* 3—5.) When Jezebel cut off the prophets of the Lord, there were a hundred that Obadiah managed to save alive by hiding them in caves. (*See I. Kings xviii.* 13.) Hence prophets, at times, were very numerous in Israel. And, no doubt, if we had all of their prophecies, we should have many volumes much larger than the Bible; but their prophecies were not all written, and from this fact, we have reason to believe that their gift was intended more for the benefit of themselves and others in their day, than for future ages.

32.—Some have supposed that after Christ came, the Christian Church would not be blessed with prophets any more; but this is a mistaken notion, for Jesus says Himself to the Jews, "Behold, I send unto you prophets, and wise men, and scribes; and some of them ye shall kill and crucify; and some of them shall ye scourge in your synagogues, and persecute them from city to city." (*Matt. xxiii.* 34.) Paul also informs the Ephesians, that when Christ "ascended up on high, He led captivity captive and gave gifts unto men." And he further states, that "he gave some, apostles; and some, prophets; and some, evangelists; and some, pastors and teachers." (*Eph. iv.* 8-11.) Prophets, then, were among the gifts which were given unto men after the ascension of our Savior: this accords with another saying of Paul, that "God hath set some in the Church, first apostles, secondarily prophets, thirdly teachers," etc.; (*I. Cor. xii.* 28.) and also when speaking of the diversity of gifts imparted to the Church by the Spirit, he says, to one is given wisdom; to another, knowledge; to another, faith; to another, *prophecy,*" etc. From these passages we learn that prophets were just as much intended for the Christian Church as teachers, pastors, wisdom, knowledge, faith or any other gift. And yet, those who profess to have the Christian religion exclude prophets from their churches; with the same propriety, they might exclude the gifts of wisdom, knowledge, faith, teachers, pastors and every other gift promised in the gospel.

33.—We shall now show that prophets and all other officers, or gifts, are indispensably necessary, as expressed by Paul, "For the perfecting of the saints, for the work of the ministry, for the edifying of the body of Christ, till we all come in the unity of the faith, and of the knowledge of the Son of God, unto a perfect man, unto the measure of the stature of the fullness of Christ: that we henceforth be no more children, tossed to and fro, and carried about with every wind of doctrine, by the sleight of men and cunning craftiness, whereby they lie in wait to deceive; but speaking the truth in love, may grow up into Him in all things, which is the head, even Christ; from whom the whole body fitly joined together and compacted by that which every joint supplieth, according to the effectual working in the measure of every part, maketh increase of the body unto the edifying of itself in love." (*Eph. iv.* 12-16.) The object, then, of these officers and gifts, is first, "*for the perfecting of the Saints;*" secondly, "for the work of the ministry," and thirdly, "for the edifying of the body of Christ." We now ask, all Christendom who profess to be Saints, whether they are perfect or imperfect? The general answer is, "we are imperfect." How do you expect to become perfect, if you do away out of your churches inspired apostles, prophets, and other officers? These are the only gifts and officers by which the Saints can be perfected. Have you got them in your midst? Millions answer "no we do not believe in prophets in our day." But do you believe in "pastors and teachers?" O yes, they are necessary Who told you to reject the most important gifts of the church and to retain the rest? No one has told us to do this but our ministers, and they must be good men, and they say that apostles and prophets are no longer necessary, but that evangelists, pastors and teachers are And then do you think your ministers are good men when they do away the plan established for the perfecting of the Saints, and substitute the plans of men in its stead? Does not Paul declare that any man or angel shall be cursed who preaches a different gospel from the one he preached? And did he not include in his gospel all these gifts for the perfecting of the Saints? Most certainly he did; and if your ministers teach you differently they are cursed and all that follow their teachings will be cursed. Know assuredly that there never was any other plan adopted in the gospel to perfect the Saints than through apostles, prophets and other gifts. Do you need "the work of the ministry?" All answer, yes. Remember, then, that "for the work of the ministry," apostles and prophets, are declared to be as necessary as pastors and teachers. If one is unnecessary, all are unnecessary, and the work of the ministry must cease. On the other hand, if one is necessary, all are necessary, that the work of the ministry may continue. If God has authorized teachers among the churches of Christendom, He must likewise have authorized apostles and prophets; if He has not the latter, He has not the former; and if He has neither, He has no Church on the earth. Again, does the Church need to be edified in these days? Most certainly. What is God's plan to edify the Church? Paul says, that He gave, not only pastors and teachers, to edify them, but also apostles and prophets. Where these officers have no existence there can be no edification of the Church. Any other plan of edification, however great and magnificent, will not do. God's plan is, not only superior to all others, but it is the only plan ordained "for the edifying of the body of Christ." Thus we see, that without inspired apostles, prophets, etc., there can be no work of the ministry—no edification of the body of Christ —no perfecting of the Saints—and consequently no Church.

34.—But Paul did not leave us ignorant with regard to further duties of these inspired officers. He says that they are necessary to prevent the Church from being "tossed to and fro" like children and to keep them from being "carried about by every wind of doctrine, by the sleight of men and cunning craftiness, whereby they lie in wait to deceive." The great reason why the millions are carried away and tossed about with the false and soul-destroying doctrines of the Papists and Protestants is, because they have not inspired apostles and prophets among them, and, therefore, without this great preventative, the cunning craftiness of men overpowers them, and they follow the corrupt impositions of modern religionists.

35.—These gifts were never intended to be done away from the Church in this state of existence, as we have already proved in the first chapters of this series. And Paul corroborates this when he says, they were given "for the perfecting of the Saints, for the work of the ministry and for the edifying of the body of Christ; *till we all come in the unity of the faith and of the knowledge of the Son of God, unto a perfect man, unto the measure of the stature of the fullness of Christ.*" In what state will all the Saints come in the unity of the faith? When will they all come in the unity of the knowledge of the Son of God? When will they all be perfect men? When will they all come unto the measure of the stature of the fullness of Christ? The answer to all these questions is given by Paul when he says, that when that which is perfect is come, the Saints are to see the Lord face to face, and know as they are known, and see as they are seen. Consequently, it will be in the next state of existence, and not in this. Therefore, in this state of existence, as the Church is imperfect and needs edifying, apostles, prophets, teachers and all other gifts which Jesus has given or promised, are indispensably necessary to accomplish that great and important work which cannot possibly be accomplished in any other way.

36.—In the foregoing, it will be seen, that new revelation is the very life and soul of the religion of heaven—that it is indispensably necessary for the calling of all officers in the Church—that without it, the officers can never be instructed in the various duties of their callings—that where the spirit of revelation does not exist, the Church cannot be comforted and taught in all wisdom and knowledge—cannot be properly reproved and chastened according to the mind of God—cannot obtain promises for themselves, but are dependent upon the promises made through the ancients. Without new revelation the people are like a blind man groping his way in total darkness, not knowing the dangers that beset his path. Without prophets and revelators, darkness hangs over the future—no city, people or nation, understand what awaits them. Without new revelation, no people know of the approaching earthquake—of the deadly plague—of the terrible war—of the withering famine—and of the fearful judgments of the Almighty which hang over their devoted heads. When the voice of living prophets and apostles are no longer heard in the land—there is an end of perfecting and edifying the Saints—there is a speedy end to the "work of the ministry"—there is an end to the obtaining of that knowledge so necessary to eternal life—there is an end to all that is great, grand and glorious, pertaining to the religion of heaven—there is an end to the very existence of the Church of Christ on the earth—there is an end to salvation in the celestial kingdom. Awake then, oh, ye slumbering nations—awake from the slumber of death and Christ shall give you light by the revelations of the Holy Ghost!

## CHAPTER III.

### THE BIBLE AND TRADITION, WITHOUT FURTHER REVELATION, AN INSUFFICIENT GUIDE.

1.—In the former chapters of this series it has been proved that more revelation is neither unscriptural nor unreasonable, but indispensably necessary to the very existence of the Church of God on the earth. In this chapter it will be shown that without further revelation the Bible is an insufficient guide. That part of the Bible called the New Testament was written many years after the establishment of the Christian Church. How was the Church founded and governed before the New Testament was written? Answer: by the revelations of Christ and of the Holy Spirit, speaking through the apostles and prophets. These revelations were verbal, and not written: were delivered by word of mouth, and not with pen and ink. Large and numerous churches were established in Palestine, in Asia, in Europe and among the various nations of the eastern hemisphere, which were abundantly blessed with revelations, with prophecies, with dreams and visions, with the ministry of angels, and with the miraculous powers and manifestations of the Holy Spirit; and yet they had not the writings of the New Testament.

2.—If the Church could be founded and grow and flourish, and be perfected without the New Testament writings; if she could, through verbal revelation, learn every principle of doctrine, and be taught in every duty, during the most of the first century, the same gift of revelation and prophecy could have instructed her in all succeeding generations, even though the New Testament had never been written. If inspired apostles, prophets and other officers could perfect the Saints in the first century, surely the same kind of officers could perfect them in all future ages. Written revelations were never intended to supersede verbal and continued revelation through the living ministry. If the Church of Christ had continued on the earth, successive apostles and prophets would have continued with her, endowed with all the powers and gifts of the first; and the revelations in each successive generation would have been equally sacred with those given at the first; and there would have been no such thing thought of *as the canon of scripture being full and complete.*

3.—There are many things practiced by both Romish and Protestant churches which the scriptures do not clearly reveal, therefore they must both of them consider that the scriptures are not a sufficient guide. We are informed in scripture that marriage is ordained of God, but we are not informed in the scripture who has the right to officiate in this ceremony. Who can tell from the New Testament anything about the order to be observed in relation to this subject? We read that "what God hath joined together let no man put asunder;" but through what particular office does God join together the sexes in matrimony? Can laymen officiate? Can those out of the Church officiate? Can a woman officiate? Can the parties join themselves together in matrimony, in the name of the Lord? Who can answer these questions from the Bible alone? No one. The Bible does not guide the Church in this important ordinance.

4.—Who can tell from the Bible whether Teachers and Deacons have authority to baptize, or not? Baptism is an important ordinance, and should be administered by proper authority, but can any one in the Church administer it? Can private members baptize? Can women baptize? Does the Bible anywhere forbid them, or say that they are not authorized? John the Baptist, who held the Priesthood of Aaron, had authority to baptize. Apostles, Elders and Evangelists baptized. Did the authority extend to any lower officers or members? The Bible does not inform us; therefore the Bible is not a sufficient guide.

5.—Again, what officers in the Curch have a right to lay on hands for the gift of the Holy Spirit? Can any but apostles administer the Spirit by this sacred ordinance? Ananias was sent to Paul to baptize him, and lay his hands upon him, that he "might be filled with the Holy Ghost." Was Ananias an apostle? or did he hold some lower office? Philip could baptize the Samaritans, while Peter and John laid hands upon both men and women for the gift of the Holy Ghost. The great question is, can any but apostles lay on hands in the ordinance of confirmation? The Bible does not answer this question, therefore the Bible is not a sufficient guide.

6.—It is admitted that the Lord's supper is a divine ordinance; but who is authorized to break the bread and bless it, and also the wine, and administer it to the Saints? Can Teachers or Deacons do this with authority? Can private members or women administer in this solemn ordinance? There is nothing in the New Testament that either authorizes or forbids them to do it. Can any one, without being instructed by new revelation, administer the Lord's supper in His name, with His authority, and by His sanction? The Bible does not answer this question, therefore the Bible is not a sufficient guide.

7.—In what particular points does a Teacher's duty differ from a Deacon's? Wherein do the duties of Elders, Evangelists and Pastors differ? What authority has one that the others do not possess? All these are questions which the Bible does not plainly answer, yet to be a sufficient guide, it should answer all such questions definitely.

8.—Is infant baptism right or wrong? Does the Bible anywhere teach infant baptism by command or example? If infant baptism be right, the Bible has not informed us of it, therefore it must be an insufficient guide. If infant baptism be wrong, at what age should children be baptized? Upon this question the Bible also is silent,

9.—Should the members or officers of the Church lay their hands upon little children, and pray for them, and bless them after the example that Jesus has given or not? This is a question that cannot be settled by the Bible.

10.—Should all the Saints wash one another's feet, or is this an ordinance limited to the apostles and officers of the Church? The Bible again is silent, and does not plainly answer the question.

11.—Again, must the seventh day or the first day of the week be kept holy unto the Lord? The New Testament does not clearly answer this question. There is rather more evidence in that book for keeping holy the Sabbath day or Saturday, than there is for keeping the first day or Sunday. The New Testament is very indefinite on this subject, and therefore it is an insufficient guide.

12.—Furthermore, where in the Bible does it say that the king and people in England ought to revolt from the Romish church, and form a church of their own by act of parliament? If the Bible were a sufficient guide, why was an act of parliament necessary as another guide to form the English church? If the Bible were a sufficient guide, why was another book made, called the "Book of Common Prayer," and the people compelled to give heed to it under pain of banishment, and even death itself? If the articles of religion, contained in the New Testament were a sufficient guide, why were "Thirty-nine Articles" more, enforced upon the people by acts of parliament, and the people butchered and murdered because they could not conscientiously comply with them? It is certain that this newly-formed-parliament-made church considered the Bible to be very deficient as a guide, or they never would have resorted to such blood-thirsty, murderous measures to establish other books in addition to the Bible.

13.—If Protestants suppose the Bible to be a sufficient guide, as they are constantly telling their followers, will they be so kind as to point out what part of that sacred book, called Luther, Calvin, Cranmer, Wesley and hosts of others, to preach, baptize and administer many other ordinances such as the ancient Church administered? Indeed, what part of the Bible calls and commissions any of the ministers of the present day? It can be said without any fear of contradiction, that the Bible nowhere has called a single individual to the work of the ministry for the last seventeen centuries. Therefore, for the calling of the ministry, the Bible is an insufficient guide.

14.—Again, what part of the Bible has established the salaries of the different officers of the church? If it be necessary that preachers should have wages, how much shall it be? How much more shall an apostle get than a prophet? If a bishop get from ten to twenty thousand pounds for one year's preaching, how much should an inspired apostle or prophet get? Or how much should some of the lower officers have? The New Testament does not tell us the amount of wages religious hirelings should have, therefore, if it be important to know, the Bible is an insufficient guide. It says, however, that apostles should "take neither purse nor scrip," but it leaves us entirely in the dark as to how much bishops, arch-bishops and other officers should have. Would it not be a wise plan for an act of parliament to increase their wages a little, lest they suffer?. We see plainly that the Bible is not a sufficient guide in many, very many points, as the doings of the whole Protestant world most plainly declare.

15.—Let us now see whether the Roman Catholics consider the Bible a sufficient guide. They plainly tell us in their writings that they do not. So far, then, they are consistent. But what do they suppose makes up the deficiency? They answer, "TRADITION," or the "unwritten word" of God, as it was spoken by the apostles, and handed down uncorrupted to the present day. The Right Reverend Doctor Milner, a very able and learned Catholic bishop, says, "The Catholic rule of faith, as I stated before, is not merely, *the written word of God*, but *the whole word of God, both written and unwritten;* in other words, *Scripture and Tradition*, and these *propounded and explained by the Catholic church.*"\* The Catholics do not believe in any later revelations than what were given in the first age of Christianity: this may be seen in their writings. Dr. Milner, in speaking of the Papist churches, says, "It

---

\*——"End of Controversy," Letter x. p. 125.

is a fundamental maxim with them all, *never to admit of any tenet*, but such as is believed by all the bishops, and *was believed by their predecessors up to the apostles themselves.*" †
According to this, the Romanists never admit any new tenet. With their views, no revelations can be given—all things believed or received by them must be traced back through all "their predecessors up to the apostles themselves:" they are not permitted to believe any thing which their fathers were ignorant of. When any thing is presented to them, the question is not, whether it is a new revelation from God, but they immediately inquire, has it been believed by the church since the first age? If it has not, it is rejected. The Catholic church does not claim the assistance of the Spirit to reveal any thing new, "but merely," as Bishop Milner expresses himself, she claims "the aid of God's Holy Spirit, to enable her truly to decide *what her faith is, and has ever been in such articles as have been made known to her by scripture and tradition.*" ‡

16.—After revelation ceased to be given, and, consequently, the Church of Christ ceased its existence on the earth, many of the first apostates pretended that scripture and tradition were a sufficient guide, and that nothing new was needed. Irenæus, who lived in the second century, seems to have forgotten that God placed in the Church inspired men to constantly instruct her by new revelation, and like all the subsequent apostates lays great stress upon *tradition*. He says, "SUPPOSING THE APOSTLES HAD NOT LEFT US THE SCRIPTURES, OUGHT WE NOT STILL TO HAVE FOLLOWED THE ORDINANCE OF TRADITION, which they consigned to those to whom they committed the churches? It is this ordinance of *tradition*," continues he, "which many nations of barbarians, believing in Christ, follow, without the use of letters or ink." § Tertullian, who lived at the close of the same century, finding the scriptures an insufficient guide, appeals to *tradition* instead of *new revelation*. He says, "We begin, therefore, with laying it down as a maxim, that these men" (speaking of the oppo-

---
†——End of Controversy, Letter xii. p. 166.
‡——Ibid, Letter xii. p. 168.
§——Advers. Hæres., Letter iv. c. 64.

nents of his church) "ought not to be allowed to argue at all from scripture. In fact," continues he, "these disputes about the sense of scripture, have generally no other effect than to disorder either the stomach or the brain It is therefore the wrong method to appeal to the scriptures, since these afferd either no decision, or, at most, only a doubtful one. And even, if this were not the case, still, in appealing to scripture, the natural order of things requires that we should first inquire to whom the scriptures belong. From whom, and by whom, and on what occasion, and to whom that *tradition* was delivered by which we became Christians."* This author in another work,† as Dr. Milner states, "proves, at great length, the absolute necessity of admitting *tradition* no less than *scripture* as the rule of faith, inasmuch as many important points, which he mentions, cannot be proved without it."

17.—Doctor Milner, to show that the *tradition* of the apostles together with the *scriptures*, was the only rule of faith in the early ages of his church, cites us to the writings of St. Clement of Alexandria, St. Cyprian, Origen, etc., of the third century—St. Basil, and St. Epiphanius of the fourth century —and St. John Chrysostom at the beginning, and St. Vincent of Lerins, at the end of the fifth century. All these writers, instead of contending for the great and infallible guide, namely, NEW REVELATION, which instructed the Church during the first century, have contended merely for ancient scripture and tradition as their only guide—as their only rule of faith. Thus we can see, how early apostasy succeeded Christianity—we can see, how early this rule of faith was changed.

18.—If all the decrees and decisions of the pope and general councils among the Catholics be examined, it will be seen that such decrees and decisions profess to be founded, not upon *new revelation*, but upon *ancient* scripture or tradition. She professes that her general councils are guided by the Holy Ghost in ascertaining what the apostolical traditions are; but that the Holy Ghost does not give them anything new. That these are really the views of the Catholics, may be perceived on almost

---

\*——Præscrip. Advers. Hæres., edit. Rhenan, pp. 36, 37.
†——De. Corona Milit.

every page of some of their standard works. The Right Rev. Bishop Milner, in his "End of Religious Controversy," has very definitely, and at some length, set forth this view. J. Murdoch, a Roman Catholic bishop, has highly recommended a work by Joseph Mumford, entitled "QUESTION OF QUESTIONS," or "Who ought to be our Judge in all Controversies?" In this work the author states most clearly that the Roman Catholic church, "PRETENDS TO NO NEW REVELATIONS, BUT ONLY TO DECLARE CLEARLY WHAT SHE FINDS TO HAVE BEFORE BEEN REVEALED." ‡ These general councils are considered infallible, not because they are inspired with the word of God direct to themselves, for this power they deny, but because they suppose the Holy Ghost assists them to find out ancient tradition. We again quote, from the last-mentioned work.

19.—"Now to see what the councils on their part are to do; I must tell you, that their chief business is to examine the points in controversy; hearing all that occurs for the one side and the other, and permitting several replies, if any remain, in due time to be made. After this diligence is used, they consider what seems most conformable to the word of God, and every one's vote is passed upon this particular. But here I must tell you, that by the word of God, all councils, and orthodox believers have ever understood, not only God's written word, contained in scripture, but also His unwritten word made known to the church ONLY by tradition, which tradition also is, and was ever accounted by the church the very best and surest interpreter of the scripture. The votes therefore of the fathers assembled in council are demanded, not only of what they think to be conformable to God's word written in scripture, but also how conformable to God's word written in scripture, but also which they have all received from the fathers of their church, as delivered to them from their fathers for God's word, by tradition committed to their forefathers as such, from the apostles themselves." §

20.—Let no one suppose that the Catholics believe in new

---

‡——"Question of Questions," Sec. xxiv. par. 14.
§——Ibid, Sec. xix. 2.

revelation; for in the above quotation it is expressly asserted that, "the unwritten word is made known to the church ONLY by tradition," and that this tradition must come through their fathers "from the Apostles themselves." The business of the Catholic councils, then, is, not to get any word from God direct to themselves, but to determine what God said to the Apostles. That this is all that they pretend to do, is also evident from the words of Vincentius Lirinensis, as quoted by Mumford; he says, "This only, and nothing but this, the Catholic church does do by the decrees of her council; that what before they had received only by tradition from their ancestors, that now they leave consigned in authentical writing to all posterity.* Councils, then, are convened to determine traditions—they are convened to write traditions in the form of decrees. Now all this is good as far as it goes, but it stops infinitely short of the true rule of faith, established in the apostolical church, namely, DIRECT AND IMMEDIATE REVELATION through her officers, whether assembled in council or dispersed individually among the nations.

21.—That the apostate papal church does not obtain new revelation, as the apostolical church always did, is still further evident from her defining the canonical books, called scripture. This was first done at the Third Council of Carthage in the year 397. Previous to that time there had been a great variety of opinions as to what books were inspired of God. Mumford speaks thus on this subject:—"If you fly to the tradition of the church only of the first four hundred years, remember that the Council of Carthage just after the end of those years alleged the ancient tradition of their fathers, which they judged sufficient for defining our canon. They, who were so near those first four hundred years, knew far better the more universal tradition of that age, than *we* can twelve hundred years after it. True it is, (nothing being defined till then) private doctors were free to follow what they judged to be truest; and as you find them varying from our canon, some in some books, some in others: so you will find them varying from one another, and varying also from you." (meaning the Protestant canon.)

---

*——"Question of Questions," Sec. xix. par. 2.

"For in those first four hundred years, Melitus and Nazianzen excluded the book of Esther, which you add. Origen doubts of the epistle to the Hebrews, of the second of St. Peter, of the first and second of St. John; St. Cyprian and Nazianzen, leave the apocalypse or revelations out of their canon. Eusebius doubts of it." Elsewhere, he says, all those holy fathers agreed ever in this, that such books were evidently God's word, which had evidently a sufficient tradition for them: now in the days of those fathers who thus varied from one another, it was not by any infallible means made known to all, that those books about which their variance was, were recommended for God's infallible word, by a tradition clearly sufficient to ground belief; for the church had not as yet examined and defined, whether tradition did clearly enough show such and such books to be God's infallible word. But in the days of St. Austin, the Third Council of Carthage, Anno, 397, examined how sufficient or insufficient the tradition of the church was, which recommended those books for scripture, about which there was so much doubt and contrariety of opinions. They found all the books contained in our canon, of which you account so many apocryphal, to have been recommended by tradition, sufficient to ground faith upon. For on this ground (*Can.* 47.) they proceeded in defining all the books in our canon to be canonical. *Because*, say they, *we have received from our fathers that those books were to be read in the Church.* Pope Innocent the First, who lived Anno 402, being requested by Exuperius, bishop of Toulouse, to declare unto him which books were canonical, he answered, (*Ep.* 3,) that having examined what sufficient tradition did demonstrate, he sets down— *What books are received in the canon of the Holy Scriptures*, in the end of his epistle, c. 7. To wit, just those which we now have in our canon: and THOUGH HE REJECTS MANY OTHER BOOKS, *yet he rejects not one of these.*" †

22—Here is the most incontrovertible evidence that this apostate church, who define the canon of scripture at the close of the fourth century, did not believe in any inspired books being given after the first century. For if she had believed

---

† ———"Question of Questions," Sec. III. pars. 4, 12.

that any man or officer in her communion had been inspired to write the word of God, during the second, third or fourth century, she would most assuredly have incorporated such inspired writings in the *sacred canon*, but the very fact that no books were admitted by the council of Carthage into the canon, which were written after the first century, shows most conclusively that they did not consider any later books to be inspired. Here, then, is demonstrative evidence, that the apostate Romish church, during the second, third and fourth centuries were destitute of that great and infallible rule, namely, NEW REVELATION which characterized the Church in the first century, and in all previous ages whenever and wherever God had a people living in righteousness before Him.

23.—So destitute were the officers of this apostate church of the spirit of revelation that they could not tell, only through tradition, which books were sacred, and which were not, and hence there arose a great contention among them on this subject, and a great variety of opinions. At length the same contending parties meet together in the capacity of a general council, and decide which books shall be received into the canon. Recollect, dear reader, that this decision does not pretend to be founded upon *new revelation* but upon *tradition*, and tradition, too, that was so very imperfect that it led one to reject one book, and another, another; producing a great contrariety of opinions before the council met. Who can, for one moment, suppose that a council, composed of a set of contending apostates so destitute of the spirit of truth and faith, that they could not inquire of God and get a revelation upon any subject, however important—who, I say, can suppose that they could sit in judgment upon God's holy word, and infallibly decide by the aid, not of new revelation, but tradition alone, which books were the word of God and which were not? Had they believed in new revelation, and inquired of God which was His word and which was not, there would have been some confidence to be placed in their decisions; but as it is, there is scarcely any confidence whatever to be placed in them in regard to this matter. Where inspired officers, possessing power to obtain new revelation, have ceased, there infallibility has ceased, and there uncertainty and doubt must remain. Tell about the councils of the church of Rome being infallible! Who ever heard of any council being infallible where there were no prophets and revelators that could decide with a *thus saith the Lord*, and thus end all controversy? The Church of God never pretends infallibility upon any other grounds; yet, this apostate "Mother of Harlots" can, with one breath, call herself infallible and with the next breath deny new revelation.

24.—That the Romanists have continued in their apostasy until the present day is demonstrated from the fact that they have not added one single book to their canon since they first formed it. Now, if there had been any prophet or apostle among them, during the last seventeen centuries, they certainly would have canonized his epistles, revelations and prophecies as being equally sacred with those of the first century. As they have not done this, it shows most clearly, that even they themselves, do not consider that they have had apostles, prophets and revelators among them, during that long period of time. They have had, during the time, many general councils which have confirmed the old canon of scripture, but in no single instance have they confirmed any other books as the word of God, so that their canon stands now as when the council of Carthage left it, without an addition of one revelation. This confirms, beyond all controversy, the testimony of their most standard works, from which we have before quoted, wherein it is repeatedly asserted, that the "written and unwritten word of God," revealed previous to and in the first century is the *only* rule of faith, and that the church "pretends to no new revelations, but only to declare clearly what she finds to have before been revealed;" and also, that the decrees of her councils are in relation to what God said in the first century, and that they by no means admit that He has said anything of a later date; and conformably with these views, they have not admitted anything into the sacred canon as scripture, or as the Word of God, that has been written during the long period of seventeen hundred and fifty years.

25.—Upwards of two hundred and fifty popes pretend to have successively filled the chair of St. Peter. All these popes, we are told, have possessed the same authority and power as St. Peter, whom they designate as the first pope; if this really be the case, then each of these popes must have been inspired of God, and the writings of each must be equally as sacred as the writings of Pope St. Peter. Why then has the church showed such great partiality? Why has she placed Pope St. Peter's writings in the sacred canon, and left all the writings of the other popes out?

26.—Bishop Milner after having quoted many passages of scripture, and used many arguments to prove the superiority of Peter's calling to that of the other apostles, says, "That bishops in general succeed to the rank and functions of the apostles; so, by the same rule, the successor of St. Peter, in the See of Rome, succeeds to his primacy and jurisdiction."* If this be true, "that bishops in general succeed to the rank and functions of the apostles," then each bishop, as well as the pope, must be a REVELATOR; for apostles were revelators, and one of the "functions" of their office was to receive revelations; therefore, all the Roman Catholic bishops, if they succeed to the same rank, and exercise the same "functions" as apostles, must be revelators. According to this, since the first century, the Catholics must have had many tens of thousands of revelators, and yet, strange to say, none of their revelations are permitted to enter the sacred canon among other scriptures given in the first century. Here, indeed, is a strange inconsistency! Even the Catholic church herself, evidently places no confidence in the popes and bishops, the pretended successors of St. Peter and the rest of the apostles; if she did, she would have canonized their revelations along with the rest of the revelations of the New Testament. What must we conclude then, as to her bishops holding "the rank and functions of apostles?" We can but conclude that it is an *imposition—a wicked soul-destroying imposition*, practiced upon the nations by a corrupt apostate church whose officers have no more "the rank and functions of apostles", than the apostate chief priests among the Jews had. Indeed, so long as "they pretend to no new revelations," they cannot exercise the "functions of apostles.'

---

*———"End of Controversy," Letter xlvi. p. 439.

27.—It is in vain for the Romish church to pretend that the word of God, spoken to the apostles, is a sufficient guide for all future ages. It is contrary to the dealings of God in all previous dispensations. He never left His faithful people in one age dependent alone on the word spoken in a previous age. The Catholics in appealing to tradition and ancient scripture as their only rule of faith, have endeavored to justify themselves, by falsely telling the people that mankind were dependent on tradition as a rule of faith from Adam to Moses—a period of about twenty-four hundred years. One of their writers speaks thus: "The whole church through the whole world was governed by tradition ONLY, for the first two thousand years." * This is evidently false; for the whole church governed herself from Adam to Moses, by *both tradition and new revelation*. Each age, during that period, furnished the Church with revelators who delivered the word of the Lord to her, and she was governed by that word; and also by the traditions of former ages as far as they were applicable.

28 —The Church was not only governed from Adam to Moses by new revelation, but from Moses to the close of the first century of the Christian era. The word of God given in past ages, whether written or unwritten, was never considered by the true Church a sufficient rule of faith in any dispensation since the creation of man. Such an idea was never originated in the Church of God. It was the apostate Catholics that first originated the idea and by them the fatal delusion has been handed down from generation to generation; and all the children that she has brought forth, or that have left her communion, have, more or less, imbibed the same great features of the apostasy. Well might the Revelator John, speaking by the spirit of prophecy, call her "THE MOTHER OF HARLOTS AND ABOMINATIONS OF THE EARTH!"

It is her true name, for all the "HARLOTS" which she has brought forth have walked in the footsteps of their "Mother" in declaring against new revelation, and in pretending that ancient revelation was a sufficient rule of faith. It is to be expected that as is the *Mother*, so will be her *Harlot daughters*.

---

*———"Question of Questions," Sec. xix par 5.

The daughters in some respects are more corrupt than the mother; for they have limited their rule of faith much more than the mother. Pope Innocent the First, (as we have already quoted), in the year 402, sat in judgment upon the books of scripture, and rejected many of them, from a compilation in the canon. Some eleven or twelve centuries after this, one of the Harlot daughters believed that her mother had retained too much scripture in her canon: therefore, she concluded to make a new canon of her own, which she actually did do, leaving out some half a score of books which were in her mother's canon. This newly-formed canon of scripture is palmed upon the British nation and the United States as a sufficient rule of faith. It must be recollected that neither mother nor daughter was guided by new revelation in forming these two different canons of scripture. As the mother decided on the word of God by tradition, so did the daughter, and as tradition taught the mother to reject many books and receive others, so tradition taught the daughter to reject all that her mother rejected, and some half-a-score besides. After awhile this harlot daughter brings forth a numerous progeny of children, each of whom alters her creeds, so as to disagree with both mother and grandmother's creeds ; yet the church of England with all her daughters agrees in the rejection of the old canon of scripture, and in the reception of the newly-formed one.

29.—In the meantime, another harlot daughter of the Catholics—the Lutherans, formed another canon, and rejected many books that the English daughter did not. She cast out the epistle of St. Paul to the Hebrews, the epistle of St. James, the second epistle of St. Peter, the second and third of St. John, the epistle of St. Jude and the Apocalypse or Revelation. Here are seven books received into the English Bibel, not received into the Lutherans' Bible. Thus we perceive three different canons of scripture, proposed for the faith of mankind. If the Bible alone is a sufficient guide, which of these three Bibles shall we take? Shall we take the Catholic, the Lutheran or the English Bible? The Catholic Bible contains many things that the English and Lutheran do not, and the English contains many things that the Lutheran does not. Which shall we believe? If it be answered that we are to take all that God ever has revealed and caused to be written, as our rule of faith, then it will require a revelator to bring to light some twenty sacred books that are known once to have existed, but are not now to be found in either of the three Bibles mentioned above. Therefore if we are to take all of God's written word as our rule of faith, it will require another sacred canon to be made out, including all the lost books. This cannot be done by a Roman Catholic or Protestant council, for tradition will not supply lost books. It is certain that if all the written word of God is necessary to be a perfect rule of faith, that neither Catholics nor Protestants can have a perfect rule, for they have only a part of the written word of God. If it be said that a part is sufficient as a rule of faith, then a question at once arises, how large a part will suffice? One sect will answer, that part contained in the Lutheran Bible is sufficient; other sects will say no; the Lutheran Bible does not contain sufficient, but the English Bible contains enough; no, answers another class, the English Bible does not contain enough, but the Catholic Bible contains just enough; and where shall we stop? Who has light enough to determine whether the Catholic Bible, which contains far more than the other two, has one-tenth part of what is necessary for a perfect rule of faith? If part of God's word forms a perfect rule of faith, I will venture to say, that there is not a man living who is able to say what part of His word should be rejected, and what part retained, in order to form this perfect rule.

30.—In those sacred books written by prophets, seers and apostles which have not descended to our day, but which we know once existed, as their names are referred to in scripture—there may be many great and important doctrines and ordinances revealed that are not contained in our scriptures. Indeed, no one, without further revelation, knows whether even one-hundredth part of the doctrines and ordinances of salvation are contained in the few books of scripture which have descended to our times, how then, can it be decided that they are a sufficient guide? May there not be some great and important things contained "in the book of Nathan the prophet, and in the prophecy of Abijah, and in the visions of Iddo the seer and in the book of Gad the seer?" \*

31.—May there not be important doctrines contained in some of Paul's epistles which we have not got? In the last epistle which Paul wrote from Rome to the Colossians, he commanded them, "likewise to read the epistle from Laodicea." † In that which is commonly called his first epistle to the Corinthians, he says, (*Chap. v. 9.*) "I wrote unto you in an epistle." Where are these two epistles which Paul himself refers to? They are gone. There may be in these lost epistles doctrines of infinite importance which we know nothing about. That the Corinthians had been instructed in a doctrine which the whole world of Christendom are now ignorant of, is evident from a particular question which he asked them, which reads as follows: "Else what shall they do which are baptized for the dead, if the dead rise not at all? Why are they then baptized for the dead?" ‡ This doctrine of baptism for the dead must have been well understood by them, or Paul never would have asked this question without further explanations upon the subject. Now when, and in what manner was this doctrine communicated to them? It may have been fully developed to them in the epistle which he says that he had previously written to them. This doctrine may have been as important as baptism to the living. Does the written or unwritten word of God with which Christendom are acquainted, inform them any thing about how this ceremony is to be performed? Does it inform them who is to officiate? Who is to be the candidate in behalf of the dead? What classes of the dead are to be benefitted by it? Does scripture or tradition inform us in what particular baptism for the dead will affect them in the resurrection? Does it inform us whether baptism for the dead can be administered in all places, or only in a baptismal font, in a temple consecrated for that purpose? All these important questions remain unanswered by scripture and tradition. Even the Catholics them-

---

\*——II. Chron. ix. 29.—I. Chron. xxix 29.

†——Colos. iv. 16.

‡——I. Corin. xv. 29.

selves, who boast of scripture and tradition as their infallible rule of faith, cannot and do not pretend to decide these questions of doctrine.

32.—The Rev. Dr. Milner, in speaking of the Catholic church, says, "She does not dictate an exposition of the whole Bible, because she has no tradition concerning a very great proportion of it, as for example, concerning the prophecy of Enoch, quoted by Jude 14; and the BAPTISM FOR THE DEAD of which St. Paul makes mention." * If "a very great proportion" of the Bible cannot be explained for the want of sufficient tradition, then that "very great proportion" of the Bible cannot be of any use; and that very small proportion of the Bible, which tradition does explain, must be a very imperfect rule of faith. For aught the Catholics know there may be hundreds of millions of the dead that will not attain to a first resurrection, because *tradition* does not explain to them the necessity of being baptized for them. Tradition, and a small proportion of scripture that it explains, are therefore not a sufficient guide. If the Catholics had all the lost books of scripture, and a perfect tradition of all the unwritten word of God that has been spoken since the world began, then they would have a little more pretext for holding forth scripture and tradition as an infallible guide, but until then, they have no authority to preach up a part of the books of scripture, united with so little tradition, as an infallible rule of faith.

33.—We are told by the Catholics "that many, and very many of the canonical books of the scripture have quite perished, and not so much as appeared in the days of the very ancient fathers; so that nothing but the names of those books are come unto us." † It is also acknowledged by the Catholics that a very great proportion of the few books which are left cannot be explained: it is further acknowledged that the tradition of the unwritten word is so limited, that it does not give them an understanding of many points of doctrine: it is still further acknowledged that their church "pretends to no new revelation," but only to interpret, as far as the few feeble

---

\*——"End of Controversy," Letter xii. p. 169.
†——"Question of Questions," sec. 17.

glimmerings of tradition, connected with the very little scripture which they profess to understand, will enable them to do —and yet they tell us, after all these acknowledgments that their very little scripture and their very little tradition, is an INFALLIBLE RULE OF FAITH. Oh, blush for the inconsistencies of "the mother of harlots!" Her claims to infallibility are blasphemy! Oh, how could the kings of the earth and all nations have been so horribly imposed upon! But they will yet take vengeance upon her, "and shall make her desolate and naked, and shall eat her flesh and burn her with fire," for thus hath the Almighty spoken.

34.—We shall now proceed to point out a thing of infinite importance, which is necessary to the very existence of the Church of God on the earth and yet it never could be learned by either the Bible or tradition. It is this: in order that the true Church may continue its existence on the earth, it is necessary that there should be kept up a regular and constant succession of the orders of the Priesthood; this is admitted by the Catholics; and they refer to upwards of two hundred and fifty popes who have succeeded St. Peter, and to many tens of thousands of bishops who have succeeded the rest of the apostles. Now if this succession can really be proved, then the Catholics must be the only true and living church on the whole earth, and all the Protestant churches are excommunicated apostates; on the other hand, if such succession does not exist, then both the Catholics and Protestants are apostates from the apostolic Church of Christ, built up in the first century. We take the ground that there has been no regular succession of the orders of the Priesthood through the Catholic church.

35.—The first proof which we adduce against any such regular succession is the Catholic rule of faith, namely, ancient scripture and tradition. What word of God, spoken by the apostles, either written or unwritten, has pointed out either of the popes who has pretended to succeed St. Peter, during the last sixteen centuries? We defy the whole Catholic church to bring forward one word of ancient scripture, or ancient tradition, to prove that the popes of the third century, namely, Zephyrinus, Calixtus I., Urban I., Pontanius, Anthurus, Fabian, etc., were the very persons who should succeed St. Peter; if then, neither scripture nor tradition designated the persons who should hold that responsible office, how were the Catholics of the third century to know that either of the above-named persons were the right ones? Perhaps, the Catholics may answer that, though there was no scripture or tradition that pointed them out, yet the church, being infallible, were able to know the right men. We reply, that the Catholic church cannot be infallible, because she "pretends to no revelations," and as we have already seen, she ONLY pretends to be guided in all her decisions and decrees by ancient scripture and tradition and she has no scripture nor apostolic tradition to tell her who, among all the millions of the third century, are called to St. Peter's chair; therefore St. Peter's chair must remain vacated until this important question is settled. And as the Catholics, according to their own admissions, have had no new revelations for the long period of seventeen centuries, therefore St. Peter's chair must have remained vacated during that long period of time. The same reasoning will apply equally to every one of the orders of Priesthood, from St. Peter's chair down to the office of teacher or deacon. Scripture and tradition call no man by name who has lived during the last sixteen centuries; therefore the succession could not possibly continue, as there could be no possible way of finding out who were called and who were not, unless they obtained new revelation, and this would contradict what we have abundantly proved to be their rule of faith; therefore it is proved by the most incontrovertible evidence that the succession of the Priesthood could not legally and lawfully be transferred where there is no new revelation.

36.—The second proof against the Catholic succession is that through ancient scripture and tradition alone, it would be impossible for the pretended successors of St. Peter and the rest of the apostles to exercise the functions of their office. One of the chief duties of the apostles was to receive commandments and new revelations for the instruction of themselves and all the Church of God placed under their charge; and one of the chief duties of a prophet in the Christian church was to foretell future events through new revelation, and forewarn individuals as well as the church of any approaching danger. That these prophets prophesied by new revelation is clear from the following plain passages of scripture, written to the Corinthians. "How is it then, brethren, when ye come together every one of you hath a psalm, hath a doctrine, hath a tongue, hath a REVELATION, hath an interpretation?" (*Chap. xiv.* 26.) - Again, St. Paul says to them, "Let the PROPHETS speak two or three, and let the other judge. If any thing be REVEALED to another that sitteth by, let the first hold his peace. For ye may all prophesy one by one, that all may learn, and all may be comforted. And the spirit of the *prophets* is subject to the *prophets*. For God is not the author of confusion but of peace, as in all Churches of the Saints." (*Verses* 29-33.) Agabus the prophet prophesied of a famine and the Church, being forewarned, made every preparation to meet it, by sending contributions to the poor saints in other places and thus, doubtless, much suffering and misery were prevented. We can here plainly perceive the principal duties of the two first offices in the Christian church. Now if the Catholics have a succession of these offices, they must exercise the functions of them, otherwise the offices would be of no benefit. But they cannot exercise the functions and perform the chief duties of these offices, unless they obtain an abundance of new revelation and prophecies and this they could not do without violating their own rule of faith, which binds them to ancient scripture and ancient tradition as their only guide. Moreover the Catholics themselves virtually acknowledge that none of their pretended successors of the apostolical and prophetical offices, have received any revelations and prophecies from the fact that they have not admitted any of them into the sacred canon of scripture. Thus we see that ancient scripture and tradition, interpreted by the Catholic church, which they acknowledge to be their *only* rule of faith, can never qualify their pretended successors to act in the apostolical and prophetical offices. And hence, those offices have not been and could not be perpetuated in the Catholic church. And, therefore, the Catholic church cannot possibly be the Church of Christ.

37.—But if the Catholic church cannot be the Church of Christ for the want of a legal succession of the apostolical and prophetical orders of the Priesthood, her daughters the Protestants cannot be the Church of Christ for the same reason, unless God has restored the Priesthood to them by a new revelation and an authoritative ordination. But the Protestant daughters, as well as the Catholic mother, make no pretension to new revelation as is demonstrated from the fact of their admitting no more into the sacred canon of scripture. Therefore, neither the Protestant nor Catholic churches, can possibly be the Church of Christ.

38.—The same reasons that demonstrate the Catholic and Protestant churches not to be the Church of Christ, will also demonstrate that the Greek church is not the Church of Christ, therefore the Church of Christ has not existed on the eastern hemisphere during the last seventeen centuries. We shall now proceed to answer some objections.

39.—First, it is objected, that the promise of the Savior, recorded in Matthew xxviii. 16, 17, 18, 19, 20, could not be fullfilled unless the Church should continue its existence on the earth. These passages read thus:—"Then the eleven disciples went away into Galilee, into a mountain where Jesus had appointed them. And when they saw Him, they worshiped Him; but some doubted. And Jesus came and spake unto them, saying, All power is given unto me in heaven and in earth. Go ye therefore, and teach all nations, baptizing them in the name of the Father, and of the Son, and of the Holy Ghost, teaching them to observe all things whatsoever I have commanded you, and, lo, *I am with you always, even unto the end of the world.*" It is argued by the Catholics, "that the apostles themselves were only to live the ordinary term of man's life; therefore, the commission of preaching and ministering, together, with the promise of the divine assistance, regards the successors of the apostles, no less than the apostles themselves. This proves that there must have been an uninterrupted series of such successors of the apostles, in every age since their time; that is to say, successors to their *doctrine*, to their *jurisdiction*, to their *orders* and to their *mission*. Hence it follows, that no religious society whatever, which cannot trace its succession in these four points, up to the apostles, has any claim to the characteristic title, APOSTOLICAL." This argument I have given in the words of one of their learned bishops, the Right Reverend Doctor Milner. * Now if it were admitted, that this *commission* and *promise* of our Savior were intended for the successors of the apostles, (which we by no means admit) it would still be out of the power of the Catholic priests to claim the commission and promise until they could prove from scripture and tradition that each one of them were the actual persons who were to be the true successors; and this, we have already shown they cannot do. Therefore, they have no more claim to the commission and promise than the Pagan priests have. But we do not admit that the promise—"LO, I AM WITH YOU ALWAYS, EVEN UNTO THE END OF THE WORLD," had any reference to any persons whatever only the ELEVEN disciples mentioned in the sixteenth verse, who had, by a previous engagement, retired to a mountain in Galilee: they were the only persons whom He addressed and to whom He made this great promise. But, says Doctor Milner, "They were only to live the ordinary term of man's life," and consequently, he draws the conclusion that the promise could not be fulfilled to them without successors. According to this curious inference of the learned bishop, the Lord must have forsaken the eleven disciples as soon as they died; for if he admits that Jesus continued with them after the period of the death of their mortal bodies, and that He will continue with them even unto the end of the world, then what need would there be of successors in order that the promise might be fulfilled? Prove that Jesus has not been with the *eleven* apostles from the time of their death until the present time, and that He will not be with them "even unto the end of the world," and after you have proved this, you will prove that Jesus has falsified His word; for to be with the successors of the apostles is not to be with them. But whether the apostles have successors or not, Jesus will always be with them, and will bring them with Him when He shall appear in His glory and they shall sit upon thrones and judge the house of Israel, during the great millennium, while Jesus will not only be with them, but will reign with them even unto the end of the world. Therefore, there is nothing in this promise of Jesus that gives the most distant intimation that an

---

*———"End of Controversy," Letter xxviii. p. 281.

apostolical succession or Church of Christ should continue on the earth.

40.—Secondly, it is objected that if the Church of Christ has not continued, then the gates of hell must have prevailed against her; and they refer us to that cheering passage in Matthew, (xvi. 18,) which reads thus:—"And I say also unto thee, that thou art Peter; and upon this rock I will build my Church, and the gates of hell shall not prevail against it." They argue, that if the Church has ceased to exist, the gates of hell have prevailed over her and the promise of Jesus must be falsified. But we would inform the Catholics, that the Church of Christ has not ceased to exist, neither has Peter ceased his existence, but both the Church and Peter are in heaven, far out of the reach of the gates of hell, and far out of the reach of the abominable soul-destroying impositions of popery. The gates of hell have prevailed and will continue to prevail over the Catholic mother of harlots, and over all her Protestant daughters; but as for the apostolical Church of Christ, she rests secure in the mansions of eternal happiness, where she will remain until the apostate Catholic church, with all her popes and bishops, together with all her harlot daughters shall be hurled down to hell; then it shall be said, "Rejoice over her thou heaven, and ye holy apostles and prophets; for God hath avenged you on her;" and then shall be "heard a great voice of much people in heaven, saying, Alleluia : salvation, and glory, and honor, and power, unto the Lord our God; for true the righteous are his judgments: for he hath judged the great whore, which did corrupt the earth with her fornication, and hath avenged the blood of his servants at her hand." And again they shall say, "Alleluia," and her smoke shall rise up for ever and ever. And thus when the Catholics and Protestants hear all the heavens, and all the holy apostles and prophets, rejoicing over the downfall of Babylon, they will learn that the Church of Christ still exists in heaven and that the gates of hell have not prevailed against her; then they will learn where the apostolical and prophetical power rests; then they will perceive the difference between the glory of the Church of Christ and the misery and wretchedness of their own fiery torments.

41.—Many Protestants say they take the Bible as their only rule of faith; if the Bible is to be taken as our only guide, it is of infinite importance that the divine authenticity of the Bible be infallibly established. How do the Protestants prove the truth of the Bible? What evidence have they that the book of Matthew was inspired of God, or any other of the books of the New Testament? The only evidence they have is *tradition*. They have received into their canon such books only as tradition accredits to be genuine; while those books which have not a sufficiency of tradition to establish their divine inspiration, are rejected from the canon. Here then we clearly perceive that the first foundation stone of the Protestant rule of faith is tradition. Tradition alone tells them that the books of the New Testament are true and as soon as they have learned this on the testimony of tradition, they take them as a sufficient guide; hence their only rule of faith is founded on tradition; but we have already shown that tradition is a very imperfect guide. Tradition taught the Lutherans to reject *seven books* of the New Testament, which tradition taught the English to receive: and tradition taught the English to reject some half a score of books from their Bible, which tradition taught the Catholics in the third council of Carthage to receive; and tradition taught the council of Carthage to reject many books which tradition taught several of their learned bishops and others, in the second, third and fourth centuries to receive. If tradition then be so very uncertain, may it not have deceived the Catholics and Protestants as to the genuineness of many of the books which they retain in their canons? And may not this very imperfect tradition have taught them to reject many books which are equally sacred with those which they have retained? Tradition cannot give an absolute certainty as to the truth of any of those books. Great numbers of books, during the early ages, were circulated and accredited, which are now said to be apochryphal. But how, we enquire, are uninspired men, by the use of tradition alone, to select a genuine book from the midst of a numerous collection of spurious gospels, and epistles, and prophecies, which were published under the names of the apostles and under the names of other holy men cotemporary with them? It would be like the chance of drawing a prize in a lottery where there were a hundred blanks to one prize. Absolute certainty is necessary as to what is true and what is false, as to what is the word of God and what is not; for without it we may build our faith upon forged scripture and reject true scripture and be led into all kinds of error. As tradition cannot give us absolute certainty, how shall this very desirable and infinitely important knowledge be obtained? We answer, that by new revelation the genuineness of all books can be tested; and without it, uncertainty and doubt must always hang over many of them.

42.—Even though tradition could demonstrate with the greatest certainty that any or all of the books that are even received by the Catholics, were, in their original written by the persons who are represented to be their authors, yet how can it be determined that even the originals were written by divine inspiration? Several learned Protestants, such as Hooker, Chillingworth, etc., allow that scripture cannot bear testimony to the truth of its own inspiration. How are the Protestants then to know without new revelation, that any one book of the Bible was divinely inspired? How do they know but that it was merely written according to the best judgment of the author? The Bible cannot inform them until the inspiration of the Bible is established. If it be admitted that the apostles and evangelists did write the books of the New Testament, that does not prove of itself that they were divinely inspired at the time they wrote. They were men subject to like passions with other men, and liable to err only when under the direct inspiration of the Spirit. How can it be known without new revelation, that these writers did not sometimes write their own words and opinions instead of the word of the Lord as given by the Holy Ghost? Some things which Paul wrote, he acknowledges that he had no commandment of the Lord for thus writing, but gave his own judgment and his own suppositions. (See I. Corinth. vii. 6, 25, 26.) As Paul and other writers of the New Testament have not told us which part they wrote by inspiration and which part they wrote according to their own opinions and judgment, how can we make the selection of the inspired parts from the uninspired parts of each book? We answer, that tradition will never decide this important question; and therefore neither Catholics nor Protestants can know of a certainty which parts of each of the original books are actually the ideas and words given by inspiration. Neither can they know but that some whole books which they receive as scripture were written by human wisdom alone. Though scripture were allowed to bear testimony of its own inspiration, even then, there are many books in the sacred canon which do not bear any such testimony and therefore the only proof which Protestants can have of their inspiration is founded solely on tradition.

43.—If it could still further be demonstrated by tradition, that every part of each book of the Old and New Testaments, was, in its original, actually written by inspiration, still it cannot be determined that there is one single true copy of those originals now in existence. The whole Catholic and Protestant world cannot produce the original writings of one single book of either the Old or New Testament. The originals are no where to be found among Christians, Pagans, Jews or Mahometans. The original writings of Moses and the ancient prophets, it is believed by the learned, were all destroyed by the Assyrians nearly six hundred years before Christ.* We are informed in the Apocrypha, that the Prophet Esdras or Ezra was inspired to re-write all those ancient books over again; and in this manner the Jews, at the close of their Babylonish captivity, once more obtained them. These books again perished in the great persecution of Antiochus.† How the Jews were supplied with copies after that no one knows. Now the Protestants do not know that Esdras was a true prophet. Indeed, they doubt of his being a true prophet by placing his books in the Apocrypha, therefore they could not rely with confidence on any book which he should pretend to replace by inspiration.

44.—The copies which we now have of the books of Moses and other ancient prophets may be very much corrupted; we are certain that they have been added unto in a degree by some person or persons who lived many centuries after Moses; this is evident

---

\*——Brett's Dissertation in Bishop Watson's Collect. Vol. iii. p. 5.
†——Brett's Dissertation in Bishop Watson's Collect., Vol. iii. p. 5.

from the books themselves: for example, the thirty-first verse of the thirty-sixth chapter of Genesis was certainly added by some one who lived after the children of Israel had kings. It reads thus: "And these are the kings that reigned in the land of Edom, before there reigned any king over the children of Israel." Here is positive proof that the transcriber of the book of Genesis lived after the children of Israel had kings, and added these his own words to this first book of Moses. Some other person after the days of Moses added the whole of the last chapter of the book of Deuteronomy. Several other passages in the books of Moses have been added or changed since his death. Learned commentators* have agreed that similar changes or additions have been made to several other books of the Old Testament by unknown persons. Who can tell at the present day who were the persons who wrote the books of Joshua, Ruth, Judges, Esther, the book of Kings and the book of Chronicles? Were they written by inspired men? If so, what were their names, and what proofs has Christendom that they were inspired?

45.—These uncertain and altered copies of some of the books of the Old Testament were translated from the Hebrew into Greek some two or three centuries before Christ; this was called the Septuagint. But even the original copies of this translation are nowhere to be found. Such copies as the English translation was taken from, were found in many places to be very much corrupted, disagreeing among themselves, insomuch that the English translators were obliged sometimes to translate from the Hebrew which is acknowledged also to be very much corrupted. The Hebrew copies are supposed by the learned to have been altered by the wicked Jews themselves, after they rejected Christ, in order to do away the force of many predictions relating to Him. St. Chrysostom (*Homily* 9) writes thus: "Many of the prophetical monuments have perished; for the Jews being careless, and not only careless, but also impious, they have carelessly lost some of these monuments; others they have partly burned, partly torn in pieces." St. Justin, in writing against Tryphon, shows most

---

*———Boufrerius, Torniellus.

clearly that the Jews did destroy many books of the Old Testament "that the new might not seem to agree with it as it should." What confidence, then, can Catholics or Protestants have in these half-destroyed, corrupted, mutilated Hebrew manuscripts? The oldest copies of the Old Testament, whether Hebrew or Greek, which the English translators could procure, disagree with each other in many—very many places; so much so, that it was impossible for them to decide which was correct. Indeed so much corruption in the old manuscript copies was calculated to throw a mist of darkness and uncertainty over the whole of them. One of the ancient writers, Jerome, in his commentaries upon the prophets, complains of the corruption of his manuscript Greek copies. Bellarmine testifies that the Greek copies of the Old Testament are so corrupted, that they seem to make a new translation, quite different from the translations of other copies. All, therefore, is uncertainty as to the Hebrew and Greek manuscripts of the Old Testament; they can be proved to be changed, added unto and corrupted in almost every text.

46.—It is abundantly proved by various learned writers, that the Greek copies of the New Testament are awfully corrupted in almost every text. Mr. Cressy writes in these words, "In my hearing, Bishop Usher professed, that whereas he had of many years before a desire to publish the New Testament in Greek, with various lections and annotations: and for that purpose he used great diligence, and spent money to furnish himself with manuscripts: yet, in conclusion, he was forced to desist utterly, lest, if he should ingeniously have noted all the several differences of reading which he himself had collected, the incredible multitude of them almost in every verse, should rather have made men atheistical, than satisfy them in the true reading of any particular passage." * Let those who take the Bible for their only guide think of this. If the few manuscripts procured by Bishop Usher, contains in almost every verse "an incredible multitude of different readings," what grounds have Protestants for confidence in one of these readings more than in another? Out of a thousand different manu-

---

*——Exomol. Ca. 8, Nu. 8.

scripts, differing in almost every text, who can select the true one? Indeed, there would be an almost infinite improbability as to any one copy being true. Now, it was from such a mass of contradictory Greek manuscripts that the English New Testament was translated.

47.—But to say nothing of the incredible multitude of different readings in the Greek manuscripts themselves, the translators from these old manuscripts are liable to commit many errors, as is evident from the vast number of very different translations which have been made. There is no two translations that agree. This then is another prolific source of error which is calculated to throw still greater uncertainty over the present copies of the scriptures.

48.—What shall we say then, concerning the Bible's being a sufficient guide? Can we rely upon it in its present known corrupted state, as being a faithful record of God's word? We all know that but a few of the inspired writings have descended to our times, which few quote the names of some twenty other books which are lost, and it is quite certain that there were many other inspired books that even the names have not reached us.* What few have come down to our day, have been mutilated, changed and corrupted, in such a shameful manner, that no two manuscripts agree. Verses and even whole chapters have been added by unknown persons; and even we do not know the authors of some whole books; and we are not certain that all those which we do know, were wrote by inspiration. Add all this imperfection to the uncertainty of the translation, and who, in his right mind, could, for one moment, suppose the Bible in its present form to be a perfect guide? Who knows that even one verse of the whole Bible has escaped pollution, so as to convey the same sense now that it did in the original? Who knows how many important doctrines and ordinances necessary to salvation may be buried in oblivion in some of the lost books? Who knows that even the ordinances and doctrine that seem to be set forth in the present English Bible, are anything like the orginal? The Catholics and Protestants do not know, because tradition is too imperfect to give this knowledge. There can

---

*———Esdras speaks of a great number of books which we have not got.

be no certainty as to the contents of the inspired writings until God shall inspire some one to re-write all those books over again, as he did Esdras in ancient times. There is no possible means of arriving at certainty any other way. No reflecting man can deny the necessity of such a new revelation.

49.—We now appeal to the honesty, good sense and learning of all good, moral men, to testify their convictions in regard to the insufficiency of their rules of faith. Is there a man among you who has candidly examined the present confused, divided, distracted state of all Christendom, who is not thoroughly convinced that something is radically wrong? Many of you, no doubt, have, in your serious reflecting moments, looked upon the bewildered, blind, cold, formal, powerless systems of religion with which you were surrounded with feelings of sorrow and disgust. You have wished to know the truth, but alas, wherever you have turned your investigations, darkness and uncertainty have stared you in the face. The voices of several hundred jarring, contending, soul-sickening sects, were constantly sounding in your ears; each one professing to be built upon the Bible, and yet each one differing from all the rest. Under this confused state of things, you have, peradventure, involuntarily exclaimed: can the Bible be the word of God? Would God reveal a system of religion expressed in such *indefinite terms* that a thousand different religions should grow out of it? Has God revealed the system of salvation in such vague uncertain language on purpose to delight Himself with the quarrels and contentions of His creatures in relation to it? Would God think so much of fallen men, that He would give His Only Begotten Son to die for them, and then reveal His doctrine to them in a language altogether ambiguous and uncertain? Such questions, doubtless, have passed through the mind of many a religiously-inclined person. Millions have been sensible of the midnight darkness, but have not known the true cause; they have acknowledged that they could not understand a very great proportion of the Bible, yet they have believed it to be the word of God; they have wondered that the Bible should be their only rule of faith, and yet so few be able to understand it alike. Many seeing the contradictions, the vagueness, and the uncertainty of all modern religions, professing to have emanated from the same God, have been so disgusted that they have renounced the Bible as a fable invented by priestcraft; others, fearing to do this, have pored over whole libraries of uninspired commentaries, seeking after the true meaning of that which they believe God has revealed; and at last, finding the learned commentators as widely disagreed as the sects themselves, they have concluded that the Bible is a great mystery and that God did not intend to have it understood when He revealed it. Others still having a little more perseverance, and believing that God would not send a revelation which He did not wish the people to understand, have with great diligence collected vast numbers of the most ancient Greek and Hebrew manuscripts of the sacred books, but here they find themselves utterly confounded: these ancient manuscripts, which they had hopes would reveal the truth, are perverted and corrupted in almost every text, so that they find "an incredible number of different readings" on every page and almost every sentence. From this heterogeneous mass of contradictory manuscripts they give an English translation, and call it the Bible; thus leaving millions to guess out the true meaning and quarrel, and contend with each other because they do not guess alike.

50.—The true cause of all the divisions which distract modern Christendom is the want of inspired apostles and prophets: they through wickedness and apostasy, lost the key of revelation some seventeen centuries ago, since which time they have been altogether unable to open the *door of knowledge.* Satan has taken the advantage of their dark and benighted condition, and robbed the world of a great number of sacred books, corrupting those few that remained to such a degree, that he has got the whole of Christendom quarreling about their true meaning. This pleases him: he cares not how much they contend and fight about religion as long as he knows that their religion is false: neither does he care how much they are united about religion, as long as he knows that it is not of the right kind. He can tolerate, and, indeed, help his reverend ministers to promulgate all kinds of religion, except that which has true prophets and revelators in it: no other kind of religion displeases him. But for a prophet or revelator to establish a religion on the earth, is more than he can quietly put up with; it strikes a death blow to all that he has been doing since the great apostasy. He is exceedingly frightened, lest some of the old lost books of the ancient prophets and apostles should be again revealed. He is also raving mad, lest the books of the Old and New Testaments should be revealed again anew in their purity as at first—lest every point of Christ's doctrine should be again revealed in such plain, definite and positive language, that no two persons could possibly disagree upon it. This would be exceedingly dangerous to his kingdom; no wonder then, that he should be full of wrath! But the sincere, honest, humble seeker after truth, must have the privilege of finding it, and that, too, in the greatest of plainness, before the overthrow of all nations, that they, by embracing it, may escape the judgments of great Babylon. Yes! the day is come and the time is at hand when all nations are to hear the word of the Lord by the mouth of his chosen apostles and prophets to whom He hath restored the key of revelation for the last time, and for the dispensation of the fullness of times, that all things may be prepared and sealed unto the end of all things, against the day of rest for the meek of the earth.

## CHAPTER IV.

### EVIDENCES OF THE BOOK OF MORMON AND BIBLE COMPARED.

1.—The Book of Mormon claims to be the sacred history of ancient America, written by a succession of ancient prophets, who inhabited that vast continent. The plates of gold, containing this history, were discovered by a young man, named Joseph Smith, through the ministry of a holy angel, on the evening and morning of the 21st and 22nd of September, A. D. 1823. Four years after their discovery, or on the morning of the 22nd of September, 1827, the angel of the Lord permitted Mr. Smith to take these sacred records from the place of their deposit. The hill in which they were found buried, is situated in the town of Manchester, Ontario county, state of New York. With the plates were also found a Urim and Thummim. Each plate was not far from seven by eight inches in width and length, being not quite as thick as common tin. Each was filled on both sides with engraved Egyptian characters; and the whole were bound together in a volume, as the leaves of a book, and fastened at one edge with three rings running through each. This volume was something near six inches in thickness, a part of which was sealed. The characters or letters upon the unsealed part were small and beautifully engraved. Mr. Smith, through the aid of the Urim and Thummim, and by the gift and power of God, translated this record into the English language. This translation contains about the same amount of reading as the Old Testament. A large edition of this wonderful book was first published early in 1830.

2.—It may be asked, what further evidence have we that Mr. Smith saw the angel? Does the truth or falsity of the Book of Mormon depend upon his testimony alone? May not Mr. Smith be an impostor? These are questions, not only reasonable, but of the greatest importance. It certainly does not seem reasonable to many that in sending a message which is to affect the temporal and eternal welfare of all the present generation, God would give but one witness only. When God sent a prophetic message concerning the flood, He must have revealed the truth of it, not only to Noah, but to his three sons; for they all seem to have labored together in building the ark; this they would not have done unless they had been fully assured that the message was from God. If, then, it be assumed that Noah's three sons were witnesses, as well as himself, and that their united testimony was given by which the whole world was condemned and overthrown, may we not expect that a message which is to prove, if rejected, the overthrow of the present generation, will come to us, confirmed by at least, as many witnesses as there were of the flood? The Savior Himself testifies that, "As it was in the days of Noah, so shall it also be in the days of the coming of the Son of Man." If God sent four witnesses in the days of Noah, the preparatory message for the day of burning, or for the coming of the Son of Man, may also have the' same number. Although the Savior has said, that "in the mouth of two or three witnesses every word shall be established," yet that does not prohibit Him from sending more if it be necessary.

3.—That the world might have no excuse for rejec ting the Book of Mormon, the Lord did, before He sent it to them, raise up three other witnesses besides Mr. Smith, namely, Oliver Cowdery, David Whitmer and Martin Harris. These three men in company with Mr. Smith testify that, in answer to their prayers, in the year 1829, they saw an angel of God, descend from heaven, clothed with glory, and that he took the plates from which the Book of Mormon was translated, and exhibited them before their eyes, so that they saw them distinctly, and also the engravings upon them; and they further testify, that while the angel was thus showing them the plates, they heard the voice of the Lord out of the heavens, declaring that they had been translated correctly; and they further declare that the voice of the Lord commanded them to send forth their testimony, of what they had seen and heard, unto all nations, kindreds, tongues and people. In obedience to this heavenly command they have sent forth their written testimony, connected with the Book of Mormon, for the benefit of all the world.

4.—No reasonable person will say that these four persons were themselves deceived; the nature of their testimony is such that they must either be bold, daring impostors, or else the Book of Mormon is true. They testify that they saw the angel descend—they heard his voice—they saw the plates in his hand—they saw the engravings upon them as the angel turned them over, leaf after leaf—at the same time they heard the voice of the Lord out of the heavens. What greater evidence could they have? They could have had nothing that would have given them greater assurance. If they were deceived, then there is no certainty in anything. If these four men could be deceived in seeing an angel descend from heaven, on the same ground the apostles may have been deceived in seeing the Savior ascend up to heaven. These men must have had just as much assurance of what they saw, and heard, and handled, as they had of the existence of any eternal thing. And having the most perfect knowledge of the truth of the Book of Mormon, they were fully prepared to bear a bold, unequivocal, fearless testimony to all nations.

5.—Is there not a possibility that these four witnesses are all wicked impostors, who have colleagued together to deceive mankind? We answer that there would be a possibility if there were no other evidences to confirm their testimony. But when we take into consideration the boldness of their testimony, and the circumstances connected with it, there is no probability that they were wicked men. Is it probable that four men who were, for the most of their days, strangers to each other, residing in three or four different counties, should all combine together to testify that they had seen an angel and heard his voice, and also the voice of God, bearing testimony to the truth of the Book of Mormon, when no such thing had happened? Three of these witnesses, namely, Joseph Smith, Oliver Cowdery and David Whitmer, were young men, from twenty to twenty-five years of age; they were men who had been accustomed from their childhood to the peaceful avocations of a farmer's life. Unacquainted with the deceptions which are more or less practiced in large towns and cities, they possessed the open honesty and simplicity so generally characteristic of country people. Is it, in the least degree, probable that men so young and inexperienced, accustomed to a country life and unacquainted with the world at large, would be so utterly abandoned by everything that was good, so perfectly reckless as to their own future welfare, so heaven-daring and blasphemous, as to testify to all nations that which, if false, would forever seal their damnation? We have read of individual impostors, like Mahomet, who have testified to the ministering of angels, and have deceived many; but where have we ever heard of four impostors, all agreed in combining together, to originate an imposition, and afterwards to send forth their united testimony to deceive all the nations of the earth? I the history of the various false Christs and false prophets who have appeared among men, we find, as a general thing, that each one originated his own system of imposition, and then offered it to the world on his own testimony alone; but not so with the Book of Mormon, it was first confirmed by angels and the voice of the Lord to *four witnesses*, before it was suffered to be printed and offered to the world with authority. We are well aware that there have been hundreds impositions offered to the world; and it is often the case that of impostors advocate a particular system, pretending that they know it to be true; but then, if such system be traced back to its origin, it will be found that it not only originated with one man, but was first offered to the world on his testimony alone. We do not say but that the Lord may sometimes send only *one witness* to bear testimony of the truth; as examples: Lot was the only one sent to warn his kinsmen in Sodom; Jonah alone was sent to Nineveh; and John the Baptist seems to have been the only one sent to warn the Jews and prepare the way for our Savior's first coming. It is evident, then, that the truth or falsity of a message does not depend upon its number of witnesses. It may be true, though there be only one witness, and there is a still greater probability of its truth where there are several witnesses. The greater the number of witnesses, the less the liability of deception, especially when we consider that most impositions have been originated and offered to the world on the testimony of only one man. We are not aware that there ever were three, or four, or five impostors who originated an imposition, and succeeded in palming it upon the world as a message from God. Such a thing might barely be possible, but such a thing would be highly improbable.

6.—If we compare the abstract testimony of these four witnesses with the abstract testimonies of the servants of God in former ages; that is, if the testimonies alone, independent of miracles and all other evidences be compared, we shall have, in many respects, greater reasons for believing these four of modern times, than we have for believing those of ancient times. For example: who were witnesses of Christ's transfiguration on the mount at the time Moses and Elias appeared? We are informed that Peter, James and John were witnesses. But how do we know? Neither of them handed down their written testimony to that effect. Peter alone testifies of the voice that he and others heard from heaven when they were with Christ "in the holy mount" (*II. Peter i.* 18). But neither Peter, James nor John, have told us anything about the transfiguration, or about the appearance of Moses and Elias. Matthew, Mark and Luke give us a second-handed testimony to that effect. But these three, not being present at the transfiguration, could not testify as eye witnesses. Compare, then, the testimony of these three, who did not see the glorious manifestations in the mount, with the testimony of the four witnesses to the Book of Mormon, who both saw and heard, and you will be compelled to admit that the latter testimony is far greater than the former.

7.—As another example, let us compare the abstract testimony of these four witnesses with the abstract testimonies of those who professed to have seen Jesus after His resurrection. How many eye witnesses were there that beheld Jesus after His resurrection? We have the written testimony of only four, namely, Matthew, John, Paul and Peter. There is no doubt but what all the eleven saw Him, though eight out of the eleven have given us no written testimony to that effect. Mark, Luke, James and Jude, the other four writers of the New Testament, have not told us in their writings, whether they saw Him after His resurrection or not. Several women saw Him, but their written testimony has never reached our day. Paul says that He was seen, not only by all the apostles, but by "above five hundred brethren at once" (*I. Cor.* xv. 6). But none of those five hundred eye witnesses have left any written testimonies of what they saw. Hence, Matthew, John, Paul and Peter are the only persons among the great number that saw Him after His resurrection, who have handed down to our day their written testimony as eye witnesses. Therefore, when this generation can establish the writings of these four apostles to be *genuine, uncorrupted* and *translated correctly*, they will have the testimony of as many witnesses to establish the resurrection of Christ, as there was, in the first place to establish the divine authenticity of the Book of Mormon; but until then, the witnesses of the Book of Mormon will be, not only equal in number, but superior in certainty to those which this generation have of Christ's resurrection. Why is it, then, that men will believe four witnesses who lived eighteen centuries ago, and reject the same number of witnesses that have lived in their own day, who testify of things with equally as much certainty, having both seen and heard? It is because it has become popular, through tradition, to believe what their fathers believed, without at all inquiring into the strength of the evidence on which their faith is founded.

8.—Many say that they will not believe in the divine authenticity of the Book of Mormon because there is so much evil spoken against the four witnesses. Let such persons remember the sayings of our Savior: "Blessed are they which are persecuted for righteousness sake; for their's is the kingdom of heaven. Blessed are ye when men shall revile you, and persecute you, and shall say all manner of evil against you falsely for my sake. Rejoice and be exceeding glad; for great is your reward in heaven; for so persecuted they the prophets which were before you." And again, Jesus said, "Woe unto you when all men speak well of you; for so did their fathers to the false prophets." Again, He said, "Ye shall be hated of all men for my name's sake." "If they have called the Master of the house Beelzebub, how much more shall they call them of His household?" Paul testifies that the Saints "were counted the off-scouring of all things." Did the hatred, the persecutions, the revilings and the "all manner of evils" which were said against the apostles, invalidate or destroy their testimony? No: their testimony was just as true after they were spoken evil of as before. Why, then, should any reject the Book of Mormon because the four witnesses have been persecuted, and all manner of evil said against them? Is it not a presumptive evidence in favor, instead of being an evidence against the work? On the other hand, if all men spoke well of these four witnesses, would they not come under the woe of the Savior, and would they not be denounced the same as the false prophets whom the Jews spoke well of? Some may say that they believe that the evils spoken against the apostles were false, while the evils spoken against Mr. Smith and the other witnesses are true. But what evidence have they to believe that the men who accused the apostles of "all manner of evil," were liars; while those who accuse these latter-day witnesses are men of truth? Are not the latter-day accusers just as likely to be liars as the former-day ones? And are not the Latter day Saints just as liable to be falsely accused as former-day Saints? Let the accusations be ever so great, or ever so numerous, it does not destroy the truth of a message now, any more than it did anciently.

9.—If we were to admit that the sins and transgressions of Joseph Smith and the other witnesses, were as great as their enemies falsely assert them to be, (which we do in no wise admit), that would not invalidate nor destroy their testimony. When Saul, the king of Israel, through transgression, lost the spirit of prophecy, and became a murderer in his heart, by seeking the life of David, no one will pretend to say that it destroyed or even weakened the testimony that he had formerly delivered as a prophet. When David added the crime of murder to adultery, will any one pretend to say that it invalidated his testimony in relation to the truth of his former prophetic writings? The Lord appeared unto Solomon twice, (*I. Kings xi.* 9); yet even after all that, he fell into transgression and became a most abominable idolator, serving numerous gods and goddesses, that were worshiped by the heathen.\*. Now did this great crime prove that his testimony, about seeing the Lord twice, was false, and not to be depended upon? Did his wicked idolatry prove that his proverbs and other witings were not inspired of God? Did Peter's lying, cursing, swearing and denying the Christ, invalidate or destroy his testimony concerning the glorious voice he heard in the mount? If then such abominable and awfully wicked crimes, committed by ancient prophets and apostles, did not invalidate nor destroy their testimonies of what they, during their righteousness, had seen and heard, why should it be thought that the testimony of the four witnesses of the Book of Mormon could be, in the least, weakened or rendered doubtful by their transgressions and sins? If they were, through fear, to lie, curse and swear as Peter did, and to deny the Book of Mor-

---

\*——I. Kings, xi. 1-10,

mon, as Peter did the Christ, that would not prove their former testimony was false. If they were to turn away and serve other gods, and commit adultery and murder, as Solomon, David and Saul did, that would not prove that they had not seen an angel, and heard the voice of the Lord, confirming to them the truth of the Book of Mormon. If such crimes would invalidate their testimony in relation to the Book of Mormon, like crimes would equally invalidate the testimonies of ancient prophets and apostles in relation to their respective messages.

10.—No man who has any degree of the Spirit of God in his heart, can read the history of Joseph Smith, as written by himself, without being fully convinced that he was no impostor. His extreme youth at the time he received his first vision, must have precluded every idea of deception: and also, the vision was of such a nature that he could not himself have been deceived. He testifies, that when he was only in his fifteenth year, that his mind was filled with the deepest anxiety for the salvation of his soul: his attention being called to this subject in consequence of a great religious excitement which prevailed in his neighborhood, and in the surrounding country. This excitement existed to a great extent among many religious sects, but more especially among the Presbyterians, Baptists and Methodists. Many contentions existed as to which of the numerous sects was right. Four of his father's family were proselyted to the Presbyterian faith. He himself, not knowing which was right, kept aloof from all. I will here insert an extract from his history, in his own words; it reads as follows:

11.—"So great was the confusion and strife among the different denominations, that it was impossible for a person, young as I was, and so unacquainted with men and things, to come to any certain conclusion who was right, and who was wrong. My mind at different times was greatly excited, the cry and tumult was so great and incessant. The Presbyterians were most decided against the Baptists and Methodists, and used all their powers of either reason or sophistry to prove their errors, or at least to make the people think they were in error. On the other hand, the Baptists and Methodists their turn, were equally zealous to establish their own tenets and disprove all others.

"In the midst of this war and tumult of opinions, I often said to myself, what is to be done? Who of all these parties are right? or, are they all wrong together? If any of them be right which is it, and how shall I know it?

"While I was laboring under the extreme difficulties, caused by the contests of these parties of religionists, I was one day reading the epistle of James, first chapter and fifth verse, which reads, 'If any of you lack wisdom, let him ask of God, that giveth unto all men liberally and upbraideth not, and it shall be given him.' Never did any passage of scripture come with more power to the heart of man than this did at this time to mine. It seemed to enter with great force into every feeling of my heart. I reflected on it again and again, knowing that if any person needed wisdom from God I did; for how to act I did not know, and unless I could get more wisdom than I then had, would never know; for the teachers of religion of the different sects understood the same passage so differently as to destroy all confidence in settling the question by an appeal to the Bible. At length I came to the conclusion that I must either remain in darkness and confusion, or else I must do as James directs; that is, ask of God. I at length came to the determination to 'ask of God,' concluding that if He gave wisdom to them that lacked wisdom, and would give liberally and not upbraid, I might venture. So, in accordance with this my determination to ask of God, I retired to the woods to make the attempt. It was on the morning of a beautiful, clear day, early in the Spring of eighteen hundred and twenty. It was the first time in my life that I had made such an attempt, for amidst all my anxieties I had never yet made the attempt to pray vocally.

"After I had retired into the place where I had previously designed to go, having looked around me and finding myself alone, I kneeled down and began to offer up the desires of my heart to God. I had scarcely done so, when immediately I was seized upon by some power which entirely overcame me, and had such astonishing influence over me as to bind my tongue, so that I could not speak. Thick darkness gathered around me, and it seemed to me for a time as if I were doomed to sudden destruction. But exerting all my powers to call upon God to deliver me out of the power of this enemy which had seized upon me, and at the very moment when I was ready to sink into despair and abandon myself to destruction, not to an imaginary ruin, but to the power of some actual being from the unseen world, who had such a marvelous power as I had never before felt in any being. Just at this moment of great alarm, I saw a pillar of light exactly over my head, above the brightness of the sun, which descended gradually until it fell upon me. It no sooner appeared than I found myself delivered from the enemy which held me bound. When the light rested upon me, I saw two personages, whose brightness and glory defy all description, standing above me in the air. One of them spake unto me, calling me by name, and said (pointing to the other)—'This is my beloved Son, hear Him.'

"My object in going to inquire of the Lord, was to know which of all the sects was right, that I might know which to join. No sooner, therefore, did I get possession of myself, so as to be able to speak, than I asked the personages who stood above me in the light, which of all the sects was right (for at this time it had never entered into my heart that all were wrong), and which I should join. I was answered that I must join none of them, for they were all wrong, and the personage who addressed me said that all their creeds were an abomination in His sight; that those professors were all corrupt; they draw near to me with their lips, but their hearts are far from me; they teach for doctrine the commandments of men, having a form of godliness, but they deny the power thereof.' He again forbade me to join with any of them: and many other things did He say unto me which I cannot write at this time. When I came to myself again, I found myself laying on my back, looking up into heaven. Some few days after I had this vision, I happened to be in company with one of the Methodist preachers who was very active in the before-mentioned religious excitement, and conversing with him on the subject of religion, I took occasion to give him an account of the vision which I had had. I was greatly surprised at his behavior; he treated my communication not only lightly, but with great contempt, saying it was all of the devil, that there were no such things as visions or revelations in these days; that all such things had ceased with the apostles, and that there never would be any more of them. I soon found, however, that my telling the story had excited a great deal of prejudice against me among professors of religion, and was the cause of great persecution which continued to increase; and though I was an obscure boy, only between fourteen and fifteen years of age, and my circumstances in life such as to make a boy of no consequence in the world, yet men of high standing would take notice sufficient to excite the public mind against me and create a hot persecution, and this was common among all the sects: all united to persecute me. It has often caused me serious reflection both then and since, how very strange it was that an obscure boy of a little over fourteen years of age, and one, too, who was doomed to the necessity of obtaining a scanty maintainance by his daily labor, should be thought a character of sufficient importance to attract the attention of the great ones of the most popular sects of the day, so as to create in them a spirit of the hottest persecution and reviling. But strange or not, so it was, and was often a cause of great sorrow to myself. However, it was nevertheless a fact that I had had a vision. I have thought since, that I felt much like Paul when he made his defense before King Agrippa and related the account of the vision he had when he 'saw a light and heard a voice,' but still there were but few who believed him; some said he was dishonest, others said he was mad, and he was ridiculed and reviled; but all this did not destroy the reality of his vision. He had seen a vision, he knew he had, and all persecution under heaven could not make it otherwise; and though they should persecute him unto death, yet he knew and would know unto his latest breath, that he had both seen a light and heard a voice speaking to him, and all the world could not make him believe otherwise. So it was with me, I had actually seen a light and in the midst of that light I saw two personages, and they did in reality speak unto me, or one of them did; and though I was hated and persecuted for saying that I had seen a vision, yet it was true; and while they were persecuting me, reviling me, and speaking all manner of evil against me falsely for so saying, I was led to say in my heart, why persecute for telling the truth? I had actually seen a vision and 'who am I that I can withstand God?' Or why does the world think to make me deny what I have actually seen? For I had seen a vision; I knew it, and knew that God knew it, and I could not deny it, neither dare I do it; at least I knew that by so doing I would offend God and come under condemnation. I had now got my mind satisfied so far as the sectarian world was concerned, that it was not my duty to join with any of them, but continue as I was until further directed." *

12.—Now we candidly ask our readers if they can believe that a boy under fifteen years of age, would relate the foregoing vision to a Methodist minister and to his old acquaintances on purpose to bring down upon himself derision and scorn. Would he continue year after year, to affirm that he had seen a great and glorious vision, unless he had truly seen one? Would he be so fond of being hated, persecuted and ridiculed, that he would continue to testify to a heaven daring falsehood, on purpose to get the contempt and ill-will of almost every one that knew him? Where is there a circumstance recorded in the annals of history of a youth of fourteen turning an impostor, declaring that he had seen the Lord and heard his voice, and continuing to affirm the same all the days of his life, in the midst of the most distressing scenes of persecution, and finally, sealing his testimony with his blood? Such an instance cannot be found. If this obscure country youth were an impostor, is it not very strange that none of the wise men of the age are able to detect the least error in his doctrine? A wicked, corrupt impostor of fourteen years of age, must be the wonder of the world, if he could begin to originate, at that early period of his life, a religious deception that could not in its progress, be detected, but that would continue year after year, to deceive its tens of thousands. If he was sincere, then the Book of Mormon is a divine revelation and this Church must be "the only true and living Church of Christ upon the face of the whole earth," and there is no salvation in any

*——History of Joseph Smith, Millennial Star, Vol. iii., No. 2, p. 21.

other. This is an immense conclusion, but we can come to no other, the moment we admit his sincerity. Therefore the world are driven to the necessity of denouncing this obscure, illiterate country youth, as the most vile, base, arch deceiver that ever disgraced the earth, or of admitting that he was one of the greatest prophets, with the exception of the Savior, that ever lived among men

13.—But in order to prove that the four witnesses of the Book of Mormon are all impostors, it will be necessary to prove that they did not see and hear an angel—that they did not see the plates in the angel's hand—that they did not hear the voice of the Lord, declaring that they were translated correctly. All reasonable men will admit that it is impossible for any negative testimony to be found to prove *directly* that God did not send His angel to reveal and confirm the truth of the Book of Mormon; and as there is no *direct* evidence to negative their testimony and prove them impostors, therefore if it be possible to prove them such, it can only be done by some *indirect* evidence, arising from the circumstances of the case, or from the nature of the message itself, as being contradictory to some known truth.

14.—Let us enquire, first, if there be any thing connected with the circumstances that renders their testimony doubtful or improbable. Is it improbable that an angel should be sent again to our earth? We see no improbability that such an event should happen. It certainly is not an unscriptural doctrine for angels to appear. Angels appeared to Abraham and took dinner with him, an angel appeared to Jacob and wrestled with him all night; angels appeared to Lot, and lodged with him; angels appeared to Moses, to Joshua, to Manoah, to Gideon, to David, to Daniel, to Zechariah, to Joseph, the husband of Mary, to the shepherds by night, to the apostles, to Philip, to Paul, to Cornelius, and finally, Paul says, that they are "all ministering spirits sent forth to minister for them who shall be heirs of salvation." The apostles exhorted the saints not to be forgetful to entertain strangers, for some, in so doing, "had entertained angels unawares." There is nothing in the scriptures which indicates that angels will cease to appear among men, therefore, there is nothing in the circumstances of the appearance of the angel to those four witnesses that is unscriptural. And there certainly is nothing unreasonable in an angel's being sent in our day. If it was reasonable for God to send an angel to announce the birth of John the Baptist, to prepare the way for the first advent, why should it be thought unreasonable for Him to send angels to announce the great preparatory message for the second advent? Hence, the testimony of these four witnesses, concerning the appearing of an angel, is neither unscriptural nor unreasonable. Therefore, the event itself, and the circumstances connected with it, are such as do not, in the least, weaken the testimony, or render it doubtful, or improbable.

15.—Let us enquire next, if there be anything, connected with the nature of the message, that is contradictory to any known truth? This can be easily ascertained by a careful examination of the historical, prophetical and doctrinal parts of the Book of Mormon and by a faithful comparison of the same with the historical, prophetical and doctrinal truths which are already known. If, after this examination and comparison, we find irreconcilable and palpable contradictions, we should then know the four witnesses to be false in their testimony and unworthy of credit. But if, on the other hand, we find no disagreement, nor contradictions to any known truths, if we find every part of the book harmonizing with every other part, if we find nothing absurd, unscriptural, nor unreasonable, then we have no authority whatever for condemning the witnesses as impostors.

16.—If the historical part of the Book of Mormon be compared with what little is known from other sources, concerning the history of ancient America, there will be found much evidence to substantiate its truth; but there cannot be found one truth among all the gleanings of antiquity that clashes with the historical truths of the Book of Mormon.

17.—If the prophetical part of this wonderful book be compared with the prophetical declarations of the Bible, there will be found much evidence in the latter to establish the truth of the former. But though there are many predictions in the Book of Mormon, relating to the great events of the last days, which the Bible gives us no information about, yet there is nothing in the predictions of the Bible that contradicts in the least, the predictions in the Book of Mormon.

18.—If the doctrinal part of the Book of Mormon be compared with the doctrines of the Bible, there will be found the same perfect harmony which we find on the comparison of the prophetical parts of the two books. Although there are many points of the doctrine of Christ that are far more plain and definite in the Book of Mormon than in the Bible and many things revealed in relation to doctrine that never could be fully learned from the Bible, yet there are not any items of doctrine in the two sacred books that contradict each other, or clash in the least.

19.—If the various books which enter into the collection, called the Book of Mormon, be carefully compared with each other, there will be found nothing contradictory in history, in prophecy or in doctrine.

20.—If the miracles of the Book of Mormon be compared with the miracles of the Bible, there cannot be found in the former any thing that would be more difficult to believe, than what we find in the latter.

21.—If we compare the historical, prophetical and doctrinal parts of the Book of Mormon, with the great truths of science and nature, we find no contradictions, no absurdities, nothing unreasonable. The most perfect harmony, therefore, exists between the great truths revealed in the Book of Mormon and all other known truths, whether religious, historical or scientific.

22.—Here, then, we have this great message of the last days, confirmed at the very outset, by the ministry of an angel to four witnesses. These witnesses have neither of them denied the bold and fearless, though humble testimony which they have sent forth to all nations. No man living can prove that an angel did not appear to them. There is nothing in the nature of the event itself, nor in any of the circumstances connected with it, that would render it absurd, unscriptural, unreasonable or improbable. There is nothing in the historical, prophetical, or doctrinal parts of the message that contradicts each other, or any known truth through the wide field of scientific or religious knowledge. Therefore, no man living has the least authority for condemning these witnesses as impostors. Indeed, there cannot be brought the least shadow of evidence, either direct or indirect, to prove that their testimony, concerning the angel, is false. Therefore, as their testimony cannot be proved false, the Book of Mormon stands upon a foundation as firm as the rock of ages, and as secure as the throne of the Almighty. Though wicked men may invent all manner of falsehoods against the Saints and against the chosen witnesses of the Lord—though they may slander, revile and persecute them and drive them from city to city, destroying property and murdering men, women and children—though they have without the least provocation, murdered this great prophet of the last dispensation, and driven tens of thousands of the Church into the wilderness, far from the abodes of what they call civilized life;—yet they will learn that all such arguments are vain and futile, when met by stubborn facts; they will learn that such arguments are powerless when they hear the voice of witnesses, saying, we have seen, we have heard, we have handled and we know of a surety. All men among all nations, kindreds, tongues and people, are required under the penalty of eternal damnation to believe, receive and obey the Book of Mormon, unless they can prove the witnesses thereof to be impostors. And this they cannot do.

23.—It is oftentimes asked, by our opposers, if the Bible says anything about the Book of Mormon? If not, say they, we will not believe in it. Now there is nothing more inconsistent than to say we will not believe a book to be a divine revelation, unless some other inspired book has spoken of it. How did Jeremiah prove to the Jews that his book was true? Did any other inspired book speak of the writings which Jeremiah should receive? No; Jeremiah's book was not mentioned by any of the former prophets. Does any former book speak of the five books of Moses? Does any former book say anything about the book of Ezekiel, the book of Amos, the book of Joel, the book of Zechariah, the book of Malachi, the book of Matthew, the book of James or Jude, or the book of John's prophecy? Those, therefore, who would reject the Book of Mormon, because they suppose that other previously inspired books had not mentioned it, would, on the same grounds, be obliged to reject every book, both of the Old and New Testaments, for not one of them can be proved a divine revelation by the testimony of any previously written book. If, then, it can be proved by the Bible that such a book as the Book of Mormon was to be revealed in the last days, this would be an additional testimony to its truth, which none of the other inspired books have. Before we close this series, we shall show that the Bible has predicted that such a book, as the one now revealed, should be sent forth to fulfill the great events of the last days. If the ancient prophets have made such predictions, they must have considered that the message in the Book of Mormon was to be of far greater consequence as to the events and purposes which it should accomplish, than all other books that had preceded it. If they had not considered it in that light, they would not have mentioned it, and passed by in silence many other sacred books that were to be written.

21.—Have any persons ever seen the plates of the Book of Mormon, besides the four witnesses? Yes: there are eight other witnesses, who send forth their printed testimony, in connection with the Book of Mormon, unto all nations, kindreds, tongues and people. They testify that they saw and handled the plates and examined the engravings upon them, and that they had "the appearance of ancient work and of curious workmanship." They close their testimony with the following words:

"And we give our names unto the world, to witness unto the world that which we have seen, and we lie not, God bearing witness of it." Here, then, are twelve witnesses of the existence of the plates. Neither of these witnesses has ever denied his testimony to this day. Some of these witnesses have died—some have been martyred for their testimony, and one is still living. Is there a person on the earth, that can prove that these twelve witnesses did not see the plates? No, there is not. The existence of the plates, filled with engravings, is proved by twelve eye witnesses; while the correctness of their translation is proved by four eye witnesses, not only of the plates, but of the angel. Therefore, the evidences which this generation have of the divine authenticity of the Book of Mormon, and of the existence of the plates, are far greater than the evidences which they have for the truth of any of the books of the Bible. Hence, if they would be condemned for rejecting the Bible, how much more will they be condemned for rejecting the Book of Mormon which was confirmed, in its very origin, by so many witnesses?

25.—After these plates had been exhibited to a sufficient number of witnesses, they were, by the commandment of God, hid up in charge of the heavenly messenger who first revealed them, and who had, from time to time, while they were being translated, directed Mr. Smith how to preserve them from the hands of his persecutors; for persecution was so heavy upon him that he had to flee from place to place to preserve his life. A portion of these plates were sealed together, and Mr. Smith was forbidden to break the seal, or to translate them. The Book of Mormon informs us that the sealed portion of the plates contains a very great and sacred revelation, unfolding things from the beginning of the world unto the end thereof, and that it is hereafter to be revealed by the power of Christ. The plates, therefore, will no doubt be kept in charge of the heavenly messenger until the time arrives for the seal to be loosed, and for the remainder to be translated.

26.—Many suppose that if they could see the plates, it would at once convince them of the divine origin of this great and marvelous work. But, we ask such, how could they know by barely seeing the plates, whether they were of ancient or modern construction? How could they tell, by seeing the engravings upon them, that they were translated correctly? Who, among all the generations of Israel after the days of Moses, saw the tables of stone on which the law was engraved? We answer, that the tables of stone were kept in the ark in the "holy of holies," and none but the high priest had the privilege of going in there and he only once a year. It is true that the high priest could testify that he had seen the tables of stone, and the people could believe it on his testimony. When Christ arose from the dead, He did not show Himself openly, but He appeared to chosen witnesses, and commanded them to bear testimony to all nations. The people, instead of seeing the risen Savior and becoming eye-witnesses to this great and fundamental truth, had to believe it on the testimony of others. So with the plates of the Book of Mormon, instead of these being sent to every creature in all the world, the testimony of chosen witnesses is sent. And as every creature in all the world, who would not believe the chosen eye witnesses of a risen Savior were to be damned, so every living soul who rejects the testimony of the chosen eye witnesses of the ministry of the angel, confirmatory of the Book of Mormon—will be damned, for thus hath the Lord spoken.

27.—We ask this generation to bring one living witness that has seen even one of the original manuscripts of any of the books of the Bible. They cannot do it. There is not one solitary original manuscript of any book of the Bible now known among men; neither has there been any such manuscript known for very many centuries. Therefore, this generation have twelve eye witnesses of the original of the Book of Mormon, whereas they have not even one eye witness of the original of any book of the Bible. Therefore, if rejecting the evidences which we have of the truth of the Bible will bring condemnation, how much greater must be the condemnation of this generation, if they reject the far greater evidences of the Book of Mormon! O the unbelief and inconsistency of this generation! How can they escape the sword of justice which hangs over them! They are drunken in iniquity, and the spirit of deep sleep is upon them, and they know not the day of their visitation! Like beasts they will be led to the slaughter and quickly go down into the pit!

28.—As there has been no apostolical succession which has continued on the earth for the want of new revelation, as was proved in Chapter III., of this series, it may be asked, how was the authority of the priesthood restored to the earth? We answer, that it was restored by the ministry of angels. On this subject we make an extract from the history of Joseph Smith, which reads as follows: "We still continued the work of translation, when in the ensuing month, (May, 1829) we," that is Joseph Smith and Oliver Cowdery, "on a certain day, went into the woods to pray and inquire of the Lord respecting baptism for the remission of sins, as we found mentioned in the translation of the plates. While we were thus employed, praying, and calling upon the Lord, a messenger from heaven descended in a cloud of light, and having laid his hands upon us, he ordained us, saying unto us, 'Upon you, my, fellow servants, in the name of Messiah, I confer the Priesthood of Aaron, which holds the keys of the ministering of angels and of the gospel of repentance, and of baptism by immersion for the remission of sins, and this shall never be taken again from the earth, until the sons of Levi do offer again an offering unto the Lord in righteousness.' He said this Aaronic Priesthood had not the power of laying on of hands for the gift of the Holy Ghost, but that this should be conferred on us hereafter; and he commanded us to go and be baptized, and gave us directions, that I should baptize Oliver Cowdery, and that afterwards he should baptize me.

"Accordingly we went and were baptized: I baptized him first, and afterwards he baptized me: after which I laid my hands upon his head and ordained him to the Aaronic Priesthood, and afterwards he laid his hands upon me, and ordained me to the same Priesthood, for so were we commanded.

"The messenger who visited us on this occasion, and conferred this Priesthood upon us, said that his name was John, the same that is called John the Baptist in the New Testament, and that he acted under the direction of Peter, James and John, who held the keys of the Priesthood of Melchisedec, which Priesthood, he said, should in due time be conferred on us, and that I should be called the first Elder and he the second. It was on the fifteenth day of May, eighteen hundred and twenty-nine, that we were baptized, and ordained under the hand of the messenger.

"Immediately upon our coming up out of the water after we had been baptized, we experienced great and glorious blessings from our Heavenly Father. No sooner had I baptized Oliver Cowdery than the Holy Ghost fell upon him and he stood up and prophesied many things, which should shortly come to pass. And, again, so soon as I had been baptized by him, I also had the spirit of prophecy; when, standing up, I prophesied concerning the rise of the Church, and many other things connected with the Church, and this generation of the children of men. We were filled with the Holy Ghost, and rejoiced in the God of our salvation. Our minds being now enlightened, we began to have the scriptures laid open to our understandings, and the true meaning of their more mysterious passages revealed unto us, in a manner which we never could attain to previously, nor ever before had thought of."*

29.—We consider the restoration of the Aaronic Priesthood to be among some of the most important events of the last dispensation. The existence of this Priesthood in the last days is clearly predicted in ancient scripture. But as this Priesthood has not authority to administer the laying on of hands for the gift of the Holy Ghost, it may be further asked, how was the authority still further restored, namely, the apostleship, which holds the authority of the Melchisedec Priesthood? We answer, that Peter, James and John appeared as ministering angels, and conferred the apostleship upon Joseph Smith and others; after which they were authorized to confirm the Church by the laying on of hands. Thus it will be seen, that the authority of the apostles of this Church of Christ was not derived through a succession of popes and bishops in the apostate church of Rome, but it was restored direct from heaven by those who hold the keys thereof.

30.—It will be perceived from the above extract, that after John the Baptist had laid his hands upon Joseph Smith and Oliver Cowdery, and ordained them, that he commanded them to baptize each other, and then ordain each other. It may be asked, why it became necessary for them to ordain each other, when they had already received an ordination under the hands of the angel? We answer, that in the Church of God ordination always follows baptism instead of preceding it. And as they had not been baptized when the angel ordained them, it was necessary that they should be ordained after baptism, in order that they might exhibit a perfect pattern for all future ordinations. If they had not been commanded to do this, the servants of God at a subsequent period might have ventured to ordain others before baptism; and as an excuse for so doing, they would have argued that Joseph Smith and Oliver Cowdery were ordained before baptism. Hence we can see the wisdom of God in giving, at the first start, a perfect pattern, by commanding them to receive a reordination after baptism;

---

*———History of Joseph Smith, Millennial Star, Vol. iii. No. 9., p 148.

thus showing that the Priesthood, after the Church was once organized, was never to be conferred upon any unbaptized person.

31.—John the Baptist it seems was the last person who held the keys of the Aaronic Priesthood, and, therefore, he would be a suitable person to restore that Priesthood once more to the earth. In order that John might be qualified to fulfill all the duties of his mission as the Lord's messenger, God raised him with many others from the dead after the resurrection of Christ.\* It is also well known that those who die holding the Priesthood will retain the Priesthood in the future life, and will be priests after the resurrection. † John, therefore, having received an immortal body of flesh and bones, and holding the Aaronic Priesthood with the keys and power thereof, has come forth from heaven as the Lord's messenger, to restore the Priesthood to the sons of men—to prepare the way before the Lord when He shall suddenly come to His temple.

32.—That John the Baptist's mission did not close with his martyrdom is evident from the testimony of both Isaiah and Malachi. Both of these prophets have spoken of John, and of the mission which he should perform, and the great events connected with it. Isaiah says, "Comfort ye, comfort ye my people, saith your God. Speak ye comfortably to Jerusalem, and cry unto her, that her warfare is accomplished, that her iniquity is pardoned; for she hath received of the Lord's hand double for all her sins. The voice of him that crieth in the wilderness, prepare ye the way of the Lord, make straight in the desert a highway for our God. Every valley shall be exalted and every mountain and hill shall be made low: and the crooked shall be made straight, and the rough places plain and the glory of the Lord shall be revealed and all flesh shall see it together: for the mouth of the Lord hath spoken it." ‡ This prophecy is applied by the evangelists to John. § He

---

\*———See Matthew xxvii. 52, 53.

†———Revelations v. 9, 10; also xx. 6.

‡———Isaiah xl. 1-5.

§———Luke iii. 4, 5, 6. John i. 23.

was sent forth as a prophet to prepare the way before the Highest at His first coming, and His voice was heard in the wilderness to that effect; but that was only one part of His great mission, for nearly the whole of the above prophecy remains yet to be fulfilled. John's message to Jerusalem was not a proclamation such as above quoted; he did not declare to her that "her warfare is accomplished, that her iniquity is pardoned; he did not testify to Jerusalem that she had already "received of the Lord's hand double for all her sins." No, the time had not come for such comforting language to be sounded in the ears of the Jews; a long dispersion and captivity awaited them—distress and trouble for many generations because of their sins. . Moreover the mission of John was to prepare the way of the Lord, not merely for His first coming, but for that coming when "Every valley shall be exalted, and every mountain and hill shall be made low;" when "the crooked shall be made straight, and the rough places plain." The preparation for the Lord's first coming did not accomplish this; the preparation for His second coming will accomplish it. That the above prophecy had reference to the great and terrible day of the Lord, when He should appear in His glory, is clearly expressed in the above quotation: "And the glory of the Lord shall be revealed, and all flesh shall see it together." At His first coming all flesh did not see His glory: at His second coming every eye will see Him in His glory. John the Baptist, then, being "the voice of one crying in the wilderness," will act a conspicuous part in the great preparatory dispensation for the second coming of the Lord—that glorious dispensation when a message of comfort shall be sent to the dispersed afflicted Jews; when it shall be said to Jerusalem, that her iniquity is pardoned, etc. The greatness and glory of his mission extended to a period when the mountains, hills, valleys, and rough places were to feel the power of God—when a highway was to be prepared in the desert for our God—when all flesh together was to behold His glory. For this purpose he was sent from heaven in these latter times, clothed with glory and power, holding the keys of a preparatory Priesthood for the revelation of Jesus Christ, accompanied by all the powers of heaven.

33.—The Lord by the prophet Malachi says, "Behold, I will send my messenger, and he shall prepare the way before me: and the Lord whom ye seek shall suddenly come to His temple, even the messenger of the covenant whom ye delight in: behold he shall come saith the Lord of Hosts. But who may abide the day of His coming? and who shall stand when He appeareth? For He is like a refiner's fire, and like fuller's soap; and He shall sit as a refiner and purifier of silver; and He shall purify the sons of Levi, and purge them as gold and silver, that they may offer unto the Lord an offering in righteousness. Then shall the offering of Judah and Jerusalem be pleasant unto the Lord, as in the days of old, and as in former years."* The Savior applies this prediction concerning the messenger to John the Baptist.† Although John the Baptist is the messenger, yet the great preparatory work which he was to perform was only accomplished in part during his first mission. The preparatory work ascribed to the messenger was to precede the great and glorious second coming. After the messenger should prepare the way, then the Lord should suddenly come to His temple. That this had reference to His glorious appearing in flaming fire is evident from the questions asked, "But who may abide the day of His coming? And who shall stand when He appeareth?" When Christ first came He did not suddenly come to His temple—He did not come in such power and glory that the wicked could not abide His coming—He did not consume the wicked so that they could not stand before His appearing. Therefore, John the Baptist did not, in preparing the way for His first coming, complete his mission. He must, in order to fulfill the prophecy, make preparations for His second coming also; and in order to do this, the Priesthood which he held must be restored to the earth. This is evident from the fact that the sons of Levi are to be purged "as gold and silver, that they may offer unto the Lord an offering in righteousness. Then shall the offering of Judah and Jerusalem be pleasant unto the Lord, as in the days of old, and as in former years." When John filled

---

*——Malachi iii. 1, 2, 3, 4.
†——Luke vii. 27.

his first mission the sons of Levi were not purged; they did not offer unto the Lord an offering in righteousness; the offerings of that Priesthood were not pleasant unto the Lord. But when He suddenly comes to His temple, as mentioned by Ezekiel, (*xliii.* 2, 4, 5, 6, 7,) then all these things will be fulfilled; but before that day the Priesthood of Levi or of Aaron must be restored to the earth. John the Baptist, who holds that Priesthood, is the legal and proper messenger to restore it, and thus he will fulfill and accomplish the great preparatory work assigned him in relation to the second coming of the Lord.

34.—This messenger, John the Baptist, has already been sent; he descended in a cloud of light and glory; he conferred the Priesthood by his own hands upon the heads of Joseph Smith and Oliver Cowdery; and thus, after so many generations have passed away in darkness, the sons of men are once more blessed with the privilege of being baptized by men holding authority. God requires all nations, kindreds, tongues and people to repent and be baptized by the authority which He has restored to the earth through the ministry of holy angels, and if they will not do this, "they shall be damned," saith the Lord, "and shall not come into my Father's kingdom where my Father and I am."

35.—The Lord having raised up these chosen witnesses, having conferred upon them the Priesthood, and having poured out the Holy Ghost upon them, sent them forth to bear testimony. Many believed their testimony, repented and were immersed in water for the remission of their sins, and were filled with great joy. And on the sixth of April, A. D. 1830, the Church of Jesus Christ of Latter-day Saints was organized, according to the commandments of God, at the house of Mr. Whitmer, in Fayette, Seneca county, state of New York, North America. Thus was the Church of Christ once more restored to the earth, holding the keys of authority and power to bind, to loose, and to seal on the earth and in heaven, according to the commandments of God and the revelations of Jesus Christ. Yea, thus saith the Lord, this Church is "the only true and living Church upon the face of the whole earth, with which I, the Lord, am well pleased, speaking unto the Church collectively and not individually; for I, the Lord, cannot look upon sin with the least degree of allowance."* All other churches are unauthorized of God. Their "articles of religion", their creeds, their prayer books, their ordinations, their sacraments, their baptisms, their various forms of worship, their preaching and their religious assemblies are all, an abomination in the sight of heaven. There is no remission of sins, nor gifts of the Holy Ghost, nor legality of Priesthood, nor authorized ministrations, nor glory, nor salvation among them. There is no vision, nor revelation, nor angel, nor heavenly powers, nor prophet, nor revelator, nor inspiration, nor voice of God, nor any other communication from the heavenly worlds unto them. The powers of heaven and the knowledge of the true God are not known among them. This is the condition of every church throughout all Christendom: they form no part of the Church of Christ, nor of the kingdom of God. O what great reason have this generation to be thankful that God has had pity upon them in their dark, benighted and apostate condition—that He has sent His angels with a message of glad tidings—that He has set up His kingdom again on the earth, that salvation may once more be obtained by the fallen sons and daughters of men!

36.—Having demonstrated the divine authenticity of the Book of Mormon, by the testimony of four witnesses in its origin among this generation, let us next inquire whether in the progress of the work, God has raised up any other witnesses of this great and glorious book. On the eleventh day of April, in the same year that the Church was organized, Oliver Cowdery preached the first public discourse at the house of Mr. Whitmer. The same day, thirteen were baptized. In order that the reader may have some little understanding of the power of the spirit that was poured out, and the testimonies given in confirmation of this work, we make the following extract from the history of Joseph Smith.

37.—"During this month of April, I (Joseph Smith) went on a visit to the residence of Mr. Joseph Knight, of Colesville, Broom county, New York, with whom and his family I

---

*———Doctrine and Covenants, Sec. i. par. 5.

had been previously acquainted, and of whose name I have mentioned as having been so kind and thoughtful towards us while translating the Book of Mormon. Mr Knight and his family were Universalists, but were willing to reason with me upon my religious views, and were as usual, friendly and hospitable. We held several meetings in the neighborhood; we had many friends and some enemies. Our meetings were well attended and many began to pray fervently to Almighty God, that He would give them wisdom to understand the truth. Among those who attended our meetings regularly was Newe Knight, son of Joseph Knight. He and I had many serious conversations on the important subject of man's eternal salvation; we had got into the habit of praying much at our meetings and Newel had said that he would try and take up his cross and pray vocally during meeting; but when we again met together, he rather excused himself. I tried to prevail upon him, making use of the figure, supposing that he should get into a mudhole, would he not try to help himself out? And that we were willing now to help him out of the mudhole. He replied, that providing he had got into a mudhole through carelessness, he would rather wait and get out himself than have others to help him and, so he would wait until he should get into the woods by himself and there he would pray. Accordingly he deferred praying until next morning, when he retired into the woods, where, according to his own account afterwards, he made several attempts to pray but could scarcely do so, feeling that he had not done his duty, but that he should have prayed in the presence of others. He began to feel uneasy, and continued to feel worse. both in mind and body, until upon reaching his own house, his appearance was such as to alarm his wife very much. He requested her to go and bring me to him. I went and found him suffering very much in his mind, and his body acted upon in a very strange manner. His visage and limbs distorted and twisted in every shape and appearance possible to imagine, and finally, he was caught up off the floor of the apartment and tossed about most fearfully. His situation was soon made known to his neighbors and relatives, and in a short time as many as eight or nine grown persons had got together to witness the scene.

After he had thus suffered for a time, I succeeded in getting hold of him by the hand, when almost immediately he spoke to me, and with very great earnestness requested of me that I should cast the devil out of him, saying that he knew that he was in him, and that he also knew that I could cast him out. I replied, 'If you know that I can, it shall be done,' and then almost unconsciously I rebuked the devil, and commanded him in the name of Jesus Christ to depart from him, when immediately Newel spoke out and said that he saw the devil leave him and vanish from his sight. This was the first miracle which was done in this Church or by any member of it, and it was done not by man nor by the power of man, but it was done by God, and by the power of godliness: therefore let the honor and the praise, the dominion and the glory, be ascribed to the Father, Son and Holy Spirit, for ever and ever. Amen.

"The scene was now entirely changed, for as soon as the devil had departed from our friend, his countenance became natural, his distortions of body ceased, and almost immediately the spirit of the Lord descended upon him, and the visions of eternity were opened to his view. He afterwards related his experience as follows:—'I now began to feel the most pleasing sensation resting upon me and immediately the visions of heaven were opened to my view. I felt myself attracted upward, remained for some time enwrapt in contemplation, insomuch that I knew not what was going on in the room. By and by I felt some weight pressing upon my shoulder and the side of my head, which served to recall me to a sense of my situation and I found that the spirit of the Lord had actually caught me up off the floor, and that my shoulder and head were pressing against the beams.

"All this was witnessed by many, to their great astonishment and satisfaction when they saw the devil thus cast out, and the power of God and His Holy Spirit thus made manifest. So soon as consciousness returned, his bodily weakness was such that we were obliged to lay him upon his bed and wait upon him for some time. As may be expected, such a scene as this contributed much to make believers of those who witnessed it; and finally the greater part of them became members of the Church.

"Soon after this occurrence, I returned to Fayette, Seneca county.

"During the last week in May, the before-mentioned Newel Knight came to visit us at Fayette, and was baptized by David Whitmer.

"On the first day of June, 1830 we held our first conference as an organized Church. Our numbers were about thirty, besides whom many assembled with us, who were either believers or anxious to learn.

"Having opened by singing and prayer, we partook togethe of the emblems of the body and blood of our Lord Jesus Christ; we then proceeded to confirm several who had lately been baptized, after which we called out and ordained several to the various offices of the Priesthood. Much exhortation and instruction were given, and the Holy Ghost was poured out upon us in a miraculous manner—many of our number prophesied, while others had the heavens opened to their view, and were so overcome that we had to lay them on beds or other convenient places, among the rest was Brother Newel Knight, who had to be placed on a bed, being unable to help himself. By his own account of the transaction, he could not understand why we should lay him on the bed, as he felt no sensibility of weakness. He felt his heart filled with love, with glory and pleasure unspeakable, and could discern all that was going on in the room; when, all of a sudden, a vision of futurity burst upon him. He saw there represented the great work, which through my instrumentality was yet to be accomplished. He saw heaven opened, and beheld the Lord Jesus Christ seated on the right hand of the Majesty on high, and had it made plain to his understanding that the time would come when He would be admitted into His presence to enjoy his society for ever and ever. When their bodily strength was restored to these brethren, they shouted 'Ho sannah to God and the Lamb, and rehearsed the glorious things which they had seen and felt, while they were yet in the spirit." *

38.—It will be seen by the foregoing extract, that after the organization of the Church, the Lord raised up other witnesses

---

*———History of Joseph Smith, Millennial Star, Vol. iv. No. 8. page 116.

to His work. The great miracle that was wrought upon Newel Knight, and that, too, before he became a member of the Church, and in the presence of some eight or nine of his neighbors, must have given him the most perfect knowledge of the truth of the Book of Mormon; and it must also have been a convincing testimony to all who saw him; they must have seen the difference between the operation of the two powers; for both powers handled him in a most miraculous manner. Under the operation of the first, he was in the most excruciating pain: but the devil being cast out in the name of Jesus Christ, he was immediately filled with the Holy Spirit and with joy unspeakable, and was taken up by the Spirit from off the floor, and was suspended in the presence of the by-standers for some time with his head pressing against the upper floor. This great manifestation of the power of God in contrast with the power of the evil one, must have given a knowledge to those who were present, that Joseph Smith was a great Prophet and Seer, and that the Book of Mormon was a divine revelation. For the satisfaction of the reader, I will here state that I am intimately acquainted with Newel Knight, and have heard him testify many a time to this great miracle. I also, in the year 1830, visited Mr. Knight's residence in Colesville, and heard not only him, but others who saw this miracle, bear their testimony. Mr. Knight ever proved a faithful member of this Church until, after wading through many scenes of bloody persecution, he was worn out, and quietly fell asleep in Jesus. It will also be seen from the foregoing extract, that at the first conference held by this Church, on the 1st of June, 1830, that many others saw the heavens opened and beheld the glory of God. Among the number was Newel Knight. "HE SAW HEAVEN OPENED, AND BEHELD THE LORD JESUS CHRIST, SEATED AT THE RIGHT HAND OF THE MAJESTY ON HIGH." This was not a dream, but a vision, like the vision of Stephen, who on the day of his martyrdom had a similar view.

39.—Hence, after the rise of the Church, the witnesses of the truth of the Book of Mormon began to multiply. Now these persons who saw the heavens open, could not themselves have been deceived. They must be either wicked impostors, or the Book of Mormon must be a divine record; for God would not open the heavens to confirm a soul-destroying imposition. Can any man prove that Newel Knight did not have a great miracle wrought upon him? Can any one show that he was not caught up by the Spirit and suspended in the air? Can any one bring any testimony that the eight or nine witnesses, who were at that time out of the Church, did not see this miracle as testified? · Can it be proved that those who testify that they saw heaven opened are false witnesses, and that they did not see any such thing? All this must be proved or else no man living can be justified in saying that the Book of Mormon is an imposition.

40.—In the Fall of 1830, four of the Elders were sent on a mission to the extreme western frontiers of the United States, a distance of some twelve or fourteen hundred miles. Having proceeded about four hundred miles, they tarried a few weeks and preached in the northern part of the state of Ohio, many believed and were baptized, among whom was Sidney Rigdon, a celebrated preacher of the Campbellite order. The Spirit of the Lord was again poured out in a most wonderful manner, and the visions of heaven were opened unto many. In December following, Mr. Rigdon performed a journey to the state of New York, for the purpose of seeing Joseph Smith, the prophet. He prolonged his stay with him until the latter part of January, when he returned, accompanied by Mr. Smith and his family. The Prophet Joseph, by the command of God, and through the gift and power of the Holy Ghost, translated the Old and New Testaments. Sidney Rigdon assisted him as a scribe to write from his mouth, as it was given by the revelations of the Holy Spirit. And on the sixteenth day of February, in the year of our Lord eighteen hundred and thirty-two, while engaged in the work of translation, a most remarkable vision was shown to Joseph Smith and Sidney Rigdon. They both at the same time saw the heavens opened, and beheld the Lord Jesus Christ on the right hand of God, they were filled with the Holy Ghost, and the glory of the Lord shone round about them: they heard the voice of God the Father bearing record to them of His Only Begotten Son: they saw the holy angels, and the wonders of eternity were opened before them: they saw and heard many things unspeakable and unlawful to be uttered. But many great and marvelous things they were commanded to write, while they were yet in the Spirit. We here insert the following item:

41.—"We beheld the glory of the Son on the right hand of the Father, and received of His fullness; and saw the holy angels, and they who are sanctified before His throne, worshiping God and the Lamb, who worship Him for ever and ever. And now, after the many testimonies which have been given of Him, this is the testimony, last of all which we give of Him, that He lives; for we saw Him even on the right hand of God, and we heard the voice, bearing record that He is the Only Begotten of the Father—that by Him, and through Him, and of Him the worlds are and were created, and the inhabitants thereof are begotten sons and daughters unto God." *

42.—To speak of the hundreds and thousands of witnesses whom God has raised up during the last fifty years, would require a large volume, and far exceed the limits which we intended for this series. Let it suffice to observe that there are now on the earth many thousands of witnesses to whom God has revealed the truth of the Book of Mormon, by heavenly visions, by angels, by the revelations of the Holy Ghost, by His own voice, and by the miraculous gifts and powers of His kingdom. This great cloud of witnesses know with the greatest certainty that the Book of Mormon is true: they know it with as much certainty as the ancient apostles and prophets knew their respective messages to be true. The nature of their testimony is such that it precludes all possibility of their being deceived themselves. Before mankind can be justified in calling these thousands of witnesses impostors, they must prove that none of them have seen and heard as they boldly testify. This generation have more than one thousand times the amount of evidence to demonstrate and forever establish the divine authenticity of the Book of Mormon than they have in favor of the Bible. And this vast amount of evidence, not only establishes the Book of Mormon, but the Bible also, as it existed in its original. Hence, the

---

\*——Doctrine and Covenants, Sec. xcii., par. 3.

Latter-day Saints have more than one thousand times the amount of evidence to establish both the Book of Mormon and Bible than what this generation have to establish the truth of either, exclusive of our testimony.

---

## CHAPTER V.

### THE BOOK OF MORMON CONFIRMED BY MIRACLES.

1.—In the last chapter of this series, we showed that in the origin of this work, the Lord confirmed the truth of the Book of Mormon unto many witnesses in such a way, and by such means, that it was impossible for them to have been deceived; that the testimony of these witnesses stands good until it can be refuted; that no man can be justified in rejecting this testimony until he can show that it is false; that it can only be proved false in two ways, first, by showing directly that these witnesses did not see and hear as they testify; second, by showing that there is something connected with the nature of the message of which they testify, that is unreasonable, unscriptural, improbable or contrary to some known truth. Now, no one has ever attempted to bring any direct negative testimony; this, indeed, would be impossible, unless the witnesses themselves should deny their former testimony, and this they have not done. And those who have attempted to condemn their testimony from the nature of the message itself, have only exhibited their own weakness and folly. Upwards of fifty years have passed away, and no man has, as yet, been found able to prove the Book of Mormon or the testimony of its witnesses false.

2.—We will now speak of the testimony of miracles. God has wrought many great and glorious miracles by the hands of His servants in confirmation of the Book of Mormon. We humbly speak of these things, not in a boasting spirit, for we can do nothing of ourselves; but it is the Lord who has in His infinite mercy, performed many great and mighty works among this generation, through those who have believed on His name. There are two kinds of miracles, first, those wrought by the power of God; and, second, those wrought by the power of the devil. When Moses was sent with a message to the Egyptians, the Lord wrought miracles by his hand. The magicians also, at the same time, wrought miracles. When Moses cast his rod upon the ground, it became a serpent; the magicians cast their rods upon the ground and they also became serpents. Moses turned the waters into blood; the magicians did the same. Moses brought frogs in great multitude; the magicians performed the same. The miracles performed by Moses were done by the power of God; those performed by the magicians were done by the power of the devil. Some miracles performed by Moses, the magicians were not permitted to perform; but as far as the Lord suffered them to do miracles, they did precisely the same things that Moses did. The witch of Endor performed a great miracle, in bringing up Samuel from the dead, by the request of Saul, king of Israel. If this woman was possessed of an evil spirit, then we are forced to admit that the devil has great power, for she was enabled through the supernatural power by which she was influenced to detect Saul, notwithstanding he came to her in disguise. That she actually did bring up Samuel is evident from the conversation which passed between Saul and Samuel; moreover, Samuel prophesied to Saul, concerning what should befall him and all Israel; and the next day the prediction was literally fulfilled.\* It seems that the Prophet Samuel was rather displeased at being disturbed from his quiet resting place; for after the king of Israel had bowed before him, "Samuel said to Saul, why hast thou disquieted me, to bring me up?"

3.—As a further evidence that the devil can work miracles, Jesus says, "There shall arise false Christs, and false prophets, and shall show great signs and wonders; insomuch that, if it were possible, they shall deceive the very elect." † As another example of the miraculous power of the devil, we are informed that the man who possessed a legion, had been often bound

---
\*——I. Sam. xxviii.
†——Matt. xxiv 24.

with fetters and chains, and the chains had been plucked asunder by him, and the fetters broken in pieces." * The miracle of breaking chains and fetters is equal to the miracle wrought by Samson in breaking new withes and new ropes.† Jesus says, "Many will say to me in that day, Lord, Lord, have we not prophesied in Thy name? and in Thy name have cast out devils? and in Thy name done many wonderful works? And then will I profess unto them, I never knew you depart from me, ye that work iniquity." From the preceding verses, taken in connection with this, we learn, that false prophets and such as should say Lord, Lord, and do not His will, but work iniquity, were to perform wonderful works, and make great pretensions, not only before men, but before the Lord. The devil, therefore, assists those who work wickedness to perform great signs and wonderful works. If the present translation of the Bible be true, he has power to show visions, for it is said, that he showed our Savior "all the kingdoms of the world," and it is also said, that "Satan himself is transformed into an angel of light."

4. —John predicts that a certain power should arise, that should do "great wonders, so that he maketh fire come down from heaven on the earth, in the sight of men, and deceiveth them that dwell on the earth, by the means of those miracles which he had power to do in the sight of the beast." ‡ Immediately before the second coming of Christ, there is to be a general gathering of the nations against the Jews at Jerusalem: these nations will gather into the valley of Armageddon near Jerusalem, after which the Lord will destroy them. This great movement of all nations against the Jews, will be set in operation by the means of wicked miracles. John speaks of it thus: "And I saw three unclean spirits, like frogs, come out of the mouth of the dragon, and out of the mouth of the beast, and out of the mouth of the false prophet. For they are the spirits of devils, working miracles, which go forth unto the kings of the earth, and of the whole world, to gather them to the battle of

---

\*——Mark v 4.
†——Judges xvi 9-12.
‡——Matthew, vii 22, 23.
§——Rev. xiii. 13, 14.

that great day of God Almighty. Behold I come as a thief. Blessed is he that watcheth and keepeth his garments, lest he walk naked, and they see his shame. And He gathered them together unto a place called in the Hebrew tongue Armageddon."* The reason the Lord will suffer the devil to work miracles to deceive "the kings of the earth and of the whole world," is because they will previously have rejected "the everlasting gospel;" therefore the devil will deceive them, and lead them on to destruction, as he did the Egyptians. This same power is prophesied of by Paul, as follows: "And then shall that wicked be revealed, whom the Lord shall consume with the spirit of His mouth, and shall destroy with the brightness of His coming; even him whose coming is after the working of Satan, with all power, and signs, and lying wonders, and with all decciveableness of unrighteousnss in them that perish; because they received not the love of the truth, that they might be saved. And for this cause God shall send them strong delusion, that they should believe a lie, that they all might be damned who believed not the truth, but had pleasure in unrighteousness." †

5.—If the foregoing quotations be correct, we see that the devil has power to create serpents and frogs, and turn rivers of water into blood—that he has power to reveal strangers who may come in disguise, and raise up a dead prophet to converse with men here on the earth—that he has power to break chains and fetters—to transform himself into an angel of light—to show all the kingdoms of the world unto Christ—to perform great signs and wonders, and call fire down from heaven—and finally, his power is to be so wonderfully manifested, that even "the kings of the earth and the whole world" will suffer themselves to be deceived by his miracles, and be blindly led to the valley of Slaughter, where they will be consumed by the brightness of Christ's coming. All of these things the devil has done, and will do, if the English translation of the Bible be correct.

6.—It may be asked, how are we to distinguish between the miracles wrought by the power of God, and those wrought by

\*——Rev. xvi. 13-16.
†——II. Thess. ii. 8-12.

the power of Satan? We answer in the language of Paul, "he that is spiritual judgeth all things." But as the greater part of the world are not spiritual, we will point out other rules by which to distinguish the two powers. Wherever miracles are wrought by the power of God, *there* will be found a true and righteous doctrine, unmixed with error: wherever miracles are wrought by the power of the devil, *there* will be found more or less false doctrine. Wherever miracles are wrought by the servants of God, they will do them in the name of Jesus Christ, after having obeyed the ordinances of the gospel: when the servants of the devil do miracles, if they pretend to do them in the name of Christ, it will be found by examination that they have not obeyed the ordinances of Christ, and therefore he suffers the devil to deceive them; but it is oftener the case that they do not perform them in the name of Christ, neither in the way that He has appointed, as in the case of mesmerism, clairvoyance, etc. Those who do miracles by the power of God, generally have a message to publish to the people by authority from God. The most of those who do miracles by the power of the devil, pretend to no message whatever; or if they pretend to have a message to deliver to the people, it will be found, on inspection, to be mixed with error.

7.—Although the devil can work great and wonderful miracles, yet there is always something in connection with them that will enable mankind, if they are sufficiently humble, to discern that they are not of God. If it were impossible to distinguish between the two powers, then miraculous evidence would be no evidence at all in favor of divine revelation: but miracles were considered by our Savior as evidence of His own mission—hence, He says, "I have greater witness than that of John; for the work, which the Father hath given me to finish, the same works that I do bear witness of me that the Father hath sent me. And the Father Himself which hath sent me, hath borne witness of me." *

Again, Jesus said, "If I do not the works of my Father, believe me not; but if I do, though ye believe not me, believe the works, that ye may know and believe that the Father is in

---

*——John v. 36, 37.

me, and I in Him." Elsewhere He said to Philip, "Believe me for the very works' sake." And in another place He said, "If I had not done among them the works which none other man did, they had not had sin." *

8.—From all these sayings, and many others of a similar nature, we learn that miracles are considered an evidence in favor of the revealed truths of heaven, and therefore, there must be a wide difference between the manifestations of the two powers: this difference is so great, that no person can be justified in judging wrongfully in the matter: he that imputes a miracle of evil to God, or a miracle wrought by the power of the Holy Ghost to the devil, commits a sin that will not be easily forgiven. Isaiah says, "Woe unto them that call evil good, and good evil; that put darkness for light, and light for darkness." † When the Pharisees accused Jesus of working miracles by Beelzebub, he immediately tells them that the blasphemies against the Holy Ghost should not be forgiven. ‡ If miracles were not intended to convince men of the truth, Jesus never would have upbraided "the cities wherein most of His mighty works were done, because they repented not." But He pronounced a heavy woe upon Chorazin, Bethsaida, and Capernaum, because they had rejected the mighty works which He had done in them, and said, that it should be more tolerable for Tyre, Sidon, and the land of Sodom, "in the day of judgment than for them." § All these examples afford ample evidence that the two supernatural powers can be distinguished from each other with the most unerring certainty.

9.—Miracles, when taken alone, are no evidence whatever of the divine mission of any one; but when taken in connection with a pure, holy and infallible doctrine, they are evidences of the strongest kind, and, if rejected, will bring the generation among whom they are wrought under the greatest condemnation. Many prophets have been sent with a divine revelation to man, who have never wrought any miracles confirmatory of their mission, and yet the people were condemned for rejecting

---

\* ——John x. 37; 38.—xiv 11.—xv 24
† ——Isaiah v 20
‡ ——Mark iii. 22-30.
§ ——Matthew xi. 20-21.

their testimony. The Prophet Noah came prophesying of one of the most universal judgments which ever befel the human race, and the whole world were condemned for rejecting his prophecy; and yet, we have no account of his performing any miracles. Lot was sent to warn his kinsmen in Sodom of the terrible judgment about to be poured upon the city; the people were condemned for not listening to him, and yet we do not read that he performed any miracles. Isaiah and Jeremiah came with a divine mission to Israel, but we have no account of their performing any miracles until quite a number of years had elapsed from the beginning of their mission; yet, Israel were condemned for not receiving their revelations. Ezekiel did not, at first, confirm his mission by miracles. Zechariah, Malachi, and many others, did not, so far as we are acquainted, establish the divine authenticity of their books by miracles. Jonah, when sent to the great city of Nineveh, wrought no miracles, so far as history specifies, that were visible to the people of that city; yet, they received his message as divine, and repented because of his preaching. One of the greatest prophets that was ever born of a woman did no miracles to prove his divine mission. The scripture says expressly that "JOHN DID NO MIRACLE;" * and yet, the Scribes and Pharisees rejected the council of God against their own souls in rejecting John's mission.

10.—If God has, from time to time, sent prophets among men without confirming their mission by miracles, and has condemned the people or generation to whom they were sent, because they would not receive their testimony; how much more will he condemn a people or generation to whom He sends a message, confirmed by miracles? If Sodom and Gomorrha were condemned for rejecting a divine message without miracles, how much greater will be the condemnation of that people who reject the still greater testimony of miracles?

11.—From the foregoing we learn, that a prophet may be a true prophet, and yet perform no miracles; and therefore, those who have the wicked presumption to say that they will

---

†——John x. 4.

not believe in any new revelation, unless God shall confirm it by miracles, are taking a very sinful, dangerous ground; for if such wicked characters had lived at the time when God sent messages, unconfirmed by miracles, they certainly would have rejected them. We are persuaded that no person who has read the scriptures, and who has the fear of God before his eyes, would ever dare to say he would reject everything under the name of new revelation, unless God would establish it by miracles.

12.—The Lord always accompanies His word, when revealed, with sufficient testimony to prove its divine authenticity, though He does not always give the same amount of evidence. He judges man according to the testimonies which He gives; where much is given, much will be required; where but little is given, but little is required; where nothing is given, nothing is required.

13.—As we have already stated, the Lord, in His great mercy, has condescended to give miraculous evidence to establish the divine authenticity of that great and glorious revelation—the Book of Mormon. Therefore the Book of Mormon is established by far greater testimonies than many books of the Bible, which were not confirmed to the generation in which they were revealed by miraculous evidence. It is useless for our enemies to say that there have been no miracles wrought confirmatory of the Book of Mormon, when there are tens of thousands of people who can and do bear testimony as eye witnesses to the contrary. We have already related, in the last chapter of this series, the first miracle that was wrought in this Church. Out of the many thousands that have since been performed, we humbly mention the following, as published in the *Millennial Star*

14.—"A GREAT MIRACLE: NARRATIVE OF REUBEN BRINKWORTH.

"On the 2nd of July, 1839, I entered on board the *Terror*, Commodore Sir J. Franklin, being then about to set out on a voyage of discovery for a north-west passage to India. Upon returning to England, we landed at Bermuda on the 16th of July, 1843, and in the afternoon the same day a terrible thunder-storm occurred, in which I was suddenly deprived of my hearing and speech. At the same time five of my comrades, viz., John Ennis, William Collins, John Rogers, Richard King and William Simms were summoned into eternity. I remained insensible for fifteen days—perfectly unconscious of all that was passing around me; but upon the return of reason, came the dreadful conviction that I was deprived of two of my faculties. I well remember the period, and shall for ever continue to do so—language cannot describe the awful sensations that pervaded my mind when I became fully sensible of the reality of my condition. I will here remark that the subject of religion had never troubled my mind; nor did the calamity I was called to suffer awaken any feeling akin to it; nevertheless I felt a certain feeling of gratitude that I had not met with the same fate as my more unfortunate companions; yet I must, to my shame, confess that it was not directed to the Great Disposer of all events, who could have taken my life as those of my companions, had He willed it.—But it was not His design. I was spared, and am now a living witness of His loving-kindness to the most abandoned sinners, if they will turn and seek His face. At that time I was about ninteen years old. After remaining at Bermuda for about three weeks, we again set sail for England, and reached Chatham on the 14th of December. I remained there only fourteen days, after which I went to London, and by the kind assistance of some gentlemen, entered the deaf and dumb school in Old Kent Road, where I remained for ten weeks, but not liking the confinement, and being from home, I became dissatified and unhappy, and resolved to leave it, and accordingly did so. I then went to George Lock's, Oxford Arms, Silver Street, Reading, with whom I lived eighteen months, supporting myself the whole of that period upon the wages I earned on board the *Terror*. I afterwards went to Rugby, not to remain there, but on the way to my mother at Stroud, Gloucestershire.

"I will here relate a circumstance of cruelty of which I was made the sufferer· being thirsty, I stepped into a public house to get something to drink; there were gentlemen in the parlor, who, seeing that I was dumb, motioned me to them, and put many questions in writing, which I answered in the same manner. While I was thus being questioned, one of the men went out and brought in a policeman, who hauled me away to the lock-up, in which place I was kept all that night, the next day and following night, and on the morning of the second day, I was taken before a magistrate, who ordered me to be taken to a doctor, where I underwent an operation, namely, having my tongue cut in two places: he became satisfied that I was both deaf and dumb, and then I was discharged. From the treatment I had received I was determined to go to another of the magistrates of that town, to whom I related by writing what had transpired. He said very little to me, more than that he would write to London respecting it, and I have since heard from a gentleman, that the magistrate who examined me has been removed from his office. I then continued my journey to Stroud, which I reached without any other inconvenience, and remained there two days. I then went to Newport, Monmouthshire, and occupied my time in teaching the deaf and dumb alphabet for about three years, at the end of which I became acquainted with the Latter-day Saints. At that time I was lodging at a public house, kept by James Durbin, sign of the "Golden Lion," Pentonville. One of the customers of this house became acquainted with me and prevailed upon me to go to live with him and his brother, who was a member of the Latter-day Saints' Church. There I first became acquainted with the doctrines taught by this people by reading and by the means of the finger-alphabet. I continued to investigate them for about three months, when I felt convinced of the truth of those doctrines which have since become so beneficial to my temporal and eternal welfare. On the 22nd of September I had been, by means of the deaf and dumb alphabet, conversing freely with some of the Saints, and had fully determined to be baptized that evening; therefore I expressed my desire to receive the ordinance of baptism, and was taken to the canal early on the morning of the 23rd, and baptized in the name of the Father, Son and Holy Ghost; and upon my head emerging from the water, I heard the voices of persons upon the towinb path, and this was the first sound I had heard since my deprivation upon the island of Bermuda, in 1843. With my hearing came also my speech, and the first words that I uttered were—'Thank the Lord, I can hear and speak again as well as any of you.' I scarcely need state my own surprise at the moment, but such it was, and it appears marvelous in my own eyes, not that God is possessed of such power, but that He should manifest it in my behalf. I have much cause to praise Him and glorify His holy name, for in obedience to His divine commands, I not only received the remission of my sins, which I esteem above all earthly blessings, but also the removal of my deafness and dumbness; and now I can hear as distinctly and speak as fluently as I ever did, although I had been deprived of both these faculties for upwards of five years, not being able to hear the loudest noise, nor to use my tongue in speech.

'There is a mistake in the *Merlin* of the date of my landing at Bermuda: it should have been 1843 instead of 1840. The same error appeared also in the *Millennial Star*, No. 22, Vol. 10, and which was caused by extracting the account from that paper.

"The following individuals are witnesses to my baptism:

"Henry Naish,
"John Roberts,     } Members of the Church.
"John Walden,

"Jane Dunbin,
"Thomas Jones,    } Non-Members."
"Jacob Naish,

## THE BLIND HEALED.

"BERRIEN, MONTGOMERYSHIRE, NORTH WALES,
May 23rd, 1849.

"I feel it my bounden duty to make the following narrative known to the authorities of the Church of Jesus Christ, to show that the manifestations of the power of God attend this Church in the last days, as it did the Church of the early Apostles, viz: My daughter Sophia Matilda, aged eight years, was, in the month of May, 1848, afflicted in her eyes, she soon lost the sight of her left eye, and on applying to medical aid, instead of the sight being restored she immediately lost the other, the surgeons stating that the pupils were closed and feared she could never be restored to her sight. I was advised to try an eminent surgeon in Shrewsbury, in the county of Salop, where in June, 1848, I sent her and her mother, as she was now quite blind, and the poor little creature's sufferings were indescribable, though the Lord enabled her to be patient in her afflictions; she remained in Shrewsbury a fortnight but found no benefit, and as the last resource to human aid, I was advised to send her to an eminent occulist in Liverpool, Dr. Neile, under whose treatment she was relieved, and a gradual improvement took place, to our great joy, until the Autumn of the same year. I corresponded with Dr. Neile, who desired me to continue the treatment he had prescribed, but it was all to no purpose, for she relapsed into the same state as before and was in total darkness the whole of the Winter, suffering acutely, and by February of the present year, 1849, she had wasted to a mere skeleton, when my brother-in-law paid me a visit previous to his embarking to California, and told me that if I would have faith in the Lord Jesus Christ, and call for the Elders of the Church, he believed she would be healed. I also soon was enabled to believe, and obeyed the command of St. James. The Church put up their prayers for us, and I found, thanks to the Giver of all good, some improvement ere the ordinance was performed. On the following Sabbath, Elders Dudley and Richards, from Pool Quay, came to my house, performed the ordinance upon my child, the pain soon left her, and she was soon, by the power of God and the prayers of the faithful, restored to sight and health, and thanks be to Almighty God, she is still in the enjoyment of these great blessings; trusting you will rejoice in the Lord with me for His great mercies manifested to me.

"I remain, etc.
"HENRY PUGH.

"LONDON, June 9th, 1849

"Beloved President Pratt.—Not only has the power of healing been manifest upon one, but I can say, although we have not been organized into a branch one year, many have been healed. I will take the liberty of naming a few cases out of the many. Sister Emma Spiring met with an accident while frying some meat: the pan was overturned, and the boiling fat went into her eye and on her face, and from the Friday to the Sunday she could not see with the eye. I, in the name of the Lord, anointed her with oil, and laid my hands on her, and the moment I took my hands off her head, she, in the presence of a large assembly, said she could see, and all pain was gone.

"Another case was of a man by the name of Greenham, who had lost the sight of one eye I anointed him, and he received his sight, and has since come into the Church, and is a good member of the same

"W. BOOTH."

68, DEVONSHIRE LANE, SHEFFIELD,
July 10th, 1849

"April 20th.—President Dunn and I were requested to attend to the ordinances of anointing with oil and laying on of hands by Brother Jackson, who had sore eyes, he had lost the sight of one eye completely, and the other was dangerously affected, but after we had attended to the ordinance, his sight was restored immediately, and the same hour he walked through the town looking about him. He was afflicted with the same disease before he became a Latter-day Saint, and was down sixteen weeks, but the last attack he was restored the third day

J. V. LONG, Presiding Elder."

HEALING OF ONE BORN BLIND

"BRISTOL, November 25th, 1849.

"Dear President Pratt.—As you were so kind as to publish the letter I sent, dated July 9th, containing an account of the miraculous power of God, displayed in the healing of Elizabeth Ann Bounsell, which made quite a stir among the pious Christians of this city. I now venture to write to you again, and say that the above circumstance caused many to call at the house and see if it were true. And upon seeing, many rejoiced, others mocked, saying, "She would have got well if the Elders had not laid their hands upon her." Among the latter was one *would-be* great man, by the name of Charles Smith (who has written a *flimsy* tract against the Saints), who said it was not enough to satisfy him. So the mother took another of her daughters, and put her upon his knee, and said, "Sir, is that child blind?" And after he had examined her eyes, he said, "She is." "Well," said the mother, "she was *born blind:* and she is now four years old; and I am going to take her to the Elders of our Church, for them to anoint her eyes with oil and lay their hands upon her; and you can call again, when you have time, and see her with her eyes opened; for I know the Lord will heal her, and she will see." "Well," said he, "if she does ever see, it will be a great proof." Accordingly, the mother brought the child to the Elders, and Elder John Hackwell anointed her eyes, and laid hands upon her only once; and the Lord heard his prayer, so that the child can now see with both of her eyes, as well as any other person. For which we all feel thankful to our Heavenly Father, and are willing to bear testimony of it to all the world.

"Yours in the kingdom of God,

"GEORGE HALLIDAY."

P. S. We, the father and mother of the child, do here sign our names to the above, as being true.

"WILLIAM BOUNSELL,
"ELIZABETH BOUNSELL.

"No. 12, Bread-street, Bristol."

## BONES SET THROUGH FAITH.

'RUMFORD, May 1st, 1849.

"Dear Brother Gibson.—At your request, I now sit down to give you a short account of the goodness and power of God, made manifest in my behalf. About two years ago, while working at my trade of coach-builder, while assisting in removing a railway carriage, I dislocated my thigh, and was conveyed home, and my parents not being in the Church, and no Elders in the town, (viz. Sterling) medical skill was called in, but from the swelling it could not be set. I was again examined by a Dr. Jeffrey, and one Taylor of Glasgow, who said that a kind of jeal had gathered in the hip joint, and before it could be set, this must be removed by cupping; so I was cupped with twenty-four lances but it did no good, and I lingered in great pain for three weeks, when it was proposed that I should again be cupped; but I was determined that it should not be; and hearing from you, that Elder Samuel W. Richards, from America, was coming to Sterling, I told my friends that when he came, they would see the power of God, and I should be healed. Accordingly, when he came, he anointed me in the name of the Lord, and the bone went into its place, and I got up in the morning and went to my work, to the astonishment of doctors and friends. I am now a traveling Elder and have a great deal of walking, but experience no inconvenience from it. I can get a dozen witnesses to attest to the truth of this cure, both in and out of the Church.

"I remain your brother,
"JAMES S. LOW."

"LEAMINGTON, August 4th, 1849.
"Dear Brother.—While visiting the different branches in this conference, I find that the power of our God has been displayed in a wonderful manner, and that the Saints have great cause to rejoice. Scores can bear testimony to the truth of the gospel, for signs and wonders *follow them that believe.* The following cases of healing I feel impressed to send to you, and if you should deem them worthy of a place in the *Star* you can insert them.

"Sister Sarah Gorde, resident of Maxstoke, near Coleshill, on the 25th of September, 1839, had a very severe confinement, which left her in a low and afflicted state, and for the space of seven years and a half was almost in continual pain. Her blood seemed to run cold within her veins, for she was scarcely ever warm. She had two doctors in regular attendance, and sometimes three, and also applied to others; but in spite of all their exertions she found no relief. She wasted in flesh until she was reduced almost to a skeleton; her joints were dislocated from the time of her confinement; to go from home was impossible, for she could not ride without great pain, and it was with the utmost difficulty that she could get about the house. But finally a small tract fell into her hands belonging to the Church of Jesus Christ of Latter-day Saints and while reading the account of the visitation of the angel to our beloved Prophet, Joseph Smith, her heart was filled with joy; the Spirit of the living God fastened the testimony upon her mind, and she was satisfied that the day of her redemption was nigh at hand, and believed firmly that she would walk again. At this time she was ignorant of the doctrines that we preached, but she firmly believed that God had raised up Joseph to be a prophet to this generation.

"After a few days' investigation she was baptized by Elder W. Bramall in the month of April, 1847, and when she was confirmed he told her that she *should be healed according to her faith.* This promise filled her heart with joy, and in three weeks from the day and hour that she was baptized she was able to walk without pain; her joints which had been weak for so many years, became strong, and since then she has enjoyed herself and been able to fulfill the duties that devolve upon a mother with a large family.

"Also her son, John Gorde, had, when nine years old, the misfortune to dislocate his thigh. The medical fraternity were called upon, who endeavored to set it, but in consequence of it being swelled so much they were not able; and thus it remained for the space of eight years, and so powerful was its effect upon the constitution that it stopped the growth of his body; his leg hung loose, so that he could turn it any way he pleased. Finally he heard the gospel of Christ, and in one week after the baptism of his mother he was immersed in the liquid grave, and, wonderful to relate, he lost his lameness, his body began to grow, and from that time he has enjoyed good health, and from appearance no one would suppose he had ever been feeble at all.

"I remain yours in the gospel of Christ,
"ALFRED CORDON.

"NANTYGWYNITH, GEORGETOWN, MERTHYR TYDFIL,
"September 14th, 1850.

"Dear President Pratt.—I enclose a testimony of a miraculous case of healing, which has taken place a few days ago in Abercanaid; I saw the brother in his affliction, and the accompanying testimony he bore at my house, more than two miles distant from his. I send it to you with permission to do with it as you think proper.

"WM. PHILLIPS.

"*The Testimony of David Richards.*
"MERTHYR TYDFIL, Sep. 10th, 1850.

On Friday, August the 23rd, 1850, at about eleven o'clock, while I was working among the coal, a stone fell upon me about two cwt. I was carried home and the doctor who was present said he could do nothing for me, and told those around me to wrap me up in a sheet that I might die. There was a lump on my back as big as a child's head. The doctor afterwards told one of my relations, about six o'clock in the evening, that I could not recover. Elder Phillips called to see me, and attended to the ordinance of the Church for the sick, and while commanding the bones in the name of Jesus, they came together, making a noise like the crushing of an old basket; my strength returned, and now I am able to go some miles to bear my testimony to this great miracle. The doctor called to see me and was astonished, and said in the hearing of witnesses that my backbone was broken; but that it now was whole, and that I was now recovering as well as any man he ever saw. Many of our greatest enemies confessed that I was healed by the power of God, and while coming here to-day, many who heard of my accident were struck with the greatest amazement. But I thank my Heavenly Father for His kindness towards me, hoping I shall live to serve Him more faithfully henceforth than ever

"D Richards.

"Morgan Mills  "John Thomas, } Witnesses.
"Thomas Rees.  "Henry Evans.

## LEPROSY HEALED

"No. 9, Guardian Street, Springfield Lane,
"Salford, May 19th, 1849.

"Last Winter, a young woman addressed me in the Carpenter's Hall, the daughter of a fustian cutter, named Lea, residing in Cook-street, Salford, and said, her parents were desirous that I should go and see her brother who was very bad with leprosy. I went in company with one or two of my brethren. I think I never saw anything so bad as the boy was (the small pox excepted); the whole of the lower part of his face and under his chin, as well as the backs of his hands and wrists, were one entire mass of scabs, indeed you could not have inserted a needle's point, they were so thick. He was eight and a half years of age, and had been afflicted since he was six months old; they had him at the Manchester infirmary and the Salford Dispensary, and are at this time paying the surgeon's bill who attended him as a private patient. The surgeon told his parents he could do nothing for him, as the disease was too virulent for medicine to reach it. His parents told me they did not know what it was to get a regular night's rest with him, and that it frequently took three hours to wash him. The first night we went, they were not disturbed during the night, and in three weeks he was entirely free, and his flesh was renewed like that of a young child.

"John Watts.

"Borland, Fifeshire, Scotland.

"To all whom it may concern. This is to certify, that I was seized with a disease like the leprosy, in the year 1837, and tried all that I could to get a cure, but I could not, and all the doctors that I applied to could do me no good; and it continued with me over all my body until the month of September, 1843, when I went and was baptized into the Church of Jesus Christ of Latter-day Saints, by William M'Farland,

Elder of the said Church, on the 1st September, 1843, and that same night, the leprosy left me.

"Jenet Ridd.

"Witnesses, { "William M'Farland, "James Crystal, "Alexander Ridd.

"Derby, September 17th, 1849.

"Another remarkable case is that of a sister in this town, named Cumberland, who was severely afflicted inwardly, for eleven years, during which time she received medical attendance from the most eminent men of that profession; such as Dr. Heigate of Derby; Dr. Robinson of Northampton; also, under the care of the Infirmary Surgeon of Loughborough, but all to no purpose; she still got worse. Some said it was the liver complaint, others said it was a decline. She was also outwardly afflicted with a disease in her skin, and her body full of sores from head to foot, for many years. Nothing seemed to do her any good, and only death was considered could put an end to her sufferings, but to her great joy, the latter part of last year she heard the Latter-day Saints preaching the gospel, and she believed and obeyed the same, and was soon made whole, and has, from that time to this, enjoyed a goodly portion of health and strength. She is now bearing testimony of the power of God bestowed upon her, both in word and person to all around. Numbers, both in and out of the Church, are witnesses of the same; and even the unbelievers in the gospel cannot help but acknowledge that it is a great miracle. I might write for hours of such like cases, but forbear at present. Concluding with the words of Paul, 'Our gospel is not in word only but in power and much assurance.'

"As a witness of the same, I subscribe myself, yours, truly,

"John Wheeler."

"Shropshire, Shemington, near Market Drayton,
"September 9th, 1849.

"Dear President Pratt.—In June, 1848, I was called upon by Sister Walsh, to administer to her daughter, whose head was in one mass of sores, so that she could not turn it without turning her whole body. I attended to the ordinances, and in a few days she was restored, and is now a member of the Church of Jesus Christ of Latter-day Saints.

"Yours in the gospel,
"William Heywood."

## RUPTURES HEALED.

"Clackmanan, May 29th, 1849.

"In the beginning of the year 1848, in Clackmanan branch, a boy of about six years of age, a son of Brother John and

Sister Margaret Hunter, who had been given up by all medical men as incurable, and whose disease they could not understand, and who was reduced in consequence thereof almost to skin and bone, and confined to bed, was administered unto by Elder John Sharp, now gone to America, and Elder John Russell, who is still here, who anointed him with oil in the name of the Lord Jesus, and next day he was running about in good health and has continued well ever since.

"Witnesses to the above,
"JOHN HUNTER,
"JOHN RUSSELL,
"MARGARET HUNTER."

"In the month of March, this year, 1849, a young boy, son of Sister Ann Hunter, in Clackmanan, who was sorely afflicted with rupture, was anointed for the same by Elder John Russell, and next day he was quite whole, and still continues so, he was rather more than three years of age, and was born ruptured.

"Witnesses to the above,
"JOHN RUSSELL,
"DAVID RUSSELL,
"ANN HUNTER."

"WOLVERHAMPTON, January 29th, 1850.

"Sister Mary Bolland, aged 25, and residing in Pool Street, Wolverhampton, had suffered severely from a rupture ever since her confinement in the autumn of 1847, until her baptism by Elder Richard Ramsell, on the 7th of December, 1849. She had, up to the time of her baptism, been accustomed to wear a truss, or some such instrument, whereby she was enabled to get about with safety, but this she took off before she entered the water, and has ever since dispensed with it entirely, having been perfectly healed in the act of baptism; in testimony of this the undersigned witnesses subscribe their names, at the same time expressing their gratitude to Almighty God for this and the many other manifestations of His goodness which we all from time to time experience

"Yours, etc.,
"JAMES BELL.
Witnesses, "MARY BOLLAND,
"SARAH HUTCHENCE,
"OLIVIA SATERS.

### FEVERS REBUKED.

"WOOD MILL STREET, DUNFERMLINE,
"FIFESHIRE, SCOTLAND.

"To all whom it may concern. This is to certify, that I was in Borland on the 8th of January, 1849, and there was a girl by the name of Catherine Kidd, lying very bad with a fever, and was at the point of death, and there was part of her dead clothes made, waiting every moment when the breath would leave her; so I was called to see her and I went; and they asked me if I would attend to the ordinance of the Church with her, and I said that I would: so in company with Elder M'Farland, I anointed her with oil, and laid hands on her, in the name of Jesus Christ; and when I had done, I told them that she would get better, and the people that were in the house, said if she did, it would be a miracle; so from that hour she did get better, and the dead clothes were laid aside. Now for this, to our Lord and Savior Jesus Christ, be all the honor and glory, both now and forever. Amen.

Witnesses,
"WILLIAM ATHOLE MACMASTER.
"WILLAM M'FARLAND.
"MRS. M'FARLAND."

"SHEFFIELD, June 28th, 1849.

"Under date of May 2nd, 1847.—Was sent for by Mrs Rodger, to lay hands on her daughter, who had been given up by the doctors. The complaint was the typhus fever, she was reduced to a complete skeleton, her bones were ready to come through the skin, and her body had many large sores upon it. I never saw such an object of pity before. Before administering the ordinance, I preached the gospel to them, for they were out of the Church. I called on them all to kneel down, then gave her some oil internally and laid hands on her in the name of the Lord and rebuked the disease, and while I had my hands on her head I saw her well and walking about as one of the most healthy and blooming girls in that place. She commenced to amend immediately; she slept safely and soundly that night and in the morning wanted her breakfast. It came to pass as I saw it. Her mother came into the Church, but her father remains an enemy to this to work this day.

"With due respect, I am yours,
"HEZEKIAH MITCHELL.

"68, DEVONSHIRE LANE, SHEFFIELD.
May 18th, 1849.

"A little girl, the daughter of Brother and Sister Bolyn, Pinstone Street, was seized with the scarlet fever, the mother was afraid and fetched the doctor, who prepared a decoction for the child to take, but when the father came home, he put the medicine away, and procured some olive oil which was consecrated by Elders Dunn, Burgess and myself, and was then administered by the father, and the disease left her that same hour; their little boy was then seized with the same kind of fever; when the doctor came in to see the little girl, he saw her playing about with the children, and said, "Why, she is better!" "Yes, sir," said the mother, "and now the little boy's begun." "Have you given the little girl all the medicine?" "No, sir," "O well, continue to give the boy the same medicine and he will soon be better." They attended to the ordinance of healing, instituted by our Savior, and the boy was restored the same day; another of the family was then seized, and they administered the same medicine (olive oil) which procured an instantaneous cure.

"Yours in the true covenant,
"J. V. LONG, Presiding Elder."

"CHELTENHAM, August 5th, 1849.

"Dear Brother Pratt.—I write to inform you of two remarkable cases of healing which took place in the village of Barrow, in the county of Gloucester.

"First. A young female, by the name of Mary Bayliss, was very violently seized with the black fever, so that she was not expected to live. Brother and Sister Bayliss sent for a servant of God from a neighboring village, called by the name of George Curtis, who came and prayed for and laid hands upon her in the name of Jesus, and she was healed, and the next day she was up, to the astonishment of the people. This occurred on the 7th of June, 1848.

"Second. A young man, not a member of our Church, was taken ill with the black fever so violently, that all human skill was of no avail. The doctor informed his friends that he would die before morning. His mother, who was in our Church, sent for Brother Curtis, who laid hands upon him in the name of the Lord and prayed for him. He immediately began to recover and the next morning he was walking about the house, to the astonishment of his friends and neighbors. In three days he was able to go to work in the fields, rejoicing in the goodness of God. He has since joined the Church of the Saints, and bears a faithful testimony to the healing power of the gospel. Believe me to be, dear brother, yours sincerely in the cause of truth,

"JOHN ALDER.

"ST. HELIERS, August 5th.

"Sent for to visit Brother Feron's child. Found her raving in a strong fever. Administered to her The fever left and her senses returned five minutes after. Next morning she was running about the doors.

"Witnesses, "JOHN FERON.
"THERESA FERON."

## A CASE OF MIRACULOUS HEALING.

"DUNDEE, Feb. 8th, 1850.

"Dear Brother Pratt.—If you deem the following worthy of a place in the columns of the *Millennial Star*, it is at your disposal: I have a girl, aged three years, who had for eighteen months been severely afflicted with convulsive fits, to the loss of all the powers of the body and even the mind seemed in the thraldom of some great power. I had tried the wisdom of the faculty but without effect, until the child was fearful to behold, almost in continual convulsions by night and day. O the 25th of December last, Elder Hugh Findlay called and anointed her with oil in the name of the Lord and prayed for her, and from that day until now she has never had a fit, but has increased daily in strength of body and mind. These facts are known to many not belonging to our Church, and for the truth of which, witness our hands,

"JAMES DAVIDSON.
"MARIA DAVIDSON,
"HUGH FINDLAY."

## CHOLERA HEALED.

"MACCLESFIELD,
"September 28th, 1850.

"Dear Brother Pratt.—I am happy to inform you that I enjoy excellent health and good spirits, and rejoice in the work of the Lord wherein I am called to administer. Many are dying in this town of the cholera. Many of the Saints have been seized with the destroying pestilence, but all have been restored to health and strength by the power of the Priesthood. I wish to forward you some remarkable instances of healing. Sister Jane Batty was seized with Asiatic cholera, in the month of August. When I was called to administer to her, she was taken with cramp, which was followed with great pain. I laid my hands on her, and by the authority of the holy Priesthood rebuked the disease in the name of Jesus Christ; the cramp and pain immediately left her, and she was restored to health and strength.

"The next was Brother George Galley: he had a violent attack of the same disease. Elder James Galley and myself laid hands on him and administered oil, and he was immediately restored. The next is Sister Caroline Parker, who was attacked violently with the same disease of Asiatic cholera. Some of the neighbors went for the doctor, who pronounced it a desperate case, and gave some advice, after which her father, Elder Boyle and Elder James Thirt, laid their hands on her and rebuked the disease, to the great astonishment of the doctor and the neighbors; for when he came the next morning, he was surprised that she was alive. He wished her to send to his surgery for some medicine, but she told him she could walk there, therefore needed none.

"Sister Ann Markland was next attacked by the same disease. I laid hands on her in the name of Jesus Christ, and rebuked the disease, and she was immediately re-tored Her mother, Margaret, was next taken with the disorder. I administered to her in the usual way, and she was immediately restored. The next was Sister Ann Stubbs, who was violently taken with the same complaint on the 17th of September. Elder Francis Sherratt and myself administered to her, and she is restored to health and strength. These are but a few cases where the power of God has been manifested in this conference, for there are many others that are equally signalized by the divine power and blessings of God.

"JOSEPH CLEMENTS, President of the Macclesfield Conference,
"JAMES GALLEY, Secretary.

"THESE SIGNS SHALL FOLLOW THEM THAT BELIEVE."—*Mark xvi.*

"10, HENRY STREET, PARK, SHEFFIELD,
"September 9th, 1850.

"Dear Brother Pratt.—While reading over my journal, I have felt impressed to make a few extracts and forward the same to you, that if you think them worthy you may insert them in the *Millennial Star*, that the faith of the Saints may be strengthened, and the inquirers after truth satisfied that the power of God is enjoyed by *latter* as much as it was by the *former* day Saints.

"August 14th, 1849.—I was called out to see Sister Fowler, who was severely afflicted with the apparent symptoms of cholera; the attack was so severe that she was incapable of being removed from the couch on which she lay, her speech was gone, a kind of whisper was the only medium through which her ideas could be obtained. At her request Elder Hardy and I attended to the ordinance of laying on of hands, and by the prayer of faith we rebuked the destroyer in the name of Jesus Christ, and the disease disappeared. She rose up, her speech returned, and we conversed cheerfully together on the gospel, which is the power of God unto salvation, to the Gentile first, and then to the Jew.

"Sep. 4th, 1849.—Brother William Lamb came to my residence, afflicted with rheumatics, from which he had suffered three years, and having just joined the Church, and got to understand the promises, he felt sure the Lord would heal him through my administration, although he was sixty-two years of age; I therefore called upon Elder Hardy to assist in the ordinance of laying on of hands, and immediately after our hands were taken from his head, he arose up and bore testimony to the manifestation of the power of God in his behalf, declar'ng that all pain had left him, and he frequently made it a part of his testimony (before he went to Zion) to tell the people how miraculously he had been healed, at a time of life when such a change could not be expected, except through the power of God

"Oct. 27th. 1849.—I was taken ill with hoarseness and inflammation of the lungs; I continued to get worse until Friday, November the 2nd, when the erysipelas broke out of my face and head, my head and face were swelled to an enormous size, my appetite was gone, and my suffering hourly increased. I took a little herb tea, as directed in Dr. Coffin's Guide to Health, but I continued to get worse; on the 3rd my suffering became indescribable, during the night in particular, I had the most excruciating pains in the head and bowels; on Sunday morning, the 4th, my throat was almost stopped up, many of my friends then gave me up to die, but my faith was unshaken in the promises of the Almighty; I therefore sent for Elders Dunn, Hardy and Roper, and while Elder Dunn was anointing my head and face, all inflammation disappeared, I felt the pain leave as fast as his hand passed over my head, for the power of God drove all pain and disease from me, and in two hours the old skin shel'ed off my face, and I have been well ever since; and I hereby bear my testimony that immediately, on olive oil being applied to my head in the name of Jesus Christ, the pain left, all inflammation ceased, my speech was restored, in fact, my system, lungs in particular, seemed to be renewed, for I have preached five times more since than I had before, and have enjoyed much better health.

"Yours faithfully, in the new covenant,
"To President Pratt.'            J. V. LONG."

"KIRKHALL LANE,
"September 22nd, 1849.

"Dear Brother Pratt,—I wish to inform you of what I consider an incontrovertible proof of the power of God. On Sunday, the 9th inst., Sister Hart, of Bickershaw, was sick, and had the usual symptoms of cholera Brothers Afflick and Hill laid hands on her, and anointed her in the name of the Lord, when she was immediately restored, got out of bed, and joined in the fellowship meeting and bore a faithful testimony to the power of God. On Tuesday, the 11th inst., Brother James Hart came for me to go and administer to his two children who were very sick. I went with him, and found them suffering from sickness, vomiting, cramp and all the usual symptoms of cholera. The eldest, three years old, and youngest, fourteen months; they were sreeching in agony. I anointed them and rebuked the disease in the name of the Lord, when the eldest got up, and before we were aware of what she was about, ran to her grandmother, without shoes or stockings, to tell her that she was well They then confessed that children could not deceive, but that it was the power of God. Of these things numbers can testify, and I trust you will make it public to the world. Praying that the blessing of God may rest upon you, and all the Church of God.

"I remain yours in the bonds of the covenant.

"RICHARD BOOTH, President of the Leigh branch.

"P. S. These are only two out of the numerous cases in this branch. R. B."

"DERBY, September 17th, 1849.

"Beloved Brother Pratt.—On Sunday morning, September 2nd, I was called upon to go and administer to Brother Thomas Parks, a young man of this town, who was suffering under a dreadful attack of the cholera. When I first entered the room, which was about ten o'clock, he appeared as though every breath would be his last, having suffered much in cramps, purging and vomiting, from about four that morning. Shortly after I arrived, Elders Duce and Reed came, with Priest Fisher. We consecrated some oil, and administered to him in the name of the Lord, and as soon as we had taken our hands off his head, he was enabled to speak, testifying that the pain had all left him, and began to praise God, the giver of all good, that the Priesthood was given to His servants by which they could effectually administer to the children of men. In a few moments he was able to get up and put on his clothes; we left him and went to meeting. We went again to see him at night, we found him free from pain but rather weak; we administered to him again, and asked for God's blessings to attend it, and on Wednesday night following we found him at meeting, strong and well, bearing testimony of the power of God and rejoicing in the same. Henry Duce, Thomas Reed and George Fisher, with the young man's parents are witnesses of the same, and truly rejoice in the blessings of Israel's God.

"JOHN WHEELER.

15—The few cases of miracles which are here inserted, are mentioned that the reader may understand that the faith of this Church is not founded upon human testimony alone, but upon the power of God. The Latter-day Saints know that

Joseph Smith is a true prophet, and that the Book of Mormon is a divine revelation, because God has confirmed the same unto them by the miraculous manifestations of His power. The Saints among this nation have been blessed, more or less, with the miraculous signs and gifts of the Holy Spirit, by which they have been confirmed, and know, of a surety, that this is the Church of Christ. They know that the blind see, the lame walk, the deaf hear, the dumb speak, that lepers are cleansed, that bones are set, that the cholera is rebuked, and that the most virulent diseases give way, through faith in the name of Jesus Christ and the power of His gospel. These are not some isolated cases that occasionally take place, or that are rather doubtful in their nature, or that have transpired a long time ago, or in some distant country; but they are taking place at the present period; every week furnishes scores of instances in all parts of this land; many of the sick out of the Church have, through the laying on of the hands of the servants of God, been healed. It is not something done in a corner, but openly, and tens of thousands are witnesses.

16.—All mankind can prove for themselves that the Book of Mormon is a divine revelation by obeying its principles; for, if they will do so, they have the promise of certain miraculous signs; and when they themselves receive the signs, they will know for themselves and no longer be dependent on the testimony of others. The testimony of others is intended to produce faith in the hearer, and not a knowledge; but the signs which a believer receives after obedience, give knowledge: this knowledge qualifies him in his turn to bear testimony; and thus the witnesses multiply in all parts of the earth where this message is received. If Catholics, Protestants, infidels, Mahometans, Jews or heathens, will obey the Book of Mormon, miraculous signs shall follow them, and by this they shall all know that it is true. If the Book of Mormon be false, God would not confirm it unto any man by granting unto him the signs, therefore all men would know, if they did not receive the signs after having complied with its requisitions, that it was false.

17.—The Book of Mormon has now been published upwards of fifty years during which time many scores of thousands have believed and obeyed it. Now, if they had not received the promised signs, would they have continued to believe the work year after year? " If they had failed to receive the promise, would they not have pronounced it an imposition long ago? Yes: we will venture to say that if the believers in the Book of Mormon had not received the promised signs, there would not have been found in five years after it was printed one solitary soul who would have continued to believe in its divine authenticity: but the very fact that tens of thousands do remain steadfast in their belief shows most conclusively that they have found by actual experiment, that the promised signs do follow, and therefore that the Book of Mormon is of divine origin.

18.—There is no way that an imposter could more effectually destroy his own imposition than to promise miraculous signs to those who would believe in it; for when the promise was not verified, it would be known that he was an imposter. We here quote an extract from a revelation given the 22nd and 23rd of September, 1832, through Joseph the Prophet unto the Apostles in this Church: "Go ye into all the world, and whatsoever place ye cannot go into ye shall send, that the testimony may go from you into all the world unto every creature. And as I said unto mine Apostles, even so I say unto you, for you are mine Apostles, even God's High Priests, ye are they whom my Father hath given me—ye are my friends, therefore, as I said unto mine Apostles, I say unto you again, that every soul who believeth on your words, and is baptized by water for the remission of sins, shall receive the Holy Ghost, and these signs shall follow them that believe.

"In my name they shall do many wonderful works; in my name they shall cast out devils; in my name they shall heal the sick; in my name they shall open the eyes of the blind, and unstop the ears of the deaf; and the tongue of the dumb shall speak; and if any man shall administer poison unto them, it shall not hurt them; and the poison of a serpent shall not have power to harm them  *   *   Verily, verily, I say unto you, they who believe not on your words, and are not baptized in water in my name, for the remission of their sins, that they may receive the Holy Ghost, shall be damned, and shall not come into my Father's kingdom, where my Father and I am. And this revelation unto you, and commandment, is in force from this very hour upon all the world."*

If Joseph Smith had been an imposter, he never would have given utterance to the above promise, unless he were determined to immediately overthrow his own testimony in relation to the Book of Mormon; an imposter could make such a promise, but he could never fulfill it. Since this promise was made, tens of thousands have placed themselves in a position to put the promise to a test, and they have found it, to their great joy, verified.

19.—Let us next enquire how many evidences we have of the miracles done in the days of the apostles. The New Testament was written by eight men, six of whom, namely, Matthew, Mark, Luke, John, Paul and Peter, testify as eye-witnesses to the marvelous works wrought in their day. We believe that the miraculous power of God was manifested eighteen hundred years ago, because six eye-witnesses in the Church have thus testified in their writings. Have we the same amount of testimony in the Church of the Latter-day Saints? If so then the Book of Mormon has just as good claims on our faith as the New Testament. We have already given the testimony of many witnesses; and there are tens of thousands of others now living, that bear a similar testimony. Therefore, this generation have thousands of eye-witnesses in favor of the miraculous gifts and powers of the gospel, confirmatory of the Book of Mormon, to where they have one confirmatory of the apostolic mission in ancient times. The six writers of the New Testament tell us of many that were healed, but none of the persons healed have handed down their written testimony to that effect. But this generation have the testimony of thousands who have been healed of every variety of sickness and disease. If we had the testimony of the deaf and dumb, and blind and lame that were healed in ancient times, it would greatly strengthen the testimony of the six writers who have related such marvelous occurrences. What evidence have this generation that the

---

*——Doc. and Cov., section lxxxiv., paragraphs 62-75.

lame man, who sat at the beautiful gate of the temple was healed? They have the testimony of one witness, and one only, namely, the writer of the Acts. What evidence have we that the apostles spoke in tongues on the day of Pentecost? The writer of the Acts has said so, and we believe it on his testimony alone. Luke, who is supposed to be the writer of the Acts, has told us that Philip wrought great miracles in Samaria—that twelve men at Ephesus, after their baptism and confirmation, spoke with tongues and prophesied—that Peter saw a vision—that Cornelius saw an angel—that Ananias and Sapphira fell dead—that devils were cast out—that the sick were healed by handkerchiefs and aprons being taken to them from the body of Paul—and that the shadow of Peter healed many but all these things are believed merely on the testimony of one man—the writer of the Acts.

20.—Many hundreds of the servants of God among the Latter-day Saints keep journals of their travels, and of the miracles which pass under their observation. Hence the acts of the Apostles of the ninteenth century are recorded as well as the acts of those in the first century: and the miracles recorded in the latter-day *acts* are just as worthy of being believed as the miracles recorded in the former-day *Acts*. If the testimony of Luke can be depended upon, when he testifies of miracles, why should not the testimony of William Gibson, J. V. Long, Joseph Clements and hundreds of others, be depended upon when they also testify of miracles?

21.—Christendom believe in former-day miracles because it is popular; they disbelieve in latter-day miracles because it is unpopular. Popularity is among the most of men the grand test by which all doctrines are tried, received or rejected. They never once think of examining the evidence on which a doctrine is founded; but the great inquiry is, have our great and learned divines believed in it? If not, it is at once rejected. It is popular to believe in ancient Christian miracles, though only testified of by six writers of the New Testament; but it is unpopular to believe in modern Christian miracles, though testified of by tens of thousands of living eye-witnesses. So it was among the Jews, dead prophets were very much venerated and honored, and their sepulchres garnished, while living prophets were persecuted and put to death. It is very popular among Christendom to believe in the New Testament; but it is exceedingly unpopular to believe in the Book of Mormon, though it is proved to them by a thousand times more evidence than the former.

---

## CHAPTER VI.

### PROPHETIC EVIDENCE IN FAVOR OF THE BOOK OF MORMON.

1.—In the last two chapters of this series, it has been abundantly proved that the Book of Mormon has been confirmed by the voice of the Lord, by the ministry of angels, by heavenly visions or by the miraculous gifts and powers of the Holy Ghost, unto tens of thousands of witnesses. The Book of Mormon, therefore, is demonstrated by a vast amount of the most incontestable evidences such as never can be weakened or overthrown by all the powers of priestcraft, editors and the infernal regions combined. It may be ridiculed, laughed at, treated with contempt, entirely neglected, or persecuted; but all such arguments will avail nothing in the day of judgment, only to bring down upon those who reject so great a revelation still greater condemnation. Having demonstrated the divine authenticity of the Book of Mormon, we might with propriety proceed no farther in search of evidences, for all additional evidences drawn from the prophecies or any other source, can only at the most be additional demonstrations of the same great divine truth. A problem in geometry after having once been demonstrated, cannot be made any more certain by any new process of demonstration; so with this great and heavenly treasure—the Book of Mormon; if any one will follow the steps of demonstration already pointed out, they will know with the same certainty that it is a revelation from God, that a geometrician has when he follows the rules of demonstration in relation to any particular problem.

2.—The revelator John, while on Patmos, saw the restoration of the gospel to the earth; he says, "And I saw another angel fly in the midst of heaven, having the everlasting gospel to preach unto them that dwell on the earth, and to every nation, and kindred, and tongue, and people, saying with a loud voice, 'Fear God, and give glory to Him, for the hour of His judgment is come; and worship Him that made heaven and earth, and the sea, and the fountains of waters.' And there followed another angel, saying, 'Babylon is fallen, is fallen—that great city—because she made all nations drink of the wine of the wrath of her fornication.',"* When the gospel was committed unto man in the first century, it was not by the ministry of an angel, but by the person of our Lord Himself; therefore, John had no reference to the preaching of the gospel in the first century. Our Savior commanded the apostles to go into all the world and preach the gospel to every creature: this mission was fulfilled before John saw this vision, as is evident from Paul's declaration to the Colossians: (*i.* 23.) "If ye continue in the faith grounded and settled, and be not moved away from the hope of the gospel, which ye have heard, *and which was preached to every creature which is under heaven, wherefore I, Paul, am made a minister.*" At the time the apostle wrote this epistle, it seems that "every creature under heaven" had heard the gospel. It was several years after this that John "saw another angel fly in the midst of heaven, having the everlasting gospel to preach unto them that dwell on the earth, and to every nation, kindred, tongue and people." From which we learn that there was to be another period after the first century when the gospel should be again preached to every creature.

3.—We have already proved in the previous chapters of this series that immediately after the first century the whole earth became corrupted by the great "Mother of Harlots,"—that apostasy and wickedness succeeded Christianity—that, for the want of new revelation, all legal succession to the apostleship was discontinued—that the gifts and powers of the Holy Spirit ceased—and that the Church was no longer to be found on the earth: this being the case, all nations must have been

---

*———Revelation xiv., 6, 7, 8.

destitute of the everlasting gospel for many generations—not destitute of its history as it was once preached and enjoyed, but destitute of its blessings, of its powers, of its gifts, of its Priesthood, of its ordinances administered by legal authority. During this long period of darkness, no man could obey the gospel and enjoy its blessings, because no people were authorized to administer its ordinances legally; therefore, in order that mankind might again possess and enjoy the ordinances and blessings of the gospel, it became absolutely necessary that the apostleship, with every other authority which characterized the Christian church when it was before on the earth, should be restored among men. This restoration of the gospel Priesthood, with all its gifts, powers and blessings, could not take place, according to the scriptures, only by an angel coming from heaven, as Saint John has clearly predicted.

4.—That the nations have had a history of the gospel, contained in the few books of the New Testament, or in other words that they have had a history of what another people believed, obeyed and enjoyed, we by no means deny. But that the nations have actually obeyed and enjoyed the gospel for themselves, we do deny. The history of what others enjoyed is a very different thing from actual possession and enjoyment for ourselves. The history is but a dead letter, unless we can enjoy the same things. What advantage would it be to a hungry man who was ready to perish to read the history of the Savior's feeding three thousand on loaves and fishes? It would only serve to aggrevate his appetite: he himself must have food or perish. So with mankind in regard to the gospel: its history is one thing, its enjoyment is another. To read the history of others feasting on gospel blessings will not satisfy the craving anxieties of our souls; to read the history of a Christian church anciently, is calculated to give us a longing desire that a Christian church might again be restored to the earth. That the nations might not despair of ever again enjoying the gospel, the Lord left them that glorious assurance that the gospel should again be made manifest by another angel flying in the midst of heaven.

If there were a nation, kindred, tongue, or people, on the whole earth that already possessed and enjoyed the gospel, there would not be the least necessity of an angel coming with it; but the very fact that the everlasting gospel, when revealed by the angel, is to be preached "TO EVERY NATION, KINDRED, TONGUE AND PEOPLE," shows most clearly that every nation on the whole earth was entirely destitute of it. This agrees most perfectly with what we have before demonstrated: all people being without it the angel restores it for the benefit of all.

5.—The Book of Mormon contains the everlasting gospel in all its fullness; and it has been revealed to the inhabitants of our earth by an angel; it was by an angel that the apostleship and Priesthood were again restored; it was by an angel that men were called and ordained by the holy ministry, and empowered to preach, baptize and administer all the ordinances of the everlasting gospel, contained in the Book of Mormon; therefore, let all people rejoice for the gospel is once more restored to the earth; let the nations be glad that after so many generations of darkness, a Christian Church has again been organized upon our dark and benighted globe: let songs of praise and thanksgiving ascend up before God among all nations, that glad tidings of great joy have once more been sent down from heaven—that inspired apostles and prophets have once more been sent to preach, baptize, and show unto man the way of salvation.

6.—The authority, power and blessings of the gospel, having been taken away from the earth, because of apostasy and wickedness, could only be restored to man by new revelation, and such revelation must come through an angel. The Roman Catholics and Protestants do not pretend to any such restoration of the gospel by an angel, and therefore they cannot be in possession of it. The only people that do testify that the gospel has been restored to the earth by an angel, are the Latter-day Saints; therefore, if the gospel is restored, the Latter-day Saints are the only people to whom it is restored: all others testify that it has not been restored to them. If the only people who do testify to the restoration of the gospel by an angel, be impostors, then all nations must still be in darkness, without the gospel, and without a Christian church, and must remain so, until the angel is sent in fulfillment of John's prediction. The gospel is, therefore, with the Latter-day Saints, or else it is nowhere on the whole earth. But when the angel restores the gospel, he must restore it to some people; why may not the Latter-day Saints be that people? If it were restored to any other people, would the nations be any more willing to receive it than they are now? If it should be restored in the next generation, would they be any more believing than the present generation? Is there anything connected with the message which the Latter-day Saints testify that an angel has restored, that proves it not to be the message of "the everlasting gospel?" If not, then all people who resist it will most assuredly be condemned in the day of judgment for so doing.

7.—It is to be expected that when the angel restores the gospel, it will be restored in fullness, and in the most perfect simplicity and plainness, so that every point of the doctrine of Christ shall be clearly revealed, and expressed in such language, that no two persons could understand it differently. Many things, connected with the doctrine of Christ, are not clearly revealed and expressed in the English translation of the Bible: this is owing, as we have already shown in chapter III. to the loss of many of the inspired writings, and to the rejection of many sacred books by the third council of Carthage, together with those which have since been rejected by the Protestants: and also, as we have before proved, another great source of error is, that the Greek and Hebrew manuscripts, from which the Bible was translated, had become so awfully corrupted, in almost every text, that the translators were utterly at a loss to know which reading was correct. All these things, combined with the unavoidable errors of an uninspired translation, have rendered the English Bible extremely uncertain and ambiguous. This uncertainty and ambiguity have been the principal cause of all the divisions of modern Christendom. The only way to remedy this great evil, is to obtain another revelation of the gospel, free from all the corruptions and uncertainty which characterizes the English Bible. Nothing short of such a revelation can ever redeem mankind from their errors of doctrine; nothing else can be an infallible standard of the Christian religion; nothing else can reclaim them from divisions and strifes; nothing else will give certainty and stability, so necessary to the happiness and salvation of man; and nothing else could be expected in the revelation of the gospel by an angel. Such a revelation is the Book of Mormon; the most infallible certainty characterizes every ordinance and every doctrinal point revealed in that book. In it there is no ambiguity—no room for controversy—no doctrine so imperfectly expressed, that two persons would draw two different conclusions therefrom. Such a revelation was greatly needed, and such a revelation the angel has revealed.

8.—As an example of the exceeding great plainness in which the doctrine of the gospel is revealed, we quote the teachings of Jesus Christ, in relation to baptism, as given by His personal ministry, in the northern part of South America, soon after His resurrection:

"And it came to pass that he spoke unto Nephi (for Nephi was among the multitude), and He commanded him that he should come forth. And Nephi arose and went forth, and bowed himself before the Lord, and he did kiss His feet. And the Lord commanded him that he should arise. And he arose and stood before Him. And the Lord said unto him, I give unto you power that ye shall baptize this people, when I am again ascended into heaven. And again the Lord called others, and said unto them likewise; and He gave unto them power to baptize. And He said unto them, on this wise shall ye baptize; and there shall be no disputations among you. Verily I say unto you, that whoso repenteth of his sins through your words, and desireth to be baptized in my name, on this wise shall ye baptize them: behold ye shall go down and stand in the water, and in my name shall ye baptize them. And now behold, these are the words which ye shall say, calling them by name, saying, Having authority given me of Jesus Christ, I baptize you in the name of the Father, and of the Son, and of the Holy Ghost. Amen. And then shall ye immerse them in the water, and come forth again out of the water. And after this manner shall ye baptize in my name, for behold, verily I say unto you, that the Father, and the Son, and the Holy Ghost, are one; and I am in the Father, and the Father in me, and the Father and I are one. And according as I have commanded you, thus shall ye baptize. And there shall be no disputations among you, as there hath hitherto been; neither shall there be disputations among you concerning the points of my doctrine, as there hath hitherto been; for verily, verily, I say unto you, he that hath the spirit of contention is not of me, but is of the devil, who is the father of our contention, and he stirreth up the hearts of men to contend with anger, one with another. Behold this is not my doctrine, to stir up the hearts of men with anger against one another; but this is my doctrine, that such things should be done away." *

9.—Now, we ask, how any one could err in regard to the meaning of this quotation concerning the mode of baptism: no two meanings could be drawn from these definite teachings. Every other point of the doctrine of Christ is equally as plain, and as definitely expressed as this, so that there is no possible chance for any differences of opinion in doctrine. There can be no question raised as to the meaning of the doctrine in the Book of Mormon; therefore all who obtain a knowledge of its divine authenticity, are from thenceforth sure and certain upon every point of the gospel: and thus divisions, strifes, contensions, and all the evils that flow from a diversity of opinions are, among the Latter-day Saints, for ever done away. The wranglings and quarrels about the doctrines of salvation, which have distracted mankind for generations and ages, can have no place in our midst. Among us new revelation has taken the place of human creeds, and knowledge has taken the place of opinion and guess-work, and the result thereof is union, peace, and eternal life.

10.—The particular period when the angel should fly with the everlasting gospel is expressed in a part of his proclamation; he was to say, "Fear God and give glory to Him, for the hour of His judgment is come." The servants of God are empowered not only to preach "the everlasting gospel," but to proclaim to all nations that "THE HOUR OF GOD'S JUDGMENT IS COME," It is the eleventh hour, or the last time that the Lord will prune His vineyard; it is the last proclamation of the gospel that the world are to be favored with, and the last

---

†——Book of Mormon, New Edition, page 502.

time that He will call upon them to repent; if they heed the warning they shall be gathered out from among the nations, and be saved; if they heed it not, the fierce judgments of the Almighty will speedily overtake them. Let the nations know assuredly that "the hour of God's judgment is come," and that they have only one way of escape, and that is, by embracing the Book of Mormon, which contains a proclamation of mercy as well as of judgment. Let the nations hearken to the voice of mercy, while she pleads in their midst; let them bow their stubborn hearts, and forsake all their evil deeds, before justice shall make his claim; for judgment followeth quickly and lingereth not; the hour is come, and the terrible day of the Lord is at hand—a day of wrath and of great terror—a day of fierce vengeance.

11.—John predicts another great event to take place immediately after the proclamation of the everlasting gospel, namely, the downfall of great Babylon. After the first angel had finished his mission, he says, "And there followed another angel, saying, Babylon is fallen, is fallen, that great city, because she made all nations drink of the wine of the wrath of her fornication." The Revelator has told us what Babylon means in the seventeenth chapter: it is represented under the figure of a woman, called, "THE MOTHER OF HARLOTS AND ABOMINATIONS OF THE EARTH." In the first verse, this woman is represented as "the great whore that sitteth upon many waters." In the fifteenth verse, the angel said to John that, "The waters which thou sawest, where the whore sitteth, are peoples and multitudes, and nations and tongues." The Roman Catholic, Greek and Protestant church, is the great corrupt ecclesiastic power, represented by great Babylon which has made all nations drunk with her wickedness, and she must fall, after she has been warned with the sound of "the everlasting gospel." Her overthrow will be by a series of the most terrible judgments which will quickly succeed each other, and sweep over the nations where she has had her dominion, and at last she will be utterly burned by fire, for thus hath the Lord spoken. Great, and fearful, and most terrible judgments are decreed upon these corrupt powers—the nations of modern Christendom; for strong is the Lord

God who shall execute His fierce wrath upon them, and He will not cease until He has made a full end, and until their names be blotted out from under heaven.

12.—The object in sending "the everlasting gospel" among the nations of Babylon is to save a remnant by literally gathering them out of her midst. St. John says, "And I heard another voice from heaven, saying, Come out of her, my people, that ye be not partakers of her sins, and that ye receive not of her plagues; for her sins have reached unto heaven, and God hath remembered her iniquities."* Hence, there is connected with the great message of the Book of Mormon, "a voice from heaven," commanding the Saints to come out from all nations as fast as they obey the gospel message; this they have been doing for these many years, and this they will continue to do, until the work of gathering is fully accomplished. And after the Saints, who are the salt of the earth, are gathered out, those who are left will quickly perish, as did Sodom and Gomorrha. All these events are clearly revealed in the Jewish scriptures; they are also clearly revealed in the Book of Mormon, which comes, saying, that the time is at hand; it is also revealed by the voice of God from heaven, and by the ministry of angels to chosen witnesses sent forth to warn mankind for the last time.

13.—"The everlasting gospel" has been committed once more to the inhabitants of our earth for the purpose of again organizing the Christian church, or in other words, the kingdom of God, as predicted by the Prophet Daniel, who said that, "In the days of these kings, shall the God of heaven set up a kingdom, which shall never be destroyed: and the kingdom shall not be left to other people, but it shall break in pieces and consume all these kingdoms, and it shall stand for ever." † The kingdom of God set up on the earth in the first century of the Christian era, was not the fulfillment of Daniel's prophecy. His prediction reached forward to a much later period of the world, namely, to the time when the angel should bring the gospel—to the time when the great image, represent-

---

*——Revelations xviii 4, 5

†——Daniel ii. 44.

ing all the kingdoms of the world, should be complete, from the head of gold to the feet and toes of iron and clay. The kingdom or church established eighteen centuries ago, does not, by any means, correspond with the time; for the feet and toes of Nebuchadnezzar's great image were not then in existence; indeed it was many centuries after that, before the Roman empire represented by the legs of iron, became divided into feet and toes. But Daniel says to Nebuchadnezzar, "Thou sawest till that a stone was cut out without hands, which smote the image upon his feet, that were of iron and clay, and brake them to pieces" (34 *verse*) From this we learn that the feet and toes must be in existence before "the God of heaven sets up a kingdom," represented by "the stone cut out without hands," otherwise, the stone could not commence its first attack upon the feet and toes, and break them in pieces.

14.—The nations of modern Europe, including England, and the Gentile nations of America, compose the legs, feet and toes of the image, while the other portions of the image will be found mostly among the Asiatic nations. The geographical position of the image is from east to west; its head is found in Asia, and its toes in Europe and America. When the kingdom of God is set up, it must be somewhere near the western extremity of this great image, for the toes and feet are first broken by it, and afterwards all the other portions, from which we learn that its advancement is from west to east. The progress of the kingdoms of the world has been from east to west; the progress of the kingdom of God is from west to east, in a retrograde direction. This stone, according to Daniel ii. 45, is to be "CUT OUT OF THE MOUNTAIN WITHOUT HANDS." "Cut out of the mountain," signifies its location before any part of the image is broken. The present location of the Latter-day Church is in the valleys among the *Rocky Mountains:* this appears to be its appropriate position, according to prophecy. The stone is to be "cut out *without hands:*" this signifies that it is a kingdom, not formed by the will of man, but by the will of God; human wisdom has no hand in its formation; it is "the God of heaven" that sets it up, and by Him it will be sustained and never be destroyed, nor broken to pieces, nor left to other people.

15.—The kingdoms of the world made war upon the Saints of the former-day kingdom and prevailed against them, and overcame them, and rooted them out of the earth, so that the kingdom no longer existed among the nations; not so with the latter-day kingdom; for it will prevail against the kingdoms of the world until they shall, as Daniel says, "Become like the chaff of the Summer threshing floors; and the wind carry them away, that no place shall be found for them: and the stone that smote the image shall become a great mountain, and fill the whole earth" (*Daniel ii.* 35). And then shall "the kingdom and dominion, and the greatness of the kingdom under the whole heaven, be given to the people of the Saints of the Most High, whose kingdom is an everlasting kingdom, and all dominions shall serve and obey Him" (*Daniel vii.* 27). The events predicted by Daniel are the same as the events predicted by John; Daniel says a kingdom shall be set up; John tells us by what means, namely, through the everlasting gospel, revealed by an angel: Daniel says, when the kingdom of God is set up, that the kingdoms of the world shall be broken in pieces: John says, that when the everlasting gospel has been restored and preached to the nations that then is, "the hour of God's judgment"—the downfall of Babylon. Both of these writers beheld the same great events, but described them in different language. That which was predicted by these two inspired men is now being fulfilled. The angel has appeared—the gospel is restored—the kingdom is set up—its location is among the mountains, and shortly the balance of these predictions will also be fulfilled to the very letter, and not one jot or tittle shall fail, until the earth shall rest from wickedness, and "the kingdoms of this world shall become the kingdoms of our God and His Christ."

16.—In the Jewish scriptures there is no prophet who has spoken more fully and plainly concerning the great events of latter times than Isaiah. In the twenty-ninth chapter he has clearly predicted that a certain book should be revealed—that the deaf should hear the words of it—that a marvelous work and a wonder should be accomplished—that Israel should be gathered and saved—that the poor and meek should rejoice—that they who err in spirit should come to understanding—

and, finally, that the wicked should all be destroyed. In the first, and part of the second verse, the Lord threatens Ariel, or Jerusalem, with judgment: he says, "Woe to Ariel, to Ariel, the city where David dwelt! add ye year to year; let them kill sacrifices; yet I will distress Ariel, and there shall be heaviness and sorrow." After the Messiah came and was sacrificed for the sins of the world, the Jews continued to "kill sacrifices," when they should have been done away; they added "year to year" to the law of Moses, until they brought down "heaviness and sorrow," and great "distress" upon their beloved city. The Roman army encompassed the city— cast a trench about it, and, finally, brought it down "even with the ground." The principal part of the Jews perished, and a remnant was scattered among the nations, where they have wandered in darkness unto this day.

17.—The latter part of the second verse speaks of another event that should be similar to the one which was to happen to Ariel, or Jerusalem: it reads thus; "And IT shall be unto me AS Ariel." This cannot have reference to Ariel itself, but it must refer to something which should be "*As* Ariel." It would be folly to say that Ariel shall be as Ariel. Therefore the word "it" must refer to a nation that should suffer similar judgments to those which should befall Jerusalem. In the three following verses, the Lord describes more fully the second event; he says, "And I will camp against thee round about, and will lay siege against thee with a mount, and I will raise forts against thee. And thou shall be brought down, *and shalt speak out of the ground, and thy speech shall be low out of the dust, and thy voice shall be as of one that hath a familiar spirit, out of the ground, and thy speech shall whisper out of the dust.* Moreover, the multitude of thy strangers shall be like small dust, and the multitude of the terrible ones shall be as chaff that passeth away; yea, it shall be at an instant suddenly." These predictions of Isaiah could not refer to Ariel, or Jerusalem, because their speech has not been "out of the ground," or "low out of the dust," but it refers to the remnant of Joseph who were destroyed in America upwards of fourteen hundred years ago. The Book of Mormon describes their downfall, and truly it was great and terrible. At the crucifiction of Christ, "the multitude of their terrible ones," as Isaiah predicted "became as chaff that passeth away," and it took place, as he further predicts, "at an instant suddenly." Many of their great and magnificent cities were destroyed by fire, others by earthquakes, others by being sunk and buried in the depths of the earth. This sudden destruction came upon them because they had stoned and killed the prophets sent among them. Between three and four hundred years after Christ, they again fell into great wickedness, and the principal nation fell in battle. Forts were raised in all parts of the land, the remains of which may be seen at the present day. Millions of people perished in battle, and they suffered just as the Lord foretold by Isaiah—"And I will camp against thee round about, and will lay siege against thee with a mount, and I will raise forts against thee, and thou shalt be brought down, and shalt speak out of the ground," etc. This remnant of Joseph in their distress and destruction, became unto the Lord as Ariel. As the Roman army lay siege to Ariel, and brought upon her great distress and sorrow, so did the contending nations of ancient America bring upon each other the most direful scenes of blood and carnage. Therefore, the Lord could, with the greatest propriety, when speaking in reference to this event, declare that, "It shall be unto me as Ariel."

18.—One of the most marvelous things connected with this prediction is, that after the nation should be brought down, they should "speak out of the ground." This is mentioned or repeated four times in the same verse. Never was a prophecy more truly fulfilled than this, in the coming forth of the Book of Mormon. Joseph Smith took that sacred history "out of the ground." It is the voice of the ancient prophets of America speaking "out of the ground;" their speech is "low out of the dust;" it speaks in a most familiar manner of the doings of bygone ages; it is the voice of those who slumber in the dust. It is the voice of prophets speaking from the dead, crying repentance in the ears of the living. In what manner could a nation, after they were brought down and destroyed, "speak out of the ground?" Could their dead bodies or their dust, or their ashes speak? Verily, no: they can only speak by their writings or their books that they wrote, while living. Their voice, speech or words, can only "speak out of the ground," or "whisper out of the dust" by their books or writings being discovered. Therefore, Isaiah further says, in the eleventh and twelfth verses: "And the vision of all is become unto you as the words of a book that is sealed, which men deliver to one that is learned, saying, read this, I pray thee: and he saith, I cannot; for it is sealed: and the book is delivered to him that is not learned, saying, read this, I pray thee: and he saith, I am not learned."

19.—After obtaining the Book of Mormon, through the ministry of the angel, "out of the ground," Mr. Smith transcribed some of the original characters upon paper, and sent them by the hands of Martin Harris, a farmer, to the city of New York, where they were presented to Professor Anthon, a man deeply learned in both ancient and modern languages. Mr. Harris very anxiously requested him to read it, but he replied that he could not. None of the learned have as yet been able to decipher the characters and hieroglyphics which are found among the ancient ruins, in almost every part of America. The written language of ancient America is a sealed language to this generation. In the year 1841, Professor Anthon wrote a letter to an Episcopal minister, in New Rochelle, Westchester County, near New York, in answer to an inquiry made by the minister in reference to the words or characters said to have been presented to him. Professor Anthon's letter was written with permission to publish; its avowed object being to put a stop to the spread of the fullness of the gospel, contained in the Book of Mormon. We here give a short extract from it, taken from a periodical, entitled, "The Church Record," Vol. I., No. 22.

20.—"Many years ago, the precise date I do not recollect, a plain-looking countryman called upon me with a letter from Dr. Samuel L. Mitchell, requesting me to examine and give my opinion upon a certain paper, marked with various characters, which the Doctor confessed he could not decipher, and which the bearer of the note was very anxious to have explained."

Here, then, is the testimony of the learned, that a man did call upon him with "the words of a book." But the learned professor continues:

"A very brief examination convinced me that it was a mere hoax, and a very clumsy one, too. The characters were arranged in columns, like the Chinese mode of writing, and presented the most singular medley that I ever beheld. Greek, Hebrew and all sorts of letters, more or less distorted, either through unskillfulness or from actual design, were intermingled with sundry delineations of half moons, stars and other natural objects, and the whole ended in a rude representation of the Mexican Zodiac."

21.—Professor Anthon, no doubt thought that this statement would militate against the Book of Mormon; but we consider it a great acquisition of evidence, confirmatory of the truth of that book, when compared with the discoveries of the glyphs and characters among the ancient ruins of America. The celebrated antiquarian, Professor Rafinesque, in speaking of the glyphs discovered on the ruins of a stone city found in Mexico, says:

"The glyphs of Otolum are written from top to bottom, like the *Chinese,* or from side to side, indifferently, like the *Egyptian,* and the Demotic Lybian. Although the most common way of writing the groups is in rows, and each group separated, yet we find some formed, as it were, in oblong squares or tablets, like those of *Egypt.*"*

Two years after the Book of Mormon appeared in print, Professor Rafinesque, in his *Atlantic Journal* for 1832, gave the public a fac-simile of *American glyphs,* found in Mexico. They are arranged in columns, being forty-six in number. These, the learned professor denominates "the elements of the glyphs of Otolum," and he supposes that by the combination of these elements, words and sentences were formed, constituting the written language of the ancient nations of this vast continent. By an inspection of the facsimile of these forty-six elementary glyphs, we find all the particulars which Professor Anthon ascribes to the characters,

---

*——*Atlantic Journal* for 1832, by Prof. Rafinesque.

which he says "a plain-looking countryman" presented to him. The "Greek, Hebrew and all sorts of letters," inverted and in different positions, "with sundry delineations of half-moons," planets, suns, "and other natural objects," are found among these forty-six elements. This "plain-looking countryman," according to Professor Anthon's testimony, got some three or four years the start of Professor Rafinesque, and presented him with the genuine elementary glyphs years before the *Atlantic Journal* made them public; and what is still more remarkable, "the characters," Professor Anthon says, "were arranged in columns, like the Chinese mode of writing," which exactly corresponds with what Professor Rafinesque testifies, as just quoted, in relation to the glyphs of Otolum. We see nothing in Professor Anthon's statement that proves the characters presented to him to be a "hoax," as he terms it; unless, indeed, he considers their exact resemblance to the glyphs of Otolum, and their being arranged in the right kind of columns—is a "hoax." But as Joseph Smith was an unlearned young man living in the country, where he had not access to the writings and discoveries of antiquarians, he would be entirely incapable of forging the true and genuine glyphs of Ancient America; therefore we consider this testimony of Professor Anthon, coming as it does from an avowed enemy of the Book of Mormon to be a great collateral evidence in its favor. Professor Rafinesque says, as we have already quoted, that "the glyphs of Otolum are written from top to bottom, like the *Chinese*, or from side to side, indifferently, like the Egyptian." Now the most of the Book of Mormon was written from side to side, like the Egyptian. Indeed, it was written in the ancient Egyptian, reformed by the remnant of the tribe of Joseph.

22.—Isaiah says, as we have already quoted, that "The vision of all is become unto you as the words of a book that is sealed, which men deliver to one that is learned, saying, read this I pray thee: and he saith, I cannot; for it is sealed." Mark this prediction; the book itself was not to be delivered to the learned, but only "the WORDS of a book;" this was literally fulfilled in the event which has already been described, as clearly testified of, not only by the "plain-looking countryman," namely Martin Harris, but by the learned professor Anthon himself.

23.—But Isaiah informs us in the next verse (12) that the book itself should be delivered to the unlearned: he says, "and the book is delivered to him that is not learned, saying, read this, I pray thee: and he said, I am not learned." This was fulfilled when the angel of the Lord delivered the book into the hands of Mr. Smith; though unlearned in every language, but his own mother tongue, yet he was commanded to read or translate the book. Feeling his own incapability to read such a book, he said to the Lord, in the words of Isaiah, "I AM NOT LEARNED." When he made this excuse, the Lord answered him in the words of Isaiah, next verse (13, 14), "Wherefore the Lord said, forasmuch as this people draw near me with their mouth, and with their lips do honor me, but have removed their heart far from me, and their fear toward me is taught by the precepts of men; therefore, behold, I will proceed to do a marvelous work among this people, even a marvelous work and a wonder; for the wisdom of their wise men shall perish, and the understanding of their prudent men shall be hid." What words could better portray the powerless apostate condition of modern Christendom than this description? and what words could be more descriptive of the "marvelous work and a wonder," than to say that "the wisdom of their wise men shall perish, and the understanding of their prudent men shall be hid? What could be more marvelous and wonderful, than for the Lord to cause an unlearned youth to read or translate a book which the wisdom of the most wise and learned could not read? Surely the Lord's ways are not as our ways, and His thoughts are not as our thoughts; for the wisdom of the world is foolishness in the sight of God; He bringeth forth by His power the hidden things of His wisdom through the meek, the simple and the unlearned, while he rejecteth the wisdom and learning of men, because of their pride and highmindedness. How marvelous and how wonderful are Thy doings, O Lord God Almighty! For Thou confoundest the wisdom and learning of men, that no flesh should glory in Thy presence! Thou exaltest the meek and the humble, that they may be taught of Thee, and know Thy ways! Glory, and honor. and wisdom, and power, and greatness of strength, and excellency of understanding be unto the Lord our God for evermore! Let all the earth fear and honor His great name, for "the hour of His judgment is come," and the times for the fulfillment of the great events of the last days, as spoken by His servants the prophets.

24.—Isaiah, in the ninth and tenth verses, has given a further description of the condition of all the nations, addressing himself to them, he exclaims—"Stay yourselves and wonder; cry ye out, and cry: they are drunken, but not with wine; they stagger, but not with strong drink; for the Lord hath poured out upon you the spirit of deep sleep, and hath closed your eyes: the prophets and your rulers, the seers hath He covered, and the vision of all is become unto you as the words of a book that is sealed," etc. Here we perceive the dark and benighted condition of the multitude of all the nations; at the time "the words of the book" should "speak out of. the ground" "the spirit of deep sleep" was to be poured out upon them; they were to be drunken and stagger, but not with wine nor with strong drink; the prophets and seers were to be covered from them; and "the vision of all," that is, the revelations of all the holy prophets and seers, contained either in the Bible or any other place were to become as the words of the sealed Book of Mormon. If they understood "the vision of all" who have spoken in past ages by the spirit of prophecy, they would not be "drunken," nor "stagger," nor be in a "deep sleep," but all nations are drunken with the wine of the wrath of the fornication of great Babylon; they see not neither do they understand the judgments which are about to befall them. As the learned Professor Anthon could not read "the words of the book" presented to him, because it was a sealed book—a language not understood by the learned, so with "the multitude of all the nations" in regard to "the vision of all the prophets and seers;" they are covered; they are not understood any more than the words of the sealed book were understood by the learned. When the events of the scripture prophecy are so clearly fulfilled, before their eyes, they will not even then perceive it; when the wisdom of the wise and learned perishes, and "a marvelous work and a wonder" is performed in causing the unlearned to read the book. the nations will not take it to heart; though, as Isaiah says, they will "stay themselves and wonder," and "cry out, and cry," because of the book which "speaks out of the ground;" yet, because they are drunken with every species of wickedness and abominations, and because they draw near to the Lord with their mouths, and with their lips, while their hearts are removed far from Him, and because they are taught by the precepts of men they will reject it, and in so doing, they will reject the Lord's great and last warning message to man, and bring upon themselves swift destruction. Because they despise so great a work, they "shall be visited," as Isaiah says, "with storm and tempest," and "earthquakes," "and the flame of devouring fire."

25.—As another evidence that the book of which Isaiah speaks was to come forth in latter times, he says in the seventeenth verse, "Is it not yet a very little while, and Lebanon shall be turned into a fruitful field, and the fruitful field shall be esteemed as the forest?" 18th verse: "And in that day shall the deaf hear the words of the book, and the eyes of the blind shall see out of obscurity, and out of darkness." This book could not mean the New Testament, for when that was written it was about the time that Lebanon was to be forsaken by the Jews and become a desolation, a forest, or wilderness for many generations. "Upon the land of my people shall come up thorns and briers." (*Isaiah xxvii.*, 13.) Hence the land of Palestine, which includes Lebanon, was, when the New Testament was written, about to be cursed. But immediately after the unlearned should read the book, "Lebanon shall be turned into a fruitful field, and the fruitful field shall be esteemed as the forest." The book, therefore, that Isaiah prophesies of, is to come forth just before the great day of the restoration of Israel to their own lands; at which time Lebanon and all the land of Canaan is again to be blessed, while the fruitful field occupied by the nations of the Gentiles, "will be esteemed as a forest;" the multitude of the nations of the Gentiles are to perish, and their lands which are now like a fruitful field, are to be left desolate of inhabitants, and become as Lebanon has been for many generations past; while Lebanon shall again be occupied by Israel, and be turned into a fruitful field. These great events could not take place until the Lord should first bring forth a book out of the ground.

26.—"*And, in that day, shall the deaf hear the words of the book.*" This has already been literally fulfilled. Those who were so deaf that they could not hear the loudest sound, have had their ears opened to hear the glorious and most precious words of the Book of Mormon, and it has been done by the power of God and not of man. "*And the eyes of the blind shall see out of obscurity and out of darkness.*" This has also been literally fulfilled, as abundantly testified of in the fifth chapter of this series. "*The meek also shall increase their joy in the Lord.*" Now during the long night of darkness there have been some, humble, meek persons who have had a degree of light; but as the church of Christ had fled from the earth there was no one that had authority to baptize or administer the ordinances of the gospel to those meek persons; therefore their joy was imperfect: but Isaiah says, when the book is revealed, "the meek shall increase their joy in the Lord." This is what the book is calculated to produce; for by its contents the meek learn that the time is at hand for them to inherit the earth, according to the blessings of our Savior on the Mount: "Blessed are the meek, for they shall inherit the earth." This will be fulfilled after all the wicked nations are destroyed. "And the poor among men shall rejoice in the Holy One of Israel." This also is promised as a result of the revelation of the book, and the means by which it is to be effected is by a general overthrow of the wicked; as, says Isaiah: "For the terrible one is brought to nought, and the scorner is consumed, and all that watch for iniquity are cut off; that make a man an offender for a word, and lay a snare for him that reproveth in the gate, and turn aside the just for a thing of naught." O how plainly it is declared that judgment was soon to fall upon all the wicked after the appearance of this book—this marvelous work and a wonder! And O how plainly it is also declared that the deaf, the blind, the meek and the poor among men were to be greatly benefitted by the book!

27.—After Isaiah had foretold the great change that was to happen to Lebanon, to the deaf, etc., when the book should be revealed, he then describes more particularly the great benefit the book should be to the house of Jacob. He says, "Therefore, thus saith the Lord, who redeemed Abraham, concerning the house of Jacob, Jacob shall not now be ashamed, neither shall his face wax pale. But when he seeth his children, the work of mine hands in the midst of him, they shall sanctify my name, and sanctify the Holy One of Jacob, and shall fear the God of Israel." The house of Jacob has been made ashamed, and his face has waxed pale, ever since he was driven away from Lebanon or Canaan, but the Lord has now brought forth out of the ground a book which shall, accompanied by His power, restore the tribes of Jacob from the four quarters of the globe, and establish them n the land of Palestine and Lebanon forever; and His holy name they shall no more profane, but shall be a righteous people throughout all their generations, while the earth shall stand, and they shall possess their promised land again in eternity, never more to pass away; therefore, they shall never again be made ashamed. It is in vain for the Gentiles to seek the conversion of Jacob, and to bring about their great redemption, only in the way that the Lord God of Israel hath predicted and appointed: they may call meetings and conventions to convert the Jews, but let them know assuredly that the book spoken of by Isaiah is to accomplish the salvation of the house of Jacob, and bring about the restoration of all Israel, while the Gentiles who will not receive it and be numbered and identified with the house of Jacob, must surely perish, yea, and they shall be utterly wasted with storm and tempest, with earthquakes and famine, with the flame of devouring fire, and their fruitful lands shall be esteemed as a forest, while Jacob shall dwell in safety for ever.

28.— Isaiah describes another event which follows the revelation of the book: he says, "They also that erred in spirit, shall come to understanding, and they that murmured shall learn doctrine" (*verse* 24). The meek of the earth who erred in spirit, because "the fear of the Lord was taught by the precept of men" should come to understanding. Oh, how precious must be the contents of a book which shall deliver us from all the errors taught by the precepts of uninspired men! Oh, how gratifying to poor, ignorant, erring mortals who have murmured because of the multiplicity of contradictory doctrines that have perplexed and distracted their minds, to read the plain, pure and most precious word of God, revealed in the Book of Mormon! It is like bread to the hungry—like the cool refreshing fountain to him that is ready to perish with thirst. Lift up your heads ye meek of the earth; let the poor among men rejoice in the Holy One of Israel; let them that have erred in spirit and stumbled in judgment, drink from the fountain of understanding; let all that have murmured because of the uncertainty of the precepts of men, read the words of the book, and they "shall learn doctrine;" let the humble and contrite in heart among all nations be exceedingly glad, for the hour of their redemption from Babylon is at hand; let all Israel praise the God of their fathers in songs of everlasting joy; for that which He spake by the mouth of their prophets, concerning their restoration to their lands is at hand to be fulfilled; already has the book which Isaiah said should accomplish your restoration and turn Lebanon into a fruitful field, made its appearance; and it truly is "a marvelous work—even a marvelous work and a wonder!" Let Zion awake again, and put on her strength as in days of old; let the servants of our God shout praises unto the Holy One of Zion; let them shout among the chief of the nations, and sing with gladness for Jacob, for he shall come in his appointed times, and none shall hinder. Lo! he shall come and sing in the hight of Zion, and the high places of the earth shall be glad for him, and the everlasting hills shall tremble with joy.

29.—Ephraim, the Lord's first-born, shall be like a mighty man, and his heart shall rejoice as through new wine; for he shall crown the tribes of Israel with glory, and his birthright shall never be wrested from his hand; his dwellings shall be in the fat valleys, and his seed shall cover the hills; he shall put forth his branches in all directions, and many shall repose in the shade thereof; with him is the key of hidden mysteries—the mysteries of ancient times; he shall unlock the sacred archives of heaven, and the skies shall pour down righteousness, like rain; the bowels of the earth shall open, and shall disclose the wonders of ages unknown. By him Zion shall be built, and her dwellings shall be encircled with glory; her light shall be as the sun, and her beauty as the morning; her tabernacles shall be as the dwelling places of the Most High, and in her palaces kings shall arise and worship; her children with one heart shall look upward, while the Zion that is above shall look downward; then the heavens and the earth shall meet, and all the creations shall shake with gladness; then the union of all dispensations will be completed, and the royal families of heaven and earth will be one from henceforth, even for evermore. This is the blessing of the children of Zion, and the glory of Ephraim the Lord's servants. The children of Manasseh shall assist Ephraim, and in all his glory they shall be glorified.

30.—The records of Manasseh in the hands of Ephraim shall gather out the Lord's elect from the four winds, from one end of the earth to the other. The Book of Mormon is the record of Manasseh; it is now in the hands of Ephraim, who have been for many generations, as the Prophet Hosea said, "mixed among the people." By them will the Lord "push the people together to the ends of the earth," even by the children of Ephraim, who is the Lord's first-born in this great latter-day work. The American Indians are partly of the children of Manasseh; though many of them are of Ephraim, through the two sons of Ishmael, who came out of Jerusalem six hundred years before Christ, and some of Judah, through the loins of David and the kings that reigned over Jerusalem. When Zedekiah, king of Judah was carried away captive into Babylon, the Lord took one of his sons, whose name was Mulok, with a company of those who would hearken unto His words, and brought them over the ocean, and planted them in America. This was done in fulfillment of the 22nd and 23rd verses of the seventeenth chapter of Ezekiel, which read thus: "Thus saith the Lord God, I will also take of the highest branch of the high cedar, and will set it: I will crop off from the top of his young twigs a TENDER ONE, and will plant it upon an high mountain and eminent; in the mountain of the hight of Israel will I plant it; and it shall bring forth boughs, and bear fruit and, be a goodly cedar; and under it shall dwell all fowl of every wing, in the shadow of the branches thereof shall they dwell." By reading this chapter, it will be seen that the Jews were the "high cedar," that Zedekiah the king was the "highest branch," that the "tender one" cropped off from the top of his young twigs, was one of his sons, whom the Lord brought out and planted him and his company upon the choice land of America, which He had given unto a remnant of the tribe of Joseph for an inheritance, in fulfillment of the blessing of Jacob and Moses upon the head of that tribe.*

31.—Jacob being a prophet, said unto his sons, "Gather yourselves together, that I may tell you that which shall befall you in the last days." He then commenced blessing them, by the spirit of prophecy, from the oldest to the youngest. The blessing of Joseph was as follows: "Joseph is a fruitful bough, even a fruitful bough by a well, whose branches run over the wall. * * * The blessings of thy father have prevailed above the blessings of my progenitors, unto the utmost bound of the everlasting hills: they shall be on the head of Joseph, and on the crown of the head of him that was separate from his brethren." (*Genesis xlix.*) Let the reader particularly notice this blessing. First, Joseph was to become very numerous: Second, his branches were to run over the wall: Third, he was to receive a blessing which was situated to the utmost bound of the everlasting hills: Fourth, Jacob declares that these blessings were greater or above those which his progenitors inherited. In the preceding chapter, Jacob predicts that Ephraim and Manasseh, the two sons of Joseph, should *become a multitude of nations.* A multitude of nations would require a large country for an inheritance. No wonder then that Jacob should prevail before the Lord, and obtain a greater blessing than Abraham and Isaac; for the land of Canaan would be altogether too small to accomodate "the multitude of the nations of Joseph," and the other tribes too; and Jacob

---

*———Genesis xlviii., and xlix; also Deuteronomy xxxiii.

foreseeing this, sought for a greater blessing than the land of Palestine, which was conferred upon his progenitors. This greater blessing is represented to be "to the utmost bound of the everlasting hills." The term *utmost bound* must have reference to the most distant portions of the earth. The geographical position of America corresponds, as to distance, with the terms of the prophecy. The range of mountains extending the whole length of the great western continent, are the longest in the whole world, and may well be designated by the Prophet Jacob as the *everlasting hills.*

32 —That Joseph might obtain the inheritance which Jacob conferred upon him, "*his branches run over the wall;*" that is, they left the main portion of the *bough* and went into some other country. They never could have had room to "become a multitude of nations" without breaking over the wall or boundaries of Palestine, and seeking the great inheritance conferred upon them, among the boundaries of the everlasting hills in America, which may well be termed the "utmost bounds" or distance from where the prophecy was uttered. On this vast continent, they could spread forth and become not only a great nation but "a multitude of nations." Asia, Africa and Europe are occupied principally by the Gentiles, and by nations who are not the descendants of Joseph. As the prophecy has not been fulfilled on the eastern hemisphere, the western hemisphere is the only part of our globe where it could be fulfilled. If we cannot find the multitude of the nations of Joseph in America, we cannot find them anywhere. But in America we truly do find several hundred nations of people who do not exhibit that diversity of character which we find distinguishing the nations of the eastern world. Their color, their features, their general physiognomy, their traditions, their manners and customs, their dialects, their general characteristics of mind, and modes of living, all proclaim that they are descended from one common origin. While their religious worship, their belief in one God, their computation of time, by the ceremonies of the new moon, their having an Ark of the covenant, their erection of a temple similar to the Jewish temple, their erection of altars, their divisions of the year into four seasons, corresponding to the Jewish

festivals, their laws of sacrifices, their ablutions and marriages, their places of refuge, their manner of conducting war, their abstaining from eating certain things forbidden by the laws of Moses, and the numerous affinities of their language to the Hebrew, all testify loudly that they are of Israelitish origin. Great numbers of writers, during two or three of the last centuries, have believed them to be Israelites, and have generally supposed them to be the nine and a-half lost tribes. But their history has spoken "out of the ground," by which we learn that they are, indeed Israel, but not the nine and a-half tribes; they are only a small remnant of one tribe, namely, of Joseph, among whom some of the tribe of Judah are mingled, through the royal seed of David.

33.—Moses, when blessing the tribes of Israel, by the spirit of prophecy, speaks in a very particular manner of the land of Joseph. And of Joseph, he said, "Blessed of the Lord be his land for the precious things of heaven, for the dew, and for the deep that coucheth beneath, and for the precious fruits brought forth by the sun, and for the precious things put forth by the moon, and for the chief-things of the ancient mountains, and for the precious things of the lasting hills, and for the precious things of the earth, and fullness thereof, and for the good-will of him that dwelt in the bush: let the blessing come upon the head of Joseph, and upon the top of the head of him that was separated from his brethren. His glory is like the firstling of his bullock, and his horns are like the horns of unicorns: with them he shall push the people together to the ends of the earth; and they are the ten thousands of Ephraim, and they are the thousands of Manasseh."\* From this we learn that Joseph was not only to inherit a land greater than the rest of the tribes, but that his land was to be peculiarly blessed. America fulfills the terms of the prophecy in every minute particular; among other favors, his land was to be blessed "WITH THE PRECIOUS THINGS OF HEAVEN." This blessing was of more importance than all the others; hence Moses places it first in the list of good things that were to be given to Joseph.

---

\*——Deuteronomy xxxiii.

34.—If the seed of Joseph were not to inherit another land separate, and at a distance from, Canaan, all these blessings would be without any meaning. If the land spoken of only meant his inheritance, joining the other tribes, why should Moses designate such great blessings upon it, and forget to say anything in reference to the particular blessings of the adjoining lands? The land of Joseph, in Palestine, seems to be about the same as the lands of his brethren; no great peculiarities seem to distinguish it from the other inheritances; therefore, the very fact that Moses speaks so definitely in his blessings upon tribes, about the *land of Joseph*, and enumerates its blessings, while he is nearly silent about the others' lands, shows, most conclusively, that the land of Joseph was to be in some other country. And as he speaks of "the chief things of the ancient mountains, and the precious things of the lasting hills," he must have reference to the same "everlasting hills," which Jacob gives to Joseph, that are said to be at the "utmost bounds." It was in this choice land, where the precious things of heaven" were to be unfolded to the multitude of the nations of Joseph.

35.—As all the tribes of Israel understood the art of writing, it is to be expected that they would keep a record or history of their nations in whatever part of the earth they might be located. When the ten tribes revolted, there were many prophets raised up among them from time to time, who wrote their prophecies as well as the prophets of Judah. If the Lord did continue to send prophets, as Elijah, Elisha and many others, among the ten tribes after their revolt, why not raise up prophets among the multitude of the nations of Joseph, after their separation from Judah? We cannot for a moment believe that a multitude of the nations of Joseph would be left destitute of the warning voice of prophecy. It would be entirely contrary to the dealings of God with both Israel and Judah. If the nations of Joseph understood the art of writing, and were to have "the precious things of heaven revealed to them," they would certainly write them, not only for the benefit of themselves, but for the benefit of future generations. This they did; and the Lord God of their fathers has now brought their history, their prophecies, their doctrines and their precious revelations from heaven to the knowledge of the people. The prophets, the seers and the revelators of the nations of Joseph have spoken "out of the ground, and their speech is low out of the dust," and their writings are now joined together with the Bible, which contains the writings of Judah, and they have become one in their testimony, declaring that the time is at hand for the restoration of the whole house of Israel to their own lands.

36.—We have already shown from Isaiah that the house of Jacob never could be restored, until God should bring forth a *book*, and that, too, "out of the ground;" and, until the deaf should hear the words of it. It will next be shown from the testimony of Ezekiel, that the book which is to perform so great a work for Israel, was really and truly to be a record of Joseph. Ezekiel says (*xxxvii*): "The Word of the Lord came again unto me, saying, Moreover, thou son of man, take thee one stick, and write upon it, for Judah, and for the children of Israel, his companions; then take another stick, and write upon it, for Joseph the stick of Ephraim, and for all the house of Israel, his compaions: and join them one to another into one stick, and they shall become one in thine hand. And when the children of thy people shall speak unto thee, saying, Wilt thou not show us what thou meanest by these? Say unto them, Thus saith the Lord God, Behold I will take the stick of Joseph which *is* [shall be] in the hand of Ephraim, and the tribes of Israel his fellows, and will put them with him, even with the stick of Judah, and make them one stick, and they shall be one in mine hand. And the stick whereon thou writest shall be in thine hand before their eyes."

37.—It was customary in ancient times to write upon parchment, and roll the same upon *sticks*, and such reading-sticks or *rolls* were called *books*. All the prophecies of Jeremiah, from the days of Josiah down to the fourth year of Jehoikim were written in one of these ROLLS (*Jeremiah xxxvi*. 1, 2). This "roll" of the writings of Jeremiah, is called a "book" in the 8th, 10th, 11th and 13th verses: hence, the terms *roll* and *book* are synonymous. If then, a reading-stick or roll, containing writings, is called a "book" we can all understand the meaning of the word of the Lord to Ezekiel: it was a clear and beautiful representation of the union of the books in the hand of the Lord. Ezekiel was commanded first, to *write* upon one stick, "for Judah and for the children of Israel, his companions." This was a representation of the Bible which is the record of Judah. "Then take another stick, and write upon it, for Joseph, the stick of Ephraim, and for all the house of Israel, his companions." This was a representation of the Book of Mormon, which is the record of Joseph written in ancient America. "And join them one to another into one stick, and they shall become one in thine hand." This was a representation of the union of the records of the two nations. In the interpretation of the meaning of the two sticks, the Lord says that He Himself "will take the stick of Joseph" and put it "with the stick of Judah." Therefore, we learn by this that the stick of Joseph was not found united with the stick of Judah by accident, but it was a work which the Lord Himself should perform. Hence, He further says, "They shall be one in mine hand." Therefore, the two writings becoming one in Ezekiel's hand, was a most beautiful representation of the two writings which should become one in the Lord's hand.

38.—Having learned by Ezekiel that the Lord God will take the stick of Joseph, and put it with the stick of Judah, and make them one in His hand; let us next inquire, what events are to follow the union of these two writings. The Lord further declares, "And the stick whereon thou writest shall be in thine hand before their eyes. And say unto them, Thus saith the Lord God, Behold, I will take the children of Israel from among the heathen, whither they be gone, and will gather them on every side, and bring them into their own land; and I will make them one nation in the land upon the mountains of Israel; and one king shall be king to them all; and they shall be no more two nations, neither shall they be divided into two kingdoms any more at all: neither shall they defile themselves any more with their idols, nor with their detestable things, nor with any of their transgressions; but I will save them out of all their dwelling places, wherein they have sinned, and will cleanse them: so shall they be my people and I will be their God." We learn from this, that the great object the Lord had in view, in bringing forth the book of Joseph, and uniting it with the Bible, is to gather Israel never more to be scattered. Thus we see that both Isaiah and Ezekiel have spoken of the same great and marvelous events; one declares that the house of Jacob should never again "wax pale" or "be made ashamed" in the day that a certain book should make its appearance; the other declares, that the whole house of Israel should be restored to its own lands, and should never again be divided into two nations, in the day that the Lord should put the writings of Joseph with the writings of Judah. Take the testimony of Isaiah and Ezekiel in connection with the testimony of Moses, concerning the "precious things of heaven," which should be given on the land of Joseph, and join this with the testimony of John concerning the restoration of the gospel by an angel, and the testimony of Daniel concerning the stone cut from the mountains without hands, representing the latter-day kingdom of God, and we have by a combination of all these testimonies, prophetic evidences of the divine authenticity of the Book of Mormon which should convince the most incredulous, and destroy atheism out of existence.

39.—Let us now hear what the Lord has said to David in relation to the salvation of Israel. David saw the long captivity of Jacob, and prayed earnestly that the Lord would show mercy to them. He prays thus: "Turn us, O God of our salvation, and cause thine anger towards us to cease. Wilt thou be angry with us forever? Wilt thou draw out thine anger to all generations? Wilt thou not revive us again, that thy people may rejoice in thee? Shew us thy mercy, O Lord, and grant us thy salvation."\* After he had thus prayed for Israel whom he saw in a long captivity, he then says, "I will hear what God the Lord will speak: for He will speak peace unto His people, and to His saints; but let them not turn again to folly." From this we perceive, that notwithstanding the Lord has been angry with Jacob for many generations, yet, He will again "SPEAK" to them. But let us read the following verses, that we may

---

\*——Psalm lxxxv.

learn in what manner He will "speak peace." "Mercy and truth are met together, righteousness and peace have kissed each other. TRUTH SHALL SPRING OUT OF THE EARTH; and righteousness shall look down from heaven. Yea, the Lord shall give that which is good; and our land shall yield her increase. Righteousness shall go before Him, and shall set us in the way of His steps." O, what a glorious answer David received to his prayer of captive Israel. He learned that the Lord would "speak peace" to them by causing "Truth to spring out of the earth," and then, and not till then, "Righteousness should look down from heaven" in behalf of captive Israel; then he learned that the land of Israel should again "yield her increase," because "the Lord should give that which is good." This agrees with what we have already quoted from Isaiah: so that both David and Isaiah saw how Israel were to be delivered. One says it shall be by truth and righteousness, combining together, truth coming out of the earth and righteousness at the same time looking down from heaven; while the other declares that Israel should "speak out of the ground," after which, Jacob should no longer be made ashamed. David says, that after "truth springs out of the earth," the land of Israel "should yield its increase." Isaiah says, that in the day that the marvelous work and a wonder is accomplished, then "Lebanon shall be turned into a fruitful field," "and the deaf shall hear the words of the book." David says, that then is the time, that "righteousness shall go before Him, and shall set us in the way of His steps." Isaiah says, "That the book shall cause those who erred in spirit to come to understanding." Every event concerning this latter-day work in behalf of Israel, which David describes in his Psalm, is also described by Isaiah; the latter gives many particulars, however, which the former does not.

Isaiah must have had reference to the same marvelous event, when he exclaims, "Drop down, ye heavens, from above, and let the skies pour down righteousness; let the earth open, and let them bring forth salvation, and let righteousness spring up together: I, the Lord, have created it." *

---

*——Isaiah xlv. 8.

40.—Never was there a work more clearly predicted than the great and marvelous work for the restitution of Israel; and never had mankind more prophetic evidences in confirmation of a revelation, than they have for the Book of Mormon. None of the books of the Old or New Testaments were prophesied of before they were revealed, whereas this great revelation of the last days has been clearly predicted by many of the inspired writers. In this respect, the Book of Mormon is confirmed by testimony to this generation, such as no other prophets could bring forward to establish their books in the day that they were given.

41.—And I now bear my humble testimony to all the nations of the earth who shall read this series of pamplets, that the Book of Mormon is a divine revelation, for the voice of the Lord hath declared it unto me. And having been commanded of the Lord, in His name, I humbly warn all mankind to repent of all their sins, to turn away from all their false doctrines, and to forsake the precepts of uninspired men. Yea, come forth with meek, humble and contrite hearts, and be immersed in water for the remission of your sins, and you shall receive the Holy Ghost by the laying on of the hands of the Apostles or Elders of this Church; and signs shall follow them that believe, as they did the believers in times of old; and all people, nations and tongues, who will not do this, shall be damned, and shall in no wise enter into the kingdom of God, for this message shall condemn them at the last day. Repent, therefore, all ye ends of the earth, for the great day of the Lord is at hand; the sword of the justice of the Eternal God will soon fall upon you except ye repent. Repent, O, ye kings and queens of the earth, for the day of the Lord's controversy with the nations has come; and thrones shall be cast down, and your kingdom shall be rent asunder, and there shall be no safety for you, unless you repent. Let the lords, and nobles, and all those in high places, repent, for calamity shall come from all quarters like a whirlwind; fear and terror shall encompass you round about, and there shall be no place of refuge for you in the day of the Lord's fierce vengeance upon Babylon. Woe unto you, ye rich men, who trade and traffic among the nations, and who have heaped up gold and silver as the dust, for except you repent, your riches shall be despoiled, your trade and traffic shall cease, and ye shall howl for the miseries that shall come upon you: repent, therefore, and gather up your riches, and flee out from among the nations, and carry your gold and silver with you unto the place of the name of the Lord of hosts, the Mount Zion, and make use of your riches as the Lord shall direct to beautify the place of the Lord's sanctuary, otherwise ye shall perish with your riches. Let all the bishops, and clergy, and priests of every denomination repent and cease to preach false doctrines, and let them be baptized and come into the Church of Christ, and seek no more to fight against the Lord's work, for unless they do this, the Lord shall visit them in swift judgment, and they shall perish quickly out of the earth; for they are the ones that have corrupted the earth with their false, vain, foolish and powerless doctrines; they are the ones who have blinded the eyes and hardened the hearts against the Lord's great and last message; therefore, except they repent, there is in reserve for them a heavier judgment, and they shall gnaw their tongues for pain. Repent, all ye inhabitants of the earth, lest the Lord shall smite you with the rod of His mouth, and with the breath of His lips consume you as stubble. Let all Israel repent, and turn unto the Lord, and gather themselves together, for the time of the fulfilling of the covenant, made with your fathers, is at hand—the time when all things are to be restored that have been spoken by the mouth of all the holy prophets since the world began—the time when the kingdom is to be restored to Israel, and the Lord God of their fathers is to reign over them in power, might, majesty and in great glory from thenceforth even forevermore.

www.ingramcontent.com/pod-product-compliance
Lightning Source LLC
Chambersburg PA
CBHW022047230426
43672CB00008B/1094